ALWAYS
FOR THE
UNDERDOG

ALWAYS FOR THE UNDERDOG

LEATHER BRITCHES SMITH AND THE GRABOW WAR

KEAGAN LeJEUNE

Texas Folklore Society Extra Book Number 23

University of North Texas Press

Denton, Texas

© 2010 Keagan LeJeune

All rights reserved.
Printed in the United States of America.

10 9 8 7 6 5 4 3 2 1

Permissions:
University of North Texas Press
1155 Union Circle #311336
Denton, TX 76203-5017

The paper used in this book meets the minimum requirements of the American National Standard for Permanence of Paper for Printed Library Materials, z39.48.1984. Binding materials have been chosen for durability.

Library of Congress Cataloging-in-Publication Data

LeJeune, Keagan, 1972–
  Always for the underdog : Leather Britches Smith and the Grabow War / Keagan LeJeune.—1st ed.
    p. cm. — (Texas Folklore Society extra book ; no. 23)
  Includes bibliographical references and index.
  ISBN-13: 978-1-57441-288-8 (hardback : alk. paper)
  1. Smith, Leather Britches, d. 1912. 2. Outlaws--Louisiana--Biography. 3. Outlaws in popular culture—Louisiana. 4. Grabow Riot, Grabow, La., 1912. 5. Grabow (La.)—History. 6. Brotherhood of Timber Workers—History—20th century. 7. Labor disputes—Louisiana—History—20th century. 8. Lumber trade—Louisiana—History—20th century. 9. Neutral Ground (La.—Social life and customs. 10. Folklore and history—Louisiana. I. Title. II. Series: Texas Folklore Society extra book ; no. 23.
  F375.S645L45 2010
  976.3'061092—dc22
  [B]   2010030471

Book design by Charles Sutherland

Always for the Underdog: Leather Britches Smith and the Grabow War
is Texas Folklore Society Extra Book Number 23.

For Melanie LeJeune and the Carmen Family

CONTENTS

List of Illustrations — IX

Preface — XI

Acknowledgments — XVII

Texas Folklore Society Statement — XIX

Introduction — 1

Chapter 1: *The Sabine River Bottom Swamp* — 13

Chapter 2: *Meanness, Just across the River* — 25

Chapter 3: *No Man's Land* — 45

Chapter 4: *Shot a Chicken's Head Clean Off* — 59

Chapter 5: *Always for the Underdog* — 76

Chapter 6: *The Grabow War* — 94

Chapter 7: *They Didn't Give the Man a Chance* — 118

Chapter 8: *The Outlaw Applied* — 154

APPENDIX A	173
APPENDIX B	175
NOTES	179
BIBLIOGRAPHY	201
INDEX	219

LIST OF ILLUSTRATIONS

Following page 138

1 Map of area

2 Louisiana longleaf pine

3 Carson logging camp

4 Felling trees near Lake Charles

5 Typical wood crew

6 John Henry Kirby speaking in DeRidder

7 Company office for mill at Carson

8 Co. K First Infantry

9 Union prisoners in Lake Charles jail

10 Portrait of Judge Overton

11 Union prisoners at the big dinner

12 Sketch of Ben Myatt

13 Leather Britches's tombstone

14 Leather Britches's tombstone with flowers

15 Burks House

16 Outlaw parade for Merryville Heritage Festival

17 Amarillo Slim, member of No Man's Land Gang
18 Pioneering couple, members of No Man's Land Gang
19 Reverend Devil, member of No Man's Land Gang
20 Beginning of a shootout skit at Merryville Heritage Festival
21 Reverend Devil during a skit
22 "Gang Wardens" parade float
23 Wanted poster

PREFACE

Does America possess enough unity and shared history for large cultural values and myths to pervade all levels of society? Does the country possess enough similarity for a few key concepts to make a noticeable impact on the minds of the American population? If so, what concepts and values are broad enough to reach all Americans, yet powerful enough to direct them? For some folklorists, the question is an intriguing one. In fact, it becomes the most important.[1] Discovering which shared beliefs exist in the American mind-set could yield incredible insight about the essence of being American, about the cornerstones of American culture. If these shared beliefs exist, we must ask a second question. What stories or which figures could communicate those beliefs and resonate with members of such a diverse group? Certain folklorists have suggested a few possibilities.

Many folklorists turn to "America: The Land of Opportunity" as the most pervasive national belief. Could this idea touch the soul of every American? Could this value shape a national mind-set? The suggestion seems reasonable, especially as one considers that many scholars argue that this single core idea manifests in a variety of forms: "The Promised Land, The Earthly Paradise, Manifest Destiny, The Garden of Eden, Land of the Free and Home of the Brave."[2] Beverly Stoeltje, a noted folklorist, claims that Americans envision America as a land of opportunity by continually creating the myth of the frontier for each new generation. Offering a new home, a new place to conquer, a new prospect for discovery and progress—the myth of the frontier presents

America as a land of perpetual opportunity, a land of continual promise. In her argument, the recent frontier of space replaces the old frontier of the West, and this notion of the continual frontier "tells the story of the sociopolitical process known as exploration and Conquest of the Unknown, the nucleus of the Progress of Western Civilization."[3]

If this pattern serves as "the nucleus of the Progress of Western Civilization," one wonders about the consequences. Undoubtedly, conquering the unknown implies violence. If in the American context this process of conquest is settling the frontier, students of the past can hardly debate the role of violence. In American history books and other records, the strong and the rugged clear out the trees, break the soil, tame the untamed. The rough and the tough settle the West. The aggressive and the hardy forge ahead until they hit the ocean. Consequently, the frontier remains unchanged until that person with enough grit and toughness arrives. The frontier remains unsettled until the man or woman with enough daring and strength and ingenuity comes along to brave the uncharted and do the nearly impossible. At least, that's what popular consciousness would have us believe. Settlement relies on frontier independence, and this land needs the rugged individualist to bring it into the fold of civilization. In order to progress, the frontier—and America by extension—requires the rugged individual's self-reliance, his grit and toughness, and perhaps even his isolationism.

But what is the second half of the story? The frontier, even if it seems stubborn on the surface, wants to be tamed, wants to be claimed, and is always better off when it is. Like a wild stallion that develops a resilient love for the master who overcomes all to befriend the beast and tame him, the frontier waits for the right person to unfold its riches. A hardy constitution, a violent disposition, a disregard for laws, or a desire to make your own, and a proclivity for ruthlessness: these traits grew in the American mind as the stock characteristics of the frontiersman. Engrained in the country's psyche, these became the traits of the individual able to take on the frontier and tame it. But as experience teaches us, a darker side lurks. Similar to the Byronic hero whose personal code isolates him, the frontiersman's ruggedness and internal code develops into a violent disposition and refusal to be governed. His pragmatism and independence stretch to ruthlessness and lawlessness. His desire for personal liberty and free enterprise grow to beliefs in unbound personal gain and fierce competitiveness.

These ideas don't exist without opponents. Mody Boatright's 1941 "The Myth of Frontier Individualism" debunks the myth of the rugged individualist. Boatright tracks the comments made by travel writers, the memoirs of frontiersmen, and the legal actions taken by settlers of the West in order to demonstrate the great reliance on community that people on the frontier must have had.[4] In his search, he discovered that travel writers tell of early settlers building churches in great groups and that travelers went unpunished if they went into the home of an absent settler and took only the food they needed. If one reads the journals and diaries of people who lived on the frontier or have conversations with their descendants, one realizes that most people want security, happiness, and companionship. People will not tolerate a completely lawless character for long. However, one also needs to consider the preponderance of the adventurer or the rugged loner in the American mind-set, in its history, and, of course, in its folklore. Even if people have exaggerated this figure's importance, we cannot deny its popularity, and the predominance of this figure in America warrants an examination.

This train of thought led me to a section of Louisiana known as the Neutral Strip. As I read local history books and heard local legends, the popularity of this figure in the region overwhelmed me.[5] In one guise or another, the rugged individualist cropped up again and again. Perhaps its popularity connects to the region's interesting history.[6] Through the Louisiana Purchase, America in one fell swoop doubled its size and increased its natural resources, but the action also left a tiny portion of the country, Louisiana's Neutral Strip, in turmoil. For this small strip of land, the 1803 purchase did not settle all accounts.

Purchasing the territory from France, the United States faced Spain's disagreements about the new territory's boundaries. In particular, Spain and the U.S. could not agree on the western border of the territory south of the thirty-second parallel of latitude. The United States believed the new lands ended at the Rio Grande, and Spain believed their possession extended to the Calcasieu River. When no agreement could be reached, both governments removed their troops and officially formed the Free State of the Sabine, or the Louisiana Neutral Strip. As governments removed military order, many squatters and even thieves came into the area and made a home. The 1819 Adams-Onís Treaty ended the dispute and set the boundary as the Sabine River, but the brief moment in history made a lasting impact. People still see the time as instrumental in shaping the area's cultural identity. Several towns in the area celebrate the historical period with festivals, and many local authors' books focus on the outlaws who made a home in the region. The region's folklore does the same, as locals tell outlaw legends and turmoil-ridden family sagas involving the Neutral Strip.

In Louisiana's No Man's Land, as some have called it, lore connects and reconnects people to their history and unique landscape, ripe with thick forests and intricate inland waterways—a landscape outlaws turned to for cover. Town histories, family sagas, legends, and even personal accounts reinvest people along the Sabine River in this brief historical moment. Since these people's ancestors settled a region unclaimed and existing as a border even before the Louisiana Purchase, a wealth of the folklore here exhorts the frontier spirit, praises freedom, and celebrates the possibilities gained from living on the edge of civilization. Casually at dinner or during coffee, people tell stories of feuds or family conflict, but these stories end by praising the resilience of ancestors and family lines. At basketball or football games, folks laugh as they relive episodes of one rival town against another, but these accounts become more about the solidarity and stick-to-itiveness of their hometown. People tell stories of explorers, pirates, or bandits who all once roamed the area; then, they whisper about the buried treasures these people left behind, smile about the riches waiting to be had out there. Many towns in the region hold these sorts of stories. The people, and sometimes even whole towns, turn to them, especially when describing the noteworthiness of the region or when trying to market the area as a worthwhile tourist attraction.

Though folklore here is rich and various types of stories remain popular, the outlaw appears to reign above them all. In the Neutral Zone (and perhaps in most frontier regions), the outlaw—a man who lives violently—exemplifies the harsh environment that surrounds him. He wields unusual power, for legends about him offer a means of expressing and thus relieving the stress and fear that accompanies a rugged life. In this way, the outlaw offers a vicarious means of escape. Incredibly, his skill reduces the residents' worries about the danger the frontier offers, and his independence removes their frustrations brought on by social or legal obedience and by communal obligations.

Paradoxically, the outlaw figure also symbolically stresses the necessity of community. Outlaws exist independently enough to consistently tread into the unknown and conquer it, yet they are eventually conquered themselves—usually killed, captured, or driven into hiding. In the end, outlaws cease. They are too wild and isolated to survive for very long. For that same reason, outlaws need the structure and boundaries that civilization offers. In order to have something to react against, to be more than a creature alone in the wilderness, an outlaw needs a border to cross. If the outlaw covets and makes his way by stealing, not much can be gained in the wilderness. If the outlaw wants to be famous, that also requires a community to act as witness. In the end, the outlaw's rebellion appears most striking juxtaposed with civilization's conformity. In a sense, the community on the border enables the outlaw. The town offers something tangible for the outlaw to react against. It offers a clear opportunity to escape something.

However, not all outlaws are the same. Though all need something to steal, they don't all go about it in the same way. Some steal from anyone, some steal from the rich, and some steal from the rich in order to give to the poor. Members of this last group of outlaws walk a precarious line between right and wrong, and they transcend into the realm of the good outlaw, also known as the outlaw-hero. Like Robin Hood, the outlaw-hero stands as an even more potent symbol of the conflict between the wild and the tamed. He breaks only certain rules, and he directs his violence only at certain targets. He symbolizes the necessity of both worlds, the uneasy balance on the frontier, and perhaps even America's complex history.

Many outlaw legends exist in the Neutral Strip, but at least one small town in the region, Merryville, Louisiana, tells stories of a good outlaw: Leather Britches Smith. Leather Britches entered the area around 1910, long after the No Man's Land period ended but right as the timber boom that swept the South hit the area. A fugitive from East Texas, Smith quickly developed a reputation for his skill and daring. Incredible with a rifle, deadly with his two Colt pistols, Leather Britches didn't "fear nothing," folks say. He marched into town carrying his guns, sat undisturbed on the front row of the theater with his pistols in his lap, and "persuaded" locals to cook him dinner. Smith's legend, however, extends far beyond his own personal exploits. As Leather Britches roamed the woods off the Sabine River, timber barons cut trees and raked in huge profits. All the while, timber laborers worked fourteen hours a day. As Smith walked the streets of Merryville, union leaders stood on street corners rallying crowds of men to join the union. Union busters and company guards stood watch at the mills. Eventually, the tension between the union men (organized in the Brotherhood of Timber Workers) and the non-union men (backed by the Southern Lumber Operators' Association) erupted in a gun battle at the Galloway Mill located at Grabow, Louisiana. The Grabow Trial that followed became national news, and Smith landed in the middle of the entire affair. Some claim the union brought in Leather Britches to scare away opposition and scare up support, but others claim Smith simply stood up for the working man and lived free as the only man with the skill and resourcefulness to do so.

When it comes to stories about Smith, people usually make an effort to tell their own version of the outlaw legend. They correct versions they have heard or add details about how their families connect to the story. By telling their own versions of the legend, people mark themselves as informed citizens or as talented storytellers. They add credibility and longevity to their family lines or stress their families' contributions to the community. They even praise the community for being an interesting or exciting place to live. Telling the legend becomes a source of pride and a means of connecting to an important history. Today, the outlaw Leather Britches Smith functions as a cultural resource, a symbol of what Merryville and the region offers the world.

ACKNOWLEDGMENTS

This book would have been impossible to complete without the help of many people, too many to name in this short space. I owe my greatest debt of gratitude to all those narrators who sat down with me and told me their stories. I have mentioned many by name, but I would like to thank Ester Terry, Catherine Stark, Frank Hennigan, Shelley Whiddon, and Gussie Townsley for visiting with me. I am a richer man for having known them. Beyond these individual narrators, I would like to thank all those people who shared their stories with me. Thanks to the members of the No Man's Land Gang and the organizers of the Merryville Heritage Days Festival, who posed for pictures and let me mill around the grounds.

I would like to thank the Carmen family, especially Eloise Carmen, who escorted me to the home of Catherine Stark, and Bobby Carmen, who shared his knowledge with me and encouraged me throughout this process. I also want to thank Marshall, Andy, and Lee Anna for being supportive and telling me their own stories about the area.

Thanks go to the members of the Fuller family and the Nash family. I would also like to thank the Bruns, Nelson, and Nichols families. Thanks to Brent for the photographs, to Brad for all the encouragement, and to all my friends who listened to me go on about the project. Of course, I would like to thank my mother, my father, and my brothers and sister, who are always very generous with their support.

Support from McNeese State University allowed my continued work on the book. Professors John Wood, Carol Wood, and Joe Cash, who encouraged me to pursue publication, deserve a great deal of thanks.

The pleasant and diligent archivists in the McNeese State University Archives were incredibly helpful in finding material and were quite generous with their time.

I would like to thank the Lake Charles Parish Courthouse for the use of its files, and the *Lake Charles American Press* for the use of its archives.

Thanks to the editorial staff of the University of North Texas Press and to the Texas Folklore Society. I would also like to acknowledge the many people who served as readers. I would like to thank Gary Joiner, Lee Winniford, Bonnie Lovell, and Ken Untiedt, who made insightful suggestions about the book. Professors Marcia Gaudet, Barry Ancelet, and Darrell Bourque were kind enough to read an early version of this work; their comments helped it immeasurably. Two readers helped shape the work. Matt Bokovoy offered important structural suggestions, and the book is far better because of his comments. Jacob Blevins read the book in several versions, and his comments may have been the most crucial toward the book's completion.

My deepest gratitude goes to Melanie, my wife and research companion. She accompanied me on many collecting sessions, answered all the questions she could, and offered insightful suggestions during the writing of the book. She, too, read the book many times and indexed it.

TEXAS FOLKLORE SOCIETY STATEMENT

The Texas Folklore Society has a long history of publishing quality folklore scholarship of Texas and the Southwest. To date, there have been sixty-six books published under the Publications of the Texas Folklore Society series. These books are typically compilations of papers presented by members at annual meetings, collected and edited by the Secretary-Editor. Additionally, the Society has generously supported members who've completed individual works, including books in the Range Life Series of the '40s and the Paisano Book Series of the late '60s. In keeping with that tradition, the Texas Folklore Society is pleased to support the publication of Keagan LeJeune's *Always for the Underdog: Leather Britches Smith and the Grabow War*, Extra Book Number 23.

INTRODUCTION

It's early December 1998. My wife, Melanie, and I approach Merryville, Louisiana, from the south. We move north on Highway 27 past the turnoffs to small towns and then northwest on 110 through expanding pine flatwoods squared off in rows like the pristine cemeteries of soldiers. A few small creeks, more like large ditches, cut under the highway, but almost nothing interrupts the forest's progression. All that breaks this view of what will be cut is what was cut a time back or what is being cut now. Up to a few years ago, someone's cattle wandering on the highway, especially in midnight or fog, could make a drive through here dangerous. The fence law put a stop to that, but this price for safety came with some sacrificing. Now fences slice hunting grounds, and the separation of land halts hounds, hunters on foot, or ATVs. As with so many aspects of life here, progress comes with trade-offs.

As the road continues and curves into town, the place shows itself. The high school ball fields, which serve as the city's recreation fields in the summer, jut up against each other. Outfield fences of some fields curve toward outfield fences of others. Like planetary orbits around suns, the wire fences curve toward each other, almost collide, and then slope away. On the fields used by the high school, long pieces of plywood line the fences. The painted planks read "PANTHERS" or contain detailed yellow eyes staring from the plywood or bloody claws whose marks have ripped the wood. The local stadium, home of the Merryville High School Panthers, rests a little farther down the road, separated from the highway by an empty grass field used as a parking lot for Friday night home football games. Running parallel to the highway, the bleachers put their back to the road, and above them the broad sign tells the place's name, "Keener Cagle Stadium." Christian Keener "Red" Cagle—a football titan—began here in Merryville during the late 1920s, was an All-American at Southwestern Louisiana Institute and West Point, and spent time in the professional league as a New York Giant.[1] The legacy and importance of football remains, and Merryville defies classification as this Class B school fields a football team.

The school itself follows the stadium. The buildings lie on a tract of land first owned by William Marsh Rice, the founder of Rice University, which spawned the Rice Land Lumber Company. The company owns a sizable amount of nearby forests, the cutting of which funded the first buildings on the Rice campus. In 1920, the Rice Land Lumber Company donated 160 acres to the Beauregard Parish school system. From kindergarten to twelfth grade, around six hundred children fill the school. Built in 1910, the school burned on a Sunday night in January 1918. A "new" school was completed on July 17 in 1920. The school today—its classrooms, fields, gym, cafeteria, library, and other buildings—stretches over a small amount of the one hundred and sixty acres donated by Rice. Most enter the school through the circle drive that curves off Highway 110 and that arcs its way in front of the school's main auditorium before it bends back onto the road. Resting as a marker of memory and meaning, a statue of the school's mascot stands in the middle of the drive's sloping curve. Painted black with a maroon that accentuates its muscles, mouth, and eyes, a panther watches as people make their way into the school's gym.

The panther stands as an emblem of the mystery and power hidden in the piney woods. The area, the town, and the school have embraced the animal, and its form and function blaze on outfield fences, the fifty-yard line, jackets, sweatshirts, cars and trucks, in yards, and even as small decorations in homes. Moreover, the popularity of panther stories rivals the popularity of the outlaw legends in the region. The creature haunts the tales of children and teenagers, and many tell stories about the animal roaming these woods. Even though many workers for Louisiana Wildlife and Fisheries and other wildlife authorities refuse to believe any panther stalks these woods, residents still have proof. On rare nights, when a person gets in earshot of a panther prowling a part of his territory, a long scream, "wailing out like a woman who is being murdered" as they say, races through trunks of pine, slams against windows of houses, and crashes over the ears of the residents. A person told me that one time he had a panther up on his roof, but he didn't dare to walk out the door to see it up there. He knew better than to try to catch a glimpse of it. Those few people who have seen the cat for an instant before it returns to the trees are beyond lucky, or are liars. The creature's dangerous reputation seems only matched by its ability to escape capture.

A small hurricane fence marks the end of the high school's land. And that is how much of the community unfolds, one separation after another. A school stops, a cemetery starts. One house ends, another begins. Family lands cease, company lands commence. Larger divisions build the Merryville community, which becomes a patchwork of small settlements and family land: The Junction to the north, Bancroft to the south, Red Hill to the northeast, and the river bottoms to the west. People from these places constitute Merryville's official population and attend the town's high school.

When the high school's land stops, an old town cemetery begins. Started in 1909 as the gravesite connected to an early Baptist church, the cemetery near the high school occupies a special position in the town's distinctiveness. Offering a few of the first images seen when entering Merryville from the southeast, this cemetery serves as a town fixture since many of the town's central family names rest there. Moreover, since it butts up to the high school, the Merryville Cemetery exists as a potent symbol of the community's identity.

From the highway, a small dirt road gently turns off to the right and passes underneath an intricate ironworks. Wire tangles with itself until "Merryville Cemetery" laces out over a lichgate in the security and tradition of tempered steel. Two cedars, trimmed in the shape of perfect teardrops, stand off from the road and mark the cemetery's entrance. On all sides except the one that juts up against the school, trees group together, lining out rows that mark the cemetery's boundaries. Throughout the grounds, a few oaks, four or five pines, and a sycamore rise amidst the stones; they add texture, tradition, memory, and a little shade for those at rest and for those who mourn them. The graves match the oddness and variety of the timber specimens. Old marble, slate, or sandstone headstones contrast with the sleek and clean modern graves that are usually only granite or concrete plaques level with the ground.

The cemetery's front is old, the back new, and most tombstones rest manicured and attended. Not a one lies flat on the ground to be tended by a lawn mower and a gardener's quick ride around the plots. Many rest adjacent to family. A few Woodmen of the World markers formed in the image of a tree trunk speak with certainty about the area's history and economy. The place contains the graves of church members, politicians, homemakers, woodsmen, and, I would find out much later, the grave of Leather Britches Smith.

We drive by the small cemetery, and as it fades away, the Malone Lumber Mill appears. Over the years, the mill has grown, cutting down trees and people's memories of what this town once looked like. As it does, the mill exemplifies the area's commitment to progress: The mill slowly cut away the tree line of a wood that ran along the road, and most of the area's surrounding forests receive the same periodically. Here, people create work this way. Acres, in a constant state of loss and return, move back and forth between growing and being cut. After a logger grades, then cuts, a tract of trees, he burns the remnants or turns them in the soil. He plants more trees, grows them, and cuts again. As so many others have done through the years in this town and in others like it, the Malone Lumber Mill takes the town and turns it into industry, into a product to be sold and shipped, into work. Its processing of place lingers in the air and mists fine black soot over houses, cars, and yards.

The soot covers the yard and home of Eloise Carmen, Melanie's grandmother, called Grand by the family, who lives just across the street from the stacks of timber stored at the mill's back. Though some may complain of a mill in their backyards, no one knows any easy answers, especially for long, because livelihood makes its own argument, and a good one. Trees have sprouted this place, and the existence of this place promises trees. The town means that forest after forest has been and will be cut. Promises of profit and work ensure that forest after forest will grow again.

During the early 1900s, many of the permanent towns in this region formed, most the result of the booming lumber industry. As communities took hold, people thrived. Houses circled like wagons and marked a stretch of land as a family's own. Cousins became neighbors. Together, generation after generation made a life. Like church worship, settling the area involved everyone and worked best as a communal endeavor. Many settlements, especially close to the river, formed as a result of children staying close by to make a home. Eventually, whole town histories attached themselves to a handful of family names.

In the past, this approach to settlement proved a necessity. Relying on the toughness, grit, and never-say-die attitude of individuals coupled with the tenacity of family ties, people formed hamlets and settlements. Staying close to family was a pragmatic decision, the common-sense approach to raising a family. Plus, family members often proved to be the best—at least the most trustworthy—set of hands a farmer or logger could find. Even if the relative wasn't much of a worker, the money made from selling produce or timber stayed in the family and, best of all, no stranger had to step foot inside the property lines.

To this day, pockets of kin dot the area, and locales become known for the families there. Longtime family surnames serve as street names, and the phonebook's list of names and addresses tells if past generations have known a certain place as home. In this way, town names, as much as any erected wooden highway sign, stand as historical markers of the region's history as a frontier. In Merryville, this history cannot be written without Franks, Eaves, Slaydon, Hennigan, Smith, Nichols, Stark, and the like filling the pages.

Like the small road to Grand's house, other small roads with churches and homes shoot off the main street. Houses speak for themselves, and what is outside talks about what is within. Anglers' boats, tarped and ready, stand poised on the sides of houses. Front yards will hold a kennel full of Walker hounds or bird dogs or curs; backyards might have a shed for the four-wheeler or hold a garden with peas, cabbage, tomatoes. Most homes have a place to sit outside. Some of what is made by hand (a bird feeder made from a gourd, a boot scraper, a rocking chair) will sit in plain sight. In town, if a person has land, relatives might set their trailer there and live close by. In the country, the place may be fenced in for a few cattle or horses or, long ago, sheep. Most plant any large tracts of land with timber, though a few plant corn or purple hull peas.

The mill hangs on the left as my wife and I turn into Grand's driveway, flanked by the great diversity of flowers, bushes, and trees and marking the boundaries of her yard. Beginning at the edge of the road, a wide conglomeration of trees runs down the left side of the driveway and forms the first of four sides of her yard's rectangle. The trees make a hard right, run the back of her yard, and end up marking the right side of her yard as well. We sit in the car a moment. On our left, trees and shrubs sprawl together, overtake a used-up tool shed, and climb a basketball goal—its pole textured with a variegated color developed from the etchings of rust and vine. Its backboard blackens with mildew. On our right, her lawn stretches out before us. In the front yard, a huge white oak and an elderly sycamore act as magnetic poles, one to the east and one to the west, pulling the aesthetics of the lawn in two directions. Near the driveway, a small redbud near the road and an unsure pecan tree—two moons—orbit around the trunks of the oak and sycamore.

In the small, ten-foot space that occupies the in-between of the driveway and the house's north side, various flowers vie for attention. Up along the house's front, one great azalea bush blossoms out, engulfing the house's yellow boards and white windows. Near the house's side, a grand hydrangea, grown from Grand's mother's plant, competes with a yellow lily. English ivy from an aunt's wedding invades the rich tradition of the azaleas. A small gardenia shrub (cape jasmine as they call it here) hides in the backyard, but the plant's sweet and syrupy fragrance pours from the rear, grits in the teeth, and gives away its position. A rosebush rests near the door and welcomes visitors. Through the seasons, this bush stays like Job and works like Paul. All the while, Grand prunes and shows off the flowers. In April or May, this yard blooms magnificently, but few manicured yards can challenge the forest's wild and raw beauty.

Once we get out of the car and go inside, we say our hellos over a cup of coffee. Grand has prepared salad, purple hull peas, and a small roast. We share the dinner and talk about the Christmas season that will soon be upon us. People know it is only a few weeks before the holidays really hit, and the anticipation makes people giddy. People have already decided to put up lights, so a few days ago, Grand, Melanie, and I planned a drive around to see a few local Christmas lights and a living nativity scene. Only days before, I finished my semester's final exams. Since I paid little attention to the holiday while swamped with coursework, I faced a few weeks of intense Christmas spirit catch-up. A Christmas trip to see lights around town seemed to be the perfect first step.

Over dessert, Grand makes me agree to drive her dark blue Crown Victoria. After another cup of coffee, we load into the car. We drive through town first. As we drive from house to house, we point out the beauty of this simple tradition. The residents break the night with blinking colored bulbs or delicate white lights or some combination of the two. Like the small town I grew up in and other small towns that I know, a few families' homes have developed reputations for elaborate or breathtaking displays and warrant a visit every year to see their holiday lights. Melanie and Grand figure most of the town will spend one night during the season on a drive to take note.

Churches, too, make their own rounds to see lights, as many churches organize hayrides for their congregations. Some members ride and sing and other members stay home to act as audience. All that folklorists have said about such rituals apply; the carolers symbolically beg for a food item, and in return the audience symbolically complies with a gift (hot chocolate and cookies), all the while solidifying social groups, marking cultural boundaries, highlighting values, and illustrating beliefs.

In the past, we would have driven to see the community Christmas tree or planned our drive to see the lights in town so the trip would fall on the night of the lighting ceremony. For ten, twelve, or fifteen years (people can't quite remember), the local book club sponsored a

"Community Christmas Tree," and a large portion of the community participated in the event. The club placed a cut tree in the courthouse and accepted dollar donations to put a light on the tree in memory of someone. Near the end of the season, the club organized a program to light the tree. The choirs of several Baptist churches, the Pentecostal Church, and the Methodist Church performed, and people visited after the songs. Recently, interest has died down.[2] Put on by individual local churches, live nativity scenes replaced the community tree and attract people in cars and on hayrides. Instead of seeing the tree, we drive to see one of the live nativities, and on our drive we pass near the Sabine River.

A few months ago, colored by autumn, the leaves formed a kaleidoscope on the woods' dirt floor. By winter, the ground had crusted over with the brown leaves. If chill never hits quite right or for long enough, some trees hang on to green for the entire year, while their bedfellows shed off every dead thing that is a part of them. The red oaks, birches, willows, and others lose varied lengths of themselves, from leaves to finger-length twigs to arm-long sticks to whole sides of trunks. A foreboding conglomeration of rot and decay reigns below the trees. Like outlaws, legends, and even the past, ice hangs on longer in the cover of the thicket than anywhere else. When a frost comes in, amber, sienna, rust, and nearly every shade of brown reflects and refracts through the thin ice sheets, deepening the textures of leaf, bark, grass, stem, and tree. On these early winter mornings, deer will flash up off the bank of the river into the cover of subtle browns and the bone-pale shades of yellow and green.

But seasons along the Sabine mean many things. In the summer, families will waste weekends on the Sabine's stark white sandbanks edging its brown water. Mothers and fathers watch children swim. Children forget boundaries and swallow water in small swallows and gulps. Teenagers drive out in pickups and secondhand cars, meet friends, carry out ice chests and food to the river's edge, and swim or boat ride up and down the river. The water in most places usually runs no more than thirty feet, but in the middle of the river, ten, twenty, or thirty feet down, swift currents run and steal support and stability. The water's push washes out sandbars and yanks the river's formations from memory. When there's rain and the river rises, the water removes chunks of the bank, leaving a river birch, black walnut, or some other tree unearthed and fallen. Soon, the whole tree loses itself to the river, catches on the bottom somewhere downstream, wedges there, and haunts the water.

Caused by currents and debris, deeper sorrows trouble the residents who swim the river. Friends, neighbors, uncles, cousins, mothers, husbands, wives, fiancées, children: they have all been taken by the quick shift of sand at the river's bottom or something dangerous submerged. In this town and in towns up and down the river, nearly everyone has lost someone to the river. Its sandy bottom can wash away in a second. Its strong current constantly deceives swimmers. "Go with the current. Do not fight. Ease your way to the bank, and then grab hold." This is what people are told for protection. But who would not fight, especially here? And who would go with this water? Despite the danger, people still swim, ride boats, and hunt along the river. Despite the losses, time after time people wade in the river, sink waist deep to enjoy what it holds. Despite the danger, people make a living from what hides beneath the water. People winch prized black cypress logs from the river's bottom and sell them for a nice profit. Some figure a buried treasure lurks somewhere out there. Some want nothing more than fish or turtle.

The river has run in many directions, and old bends and false rivers remain as testaments to this. Some search out these small false rivers, old portions of the Sabine cut off from the main river. These sections, kept hidden, remain curved oxbows dense with fish. People prize these places, held as prime fishing spots, not only for the lunkers waiting in the bottom but also for the quiet thinking space they offer. Some people even find themselves pushing their chests through the water: arms extending from their sides, floating on the surface; their hands—palms down—skimming the dark water flowing by them; their body moving slowly, gingerly, as if each step were a danger, a discovery. In fact, that is what each step is—an exploration. Each planting of a foot reveals the secrets hidden along the bottom.

Some people know to move toward a stump, a tree trunk, a buried log they have explored before. They move toward a cypress, water reaching three feet up its trunk. They know to use their feet to inspect the base. Beneath the water, roots of the cypress curve up out of soil and then plunge down into it. As a result, a small pocket rests between the base of the trunk and the river's silt bottom. When people find these sorts of trunks, they have found what they have been searching for. They draw their shirts or towels or sacks from around their necks, push them beneath the water, and stuff them around the backside of the trunk. They use the fabric slowly to encircle the tree, close off all the openings but the one right in front of them. In this way, they make a cage. They slow themselves, control their entire bodies, bringing each individual motion into one fluid movement. Their whole selves turn into one smooth, flowing assault on the prize.

The fish remain perfectly still, and age after age the fish have learned to remain like this until the last moment. They have learned that to remain hidden earns safety. The fish will not move until fingers squeeze around their bodies or until they, thinking hands are great meals being served, strike the hands nearing them. Then, the sunken catfish thrashes, whips its tail, throws itself forward through the water. People who know pull the fish from their lairs and take them home. They hang them from a line or tree, pull off their skin with pliers, split open their bellies, filet them, fry them, and enjoy what this close connection to the river brings.

Melanie, Grand, and I aren't out for something so adventurous; still our route crosses the river. We come near the river as we drive around the town to see the lights. In this dark, it is massive and beautiful. A night's drive to see Christmas lights and nativities, though, cannot last. Christmas passes. We spend New Year's Eve chasing away night with fireworks and bonfires. In February, winter closes as basketball reaches its peak. That year, one of Merryville's varsity basketball teams makes the Lake Charles paper.[3] "Lady Panthers: Pride of Merryville," an article with a team photo and three columns, fills two-thirds of a sports page. Much of the article deals with the play of the team, but some of it says something more: "Times have been a lot better in this small sawmill town in southwest Beauregard Parish. Like the days when the mill boom of the early 1900s actually gave rise to Merryville, which is still the only other incorporated town in the parish outside of DeRidder." Then the article plummets to the problems of the present: the timber boom over, the oil boom busted, the tourism boom never quite exploding, even the added troubles of political scandals and the loss of a hospital. The author explains that a small town like Merryville gets its identity from its high school, and for now the girls' basketball team will do as a nice boost to the ego. The article lets the coach chime in, "You know what, they just don't want to lose, it's as easy as that. They will do everything they can not to lose." The author follows the coach's words with her own, "Just like the town itself."[4]

What can be said about a place in the space of a single newspaper column? What about a book-length study? I am not certain, but I do know that that year's basketball team played tough, and every girl played hard. A few girls made scoring look easy, and fans of the basketball team loved every minute. The girls seemed as fierce as panthers, and the town took great pride in it. Perhaps the writer is right, "a small town like Merryville gets its identity from its high school."

Time and the river always move, as do the seasons and colors around them. The basketball games end. With green, March and April and May break the dominant shades of red and brown. Once spring comes on, the woods thicken with leaf and vine. Trees that remained standing through the winter turn with vigor. The tops of trees unfold. Shoots and buds solidify. Beneath the trees, other more vibrant colors follow as the black-eyed Susan, goldenrod, Saint-John's-wort, and other wildflowers spread.[5] Out along the roadside or rooted in the railroad's bank, buttercups range free and thistles turn thorn and weed into flower.

The banks of the river, timber tracts and family lands, the town itself: underneath all this a low buzz reigns supreme. Frogs chirp in rain. Doves coo in morning. These bursts, though, add only treble for the insects' bass thrum, and the low vibrating tingle of insect becomes the great denominator of place. All the seasons hold the sound, but the music during the heat of the summer bellows the longest and lowest. Mosquitoes hatch out in the marshes, in still ditch water, in old tires. They hatch and swarm into town. Cicadas click out in the trees. June bugs rap on screen doors. Bees hover around ligustrum, jasmine, or some other sweet flower. Crickets cricket, and beetles beat their wings.

Residents take note of the sounds and colors of the natural world. So much of life here connects to the forest and river.

The water and timber, as do the high school and cemetery, help create the place's identity. They define the town's sense of place. Sound, weather, season, and all the other aspects of the region factor in. People attach meaning to the landscape surrounding them; their traditions involve and evolve from the environment.[6] Place directs their lives, modifies their memories, their histories. In the end, their sense of place directs their lore—shaping legends, artifacts, songs. Eventually, landscape, history, and belief coalesce into these tangible products. Leather Britches Smith, a notorious local outlaw, stands at the place's center.

CHAPTER ONE

THE SABINE RIVER BOTTOM SWAMP

In 1803, when the United States purchased the Louisiana Territory, the American and Spanish governments contested the western boundary.[1] Due to a treaty ratified after the Louisiana Purchase between Spain and the United States, this section of Louisiana experienced a brief period (about fifteen years) of military inoccupation. During this time, the area went by many names: Louisiana's No Man's Land, the Free State of the Sabine, the Devil's Play Ground, the Backdoor to the United States, the Neutral Zone, the Neutral Ground, and the Neutral Strip. This frontier region drew the attention of the adventurer, the rugged individualist, the opportunist, and the outlaw. The dynamic state of the area's frontier and the lack of order during the area's limbo created an intensity of family and clan and shaped its inhabitants' view of the world. Here, people praise the indispensable qualities of survivors (strength, size, and grit) and the tools of survival (a good dog, a good gun, and a good set of hands). Nowhere is the praise of the qualities higher than in an outlaw legend.

This topic arose one day while I watched a game of ragball—a softball with a nylon cover. My wife, Melanie, hails from Merryville, and when she still played, sometimes I sat in the bleachers and watched.

We were dating then and didn't have any children, and she still made a few trips from Lake Charles back home to Merryville so she could play the game she loves. The sport was somewhat new to me, not being from Merryville or the Neutral Strip. Of course, I had watched softball games before, but I never held a ragball until I dated a girl from Merryville. That July weekend was one of my first experiences watching a ragball game. Darrell Hieronymus, a history teacher at Merryville K-12 and my wife's former supervising teacher during her requisite student teaching practicum, sat next to me. As we chatted, I described my interest in local history and folklore. He smiled as I talked; then, he said, "You must know about No Man's Land. This area holds a special place in history." I sat there entertained as he explained the area's captivating record of the past. Next, he asked a simple question, "Have you heard of Leather Britches Smith?"

"No," I said.

"You should have. He's a fascinating figure—Merryville's most famous outlaw." He explained that Leather Britches Smith, an outlaw from East Texas, arrived around 1910, which happened to be the same time Merryville experienced a timber boom. People flocked to the area; timber mills flourished. Soon, though, mills brought unions, and the unions brought strife. For some reason that I can't remember now, my conversation with him ended as abruptly as it began, and I didn't hear the rest of his version.

Considering the casual nature of the conversation and the story's clipped form, a person could easily dismiss the whole affair as trivial. Folklore deserves close consideration, and dismissing even seemingly inconsequential stories people tell—how a place earned its name, what their first day on a job was like, a personal encounter with a ghost—can be a mistake, especially for one interested in history, culture, or community. These small stories often provide insight into people's lives. They can link to the past and they can express complex psychological beliefs. Ask people what they believe, and usually meaningless, rehearsed stock answers come dribbling out. Ask people to tell a story about a day they never will forget that has changed the way they live, and their true beliefs come bubbling to the surface.

Folklore doesn't automatically mean old and untrue; in fact, it rarely does.² Much of the knowledge disseminated through folklore has undergone rigorous tests. In a manner of thinking, every time people choose to pass on a bit of information, they weigh and judge its worth. For example, people pass down the use of the toothache tree because people have tried it, and it works, not because it doesn't. People spew proverbs in certain situations not only because they always have, but also because life has taught them such truisms are so. If we examined the routines of our daily lives, we would find folklore extending to nearly every aspect. When the daily activities link to the past, they become all the more important. Folklore, at its best, is traditional and incredibly current. Years later, I would come to realize that the talk with Darrell Hieronymus was both. That exchange in the stands served as my first brief introduction to Leather Britches. I would not think of that short conversation again until the following December.

The 1998 Christmas season in Louisiana came in as we all expected. The heat of the summer and early fall faded far enough into memory as a few cold spells swept in and stayed for a little while. Convinced of winter's hold, people kept their coats on coat racks stationed near front doors and stacked firewood on back porches. Since it felt enough like Christmas, people allowed the Christmas spirit to take hold of them. They shopped for presents, decorated their homes and yards, and threw parties. Expecting company, they also cooked, and they turned to those certain dishes reminding them of home and suitable for these holidays. That year, for the first time I spent Christmas Eve at my wife's family's celebration. Grand sat at the kitchen table, pleased that this year her family—even those daughters, sons-in-law, and grandchildren who lived out of town—came to her Merryville home to celebrate. A TV played in the living room; Christmas presents not from Santa Claus glowed under the tree. On the stove, a few large pots bubbled and filled the whole house with aromas this family associates with Christmas.

For me, as a child of a Cajun family, the thick scent of gumbo drifting through the house means cold weather and Christmas, but for my wife's family, a Louisiana family tried and true but a family in the western part of Louisiana and north of Cajun Country, chili comes with Christmas and the cold. I still remember this first Christmas Eve with her family, and I recall that moment as one of my first small experiences of culture shock. Years of marriage would mean many more: "Pluck" versus "thump," children being drug along to funeral homes versus being left at home, brown versus white chicken and dumplings, or, like tonight, gumbo versus chili for Christmas. I have to admit that their chili, hot and better than any chili my family has ever made, served as an admirable alternative to gumbo. I am smart enough never to complain about food a family member serves me, but I told my wife later how odd it was to be so shocked by what seems to be such a small part of the night. The following year, she would say the same about gumbo.

I ate two heaping servings right off the bat. Her family, like mine does with its Christmas Eve gumbo, left the pot on the stove over a tiny flame so the food stayed warm and ready. People had bowls when they first walked in the door, right after hellos. They had bowls much later in the evening after hours of talking and catching up, and they had another one at 1:00 or 2:00 A.M. when furious games of dominoes threw a hunger upon them. That was when I helped myself to my third serving. Each new bowl meant a new conversation, and I greedily took both. My father-in-law spent that morning hunting and planned to spend the next morning the same way, so part of the talk over chili concerned itself with how he fared.

A deer hunter with dogs, he ends plenty of hunts without a kill. If all goes right, the well-trained hounds grab a scent in the woods, track the deer, and run it through a trail a hunter has chosen to watch. More difficult than hunting on a stand, deer hunting with dogs yields even fewer results, but certain men in Merryville swear by it since the other methods deny them the opportunities to move around in the woods, show off their specialized dogs, and discuss all the best and worst parts at the end of the hunt. That day he didn't come home with a deer, but he still had a few stories to tell. Melanie asked about one of her favorite hounds, Bumper, an old red Walker hound with a legendary nose. Story after story followed: the deer killed that year, the times people called on Bumper to find a deer dead somewhere in the woods, someone's first hunt, someone's last, the best hunters who have roamed this area.

"This place was full of wolves and bears. Goob told Ralph Ramos [a local reporter] how he killed a ton of wolves, and Kit Carson talks about coming in here and killing a slew of bears," my wife's father said at one point in the string of tales. That night was the first time I heard the name Goob Newton, but it would become as familiar to me as the name of Leather Britches Smith.

Grown, Goob stood as an imposing figure, even though he was not a very big man. Instead, his wiry body that had seen its share of work and the gleam in his eyes struck people, impressing upon them a desire to give Goob his due respect. At seventy-four, his legs bowed from years spent on a horse, his walk slowed, his back stiffened, and his face ran with lines etched by time spent in the weather.[3] Unfortunately, Goob died before I could ever meet him, but stories about him circulate to such an extent that I suspect many who have never met him still know him. People still describe Goob's skill as hunter and woodsmen. They tell that he was an expert wolf hunter, a person who knew the "old ways," and, perhaps most importantly, an individual versed in many of the events constructing the town's history. They remember Goob's skill at telling stories and know him as a gifted storyteller, one who could and would tell nearly everything his eyes had seen. People loved that about him, and if he strayed a bit from the truth or embellished and exaggerated a bit for effect, they forgave him for it. They would just smile at his genial nature and say he could lie like anyone. With his own kind of flair, Goob told hunting stories, related incidents from his childhood, recounted the town's most important events, and regaled folks with tales of Merryville's most notorious characters. Hunters, loggers, speculators, lawmen, outlaws—all sorts of people occupied his stories. In his string of tales, these people inhabited the woods, lumber towns, turpentine camps, frontier homes; they participated in wars, industry, politics, tragedies. Goob witnessed it all, even Leather Britches Smith, a legend Goob told most vividly and one that cemented his reputation as a talker and, for that matter, probably Smith's reputation as an outlaw.

"Goob would tell those stories, too," my wife's father said. "You know, Goob would tell me about Leather Britches and all that, all the outlaws in this area."

Goob Newton, as a boy, knew how to get along in the woods and in the streets of Merryville, which in the early 1900s stood as just about the most bustling city one could hope for in this part of the world. The huge fertile tracts of timber in East Texas and Central Louisiana, especially the cypress stands down in the Sabine River bottoms, drew various people to the area: from the North timber speculators in new suits; from Fort Smith and beyond families with new dreams, sharecroppers and tenant farmers in search of new jobs and opportunities, lawmen who carried new Colts and new laws, and various badmen and outlaws looking for a new life or new opportunities.

"Yeah, they had a lot of rough people here . . . outlaws, gunfighters . . . just some rough people," an uncle added.

Melanie's brother, Marshall, jumped in. "This place was called No Man's Land because it was such a rough place."

The folklore of the region, including the legend of Leather Britches and the cycles of stories Goob told, emerge from this reputation of the region. Many residents know this reputation, and some of their self-perceptions derive from this awareness. In the talk over holiday meals, after church services, or during other occasions when people have the time to visit, like a Christmas gathering, I hear bits and pieces of this rich folk tradition—a part of the region's identity. I hear the typical boasts and praises of rugged individualism and the narratives of hunting deer or wild hogs or even foxes. I listen to the spoken chunks of a family's saga and the narratives about memorable locals.[4] I stand mesmerized as I hear the legends recounting how outlaws crossed the Sabine over and over again, back and forth from Texas to Louisiana, all the while moving to keep out of danger.

Not only have these outlaws crossed into the region for the prize of a good hiding place, but also folks have come for other equally valuable pursuits, such as land, timber, oil, and—perhaps its greatest and grandest store—its wealth of lore, including the Smith legend. That's what Ralph Ramos, a Texas reporter and local historian who crossed the border himself now and again and interviewed people from Louisiana, came in search of when he left Beaumont and East Texas and crossed the Sabine . . . when he knocked on doors, set up his recorder, and collected the stories of the longtime residents of the Neutral Strip . . . when he interviewed Dave Burges, Arch Slaydon, and Goob Newton—who all mention the dangers of the Neutral Strip and Leather Britches.

Born in Ashtabula, Ohio, Ramos did everything from wrestling to reporting before he ultimately ended up in Beaumont, Texas, around 1950. There, he settled in as a roaming reporter for the local paper, the *Beaumont Enterprise*. In this position, Ralph Ramos spent time traveling eastern Texas and western Louisiana collecting reports of hurricanes, heat waves, bear hunters, and "humble, suffering citizens," as he puts it.[5] He used most of what he collected to fill his columns, and his columns filled the pages of the *Beaumont Enterprise*. His work immensely popular, Ramos eventually turned to writing books, the first being *Rocking Texas' Cradle*.[6] The printed work (a 262-page book published in 1974 and organized in short chapters of narrated remembrances) documents the memories of "those survivors of early East Texas or their nearest descendants."[7]

During the 1970s, Ramos produced about seven articles about Leather Britches, and even today when other local papers run a story about Smith every ten years or so, many reporters return to these early *Beaumont Enterprise* articles.[8] In these, Ramos attempts to retrace Smith's past and determine his real identity. They also offer an answer to two local mysteries: the identity of the person who placed a headstone for the outlaw's grave in a local cemetery, and the identity of the person who places flowers on the tombstone each year. One article also includes a sketch of Leather Britches reproduced from a photograph preserved in the wallet of an old bounty hunter. At the culmination of his work on the outlaw, Ramos reports that Leather Britches was more than likely a man named Ben Myatt who killed his wife in Texas and fled to Louisiana for safety. In his final article on the subject, Ramos explains that descendants of the union men Smith protected marked and maintain the outlaw's grave.[9]

The articles stuck in scrapbooks and the book placed on bookcases, Ramos's work endures in the minds of residents, and when I come to hear what they know about Leather Britches, people often pull his book from the shelf. When I went to the home of eighty-two-year-old Granny Cat, she like many others directed me first to Ralph Ramos: "I looked for it [a book written by Ramos] and I can't find it," she says.

"I got a book that Ralph Ramos, and he's [Smith] mentioned in one of these articles. And it was written on him."[10] Usually, however, they offer this book with reservation, typically insisting that Ramos failed to include some detail or simply made some mistakes.

One day I sat in my office at school with a college sophomore from the area. She told me her grandmother's reaction to the Leather Britches story Ramos wrote.[11]

> My great-grandmother loved him [Ramos]. She loved his stories. . . . Whatever he said was the truth. [She pauses enough for my recognition and then she begins to speak right above a whisper.] Until he was talking about Leather Britches and he wrote the businessperson's side of it, which was a horrible person who terrorized families. She knew him and that was just [she stammers but can't do anything but put it plain] bullshit. And she never read anything he ever wrote again.

In another example, during one interview a man began his story mindful of Ramos's work. His feet on an ottoman in his front room, his body planted in his recliner, his back tilted just enough off the chair's back to guarantee that I remain engaged in what he has to say—the man started his account of the outlaw, "We don't really know who he was. Ralph Ramos . . . claimed that his name was Ben Myatt and he was [from] around somewhere near Clarksville, Texas. But there's no proof to that." People may start with Ramos's work, but they have their own bit of information to tell and often feel strongly enough about it to share.

Sometimes tellers debate dates or facts or small details, sometimes they doubt Ramos's knowledge or his desire to be accurate, and sometimes they resent his one-sided depiction of the events. Frequently, tellers simply build off his collected accounts, or only refer to them before moving to their own version. In these personal versions, along with the outlaw's exploits tellers emphasize which past family members knew the outlaw, how a family's own saga connects to the Smith legend, and how these relatives contributed to the area's history during that same time.[12] Even when people take time to correct Ramos or simply state that "he got it all wrong," they make a statement about their connection to the legend and about the legend's importance in their lives. They prove they care about the legend and care enough that someone gets it right.

To be fair, Ramos did not have Leather Britches as his main concern in the book, especially at first. A Texas reporter, he wanted to focus on early Texas settlers. His newspaper articles do focus on the outlaw, but in them, Ramos searches for the "actual legend" or the "true story." He cares less about what every person has to say and more about what those he views as credible know.

My efforts, however, focus on discussing something beyond the "true" story, though that pursuit holds value. Chasing something beyond the "true" or "definitive" legend, my work considers many versions, treats them as equally true and accurate, and focuses on the variations in them. The benefit is twofold. Since the legend exists in multiple versions, the legend functions in multiple ways and communicates multiple messages. Theoretically, variation facilitates the communication of multiple ideas more than a single "verifiable" narrative of the outlaw's life. Second, by examining multiple versions one can see which details exist universally and which emerge on an individual level.

One afternoon a few years after that Christmas, I encountered a tiny piece of local family history connected to Leather Britches and indicative of the region's cultural consciousness. Melanie and I had plans to meet a woman whose deceased husband had known something about Leather Britches. We met at the library. The woman said she was reluctant for us to come to her home, but after we visited a while, she told us she felt better about us. (I think she wasn't too sure about me. I suspect somehow on the phone I made the planned conversation seem too scary or academic.) We visited only briefly. She explained that her husband had known all about this stuff, but she just didn't know much. She did pull out a cassette tape she wanted us to have. Her brother-in-law (actually her ex-brother-in-law, which might explain why she had so little information about all of this) knew a band that made an album with an interesting song she wanted us to hear. Before she came to the library, she made a copy of the original for us. I copied the cassette jacket on the library's Xerox machine and thanked her over and over again. Before the interview was over, she realized she knew my wife's family, which I also think made her feel a little better about me. By the end of the interview, she apologized again for not having us over to her house. We couldn't listen to the tape in the library, but when Melanie and I heard it in the car, it blew us away.

Aptly entitled "Leather Britches," the song on the cassette she gave us features Sam Pruitt as lead vocalist and appears on *Something Old—Something New*, recorded and produced by Pruitt Productions. The woman I interviewed didn't have much information about the band, Sam Pruitt, nor the events that led up to the writing and recording of the song. Her brief story seems to be that Sam Pruitt, who produced the album in Georgia, traveled through the region, heard the legend, and became enamored enough with the story to turn it into a Southern rock ballad. Finding any more detailed information about the song or Pruitt proves difficult, but the song's text stands as all the information one really needs.

> *In the western part of Louisiana,*
> *way down near the Texas line,*
> *folks tell a story about old Leather Britches,*
> *a man that lived down there one time.*
>
> *He was the biggest, meanest man, Lord,*
> *that always got what he want.*
> *He was the ugliest thing that ever crawled up*
> *out of that Sabine River bottom swamp.*
>
> *He walked up to a preacher's house;*
> *he was hungry one day.*
> *He shot two chickens, told that preacher's wife,*
> *'You better cook them, girl, or you better pray.'*
>
> *He had a twelve gauge on his shoulder*
> *and two .44s on his hips,*
> *and everybody knew you didn't talk back to Leather Britches*
> *or you didn't give him no lip.*
> *They tell how he went down to Grabow,*

when the sawmills all shut down.
When the smoke cleared away in less than fifteen minutes,
forty men was dead on the ground.

He was the biggest, meanest man, Lord,
that you ever saw.
Some folks say he had a brown bear for a mama
and an alligator was his pa.

Sheriff tried for a long, long time
to track old Leather Britches down.
They searched through swamps; they searched down the highway,
but Leather Britches couldn't be found.

And then one day he was walking down
the railroad tracks leading into town
and the sheriff and his men were laying hid in the bushes,
and they shot old Leather Britches down.

If you ever travel the South Land
and you happen to pass this way,
in the small town of Merryville in Beauregard Parish
there old Leather Britches lay.

He was the biggest, meanest man, Lord,
that you ever saw.
Some folks say he had a brown bear for a mama
and an alligator was his pa.

Leather Britches he was mean,
the meanest man you've ever seen.[13]

The song does more than recount the Leather Britches Smith legend. It touches on the wildness of the Sabine, of the Neutral Zone. It hints at the influx of outlaws, and the prominence of the timber industry. In other words, the song connects to many aspects of the region's culture. In a sense, the song does exactly what the Leather Britches legend does. It becomes a repository of knowledge, a catalog of events. Of course, Smith's legend recounts his life, but it does much more than that. Smith's legend exemplifies the region itself. It expresses the core values the region holds.

In addition to Leather Britches, adventurous explorers, remnants of Jean Lafitte's privateering crew, rugged pioneering families, and even other outlaws on the run—all of these characters appear in legends told in the Neutral Strip. These legends and stories, in turn, create the perception these people have of themselves. People take pride in their family's toughness, a great-grandmother's fighting spirit, or a grandfather's skill as a gunsmith. Even in a song full of exaggeration, the residents' awareness of their history and toughness seems clear. In this way, the Neutral Strip remains. It persists through each change of season, each birth and death, each boom and bust. As it does, the place through its lore continues to celebrate strength, grit, knowledge, loyalty, and survival. The rivers, trees, and soil—place and space shape it all.

CHAPTER TWO

---·✦·---

MEANNESS, JUST ACROSS THE RIVER

A few days later, Melanie and I found ourselves with plans for another trip scheduled for the days between Christmas and New Year's. Grand decided taking a trip to Newton, Texas, to see the Christmas lights was in order. During any typical Christmas season, some people in Merryville will decide to cross the Louisiana-Texas border, "the River" as they say, to see the town lights of Newton, the county seat of Newton County, Texas. This trip exists as somewhat of a local Christmas tradition and seemed to be my initiation rite. My acceptance of chili as a holiday meal no doubt won her favor. Hearing of my interest in Leather Britches Smith, Grand also decided I should talk to a few people in town versed in "all about the history of Merryville" and bound to know some of the details surrounding the outlaw. We drove for a while, and then we came to the border. We crossed the Sabine to head over to Newton. Even at night, we could feel ourselves crossing and could see the thickets of growth teeming off its banks.

Many places right off the river are swamps or thickets with a fair amount of vegetative diversity: black willow, river birch, others from the beech family, swamp black gum, red oak, white oak, red gum, swamp red maple, cypress before most of it was cut, and pine (the indigenous varieties of longleaf and loblolly and the fairly recently introduced variety of slash pine).[1] Especially in the section of river running through No Man's Land, swamp vegetation or dense brush flourishes on much of the riverbank and provides plenty of game for hunting, choice opportunity for hiding, and impressive natural defenses.[2] These special sections of woods close to the river remain, and in them, growth has somehow held on to the past or convinced the people around them to preserve the past there. The Sabine River, especially because it still holds parts like these, may be even more important to the region's cultural landscape than the timber or the pinewoods.

The river basin runs about three hundred miles. It stretches southeasterly through Texas, and turns at Logansport, Louisiana, to head south to the Gulf of Mexico.[3] Currently, the Sabine River acts as Louisiana's and the region's current western border.[4] The river, however, has been a prominent landmark before its official status as a boundary and even before European settlement helped shape the area's distinct contemporary folk culture.[5] Geographic borders may stand as legal markers, but they often function more prominently as mental markers, as powerful delineations of identity.[6] Often, people living on the "fringe of society" (I hesitate using the phrase) develop an identity from this experience.[7] They see themselves as isolated, sometimes even forgotten or excluded, but they also see themselves as independent, sometimes even adventurous and resourceful.[8] More importantly, they see themselves as split in two, as members of two communities, or as people who can operate in two worlds.[9] Equally civilized and untamed, simultaneously community members and isolationists, people here often move in and out of personal definitions.[10]

Since borders are often hostile, rugged, violent places, the people who cross them are often dangerous, rugged, and violent people.[11] The border the Sabine River creates is punctuated by danger and strife.[12] Violent tales of feuds and outlaws use it as a backdrop, and horrific stories of drowning and murder employ it as a setting.[13] Personal narratives have loved ones crossing it to escape a bad marriage or find a new start. As a rite of passage to mark a person's crossing into a time of independence, a teenager sometimes will make his or her first unchaperoned trip into Texas. The river, as a result, becomes a crucial part of these residents' lives.

The Sabine's long-standing and symbolic role as a line in the sand—one side ensuring punishment and the other promising freedom—tied Smith to its banks. In the past, when facing a crime, outlaws crossed the Sabine from one jurisdiction to another as a sure way to avoid capture. The river offered a similar safe haven for Leather Britches Smith. Many claim Leather Britches to have been a Texas outlaw who crossed the river to escape justice and, on some occasions, crossed back into Texas during his career to escape pursuers in Louisiana. In fact, one person, using the area's own brand of border logic, perfectly explained the relationship between the outlaw and the river: "Of course [his meanness] followed him across because it's just across the river." In this way, Smith and the Sabine connect; the legend and the landscape intertwine.[14]

This intersection begins with the controversy over Smith's start. As is the case with many outlaws, Smith's actual identity—his true past and his real name—sparks debate, and conversations about Smith often speculate about it. Was he really from Texas? Was he Ben Myatt, already wanted by Texas law for violent crimes? Did his meanness follow him across the river? Answers vary, and in these accounts of the outlaw's life, possibilities abound about his actual name and past. In them, even his nickname inspires controversy. Some say he was a simple drifter whose past cannot be traced. Others claim him to be Ben Myatt who adopted the alias Leather Britches Smith. Some think his real name was Charles Smith, who simply had Leather Britches as a nickname. Some people say Charles Smith was Ben Myatt's assumed name. Still others think Charles Smith, since it is obviously a common name, is an assumed name as well, and the unidentified outlaw simply added Leather Britches to this already fake name. Finally, some go as far as claiming another Leather Britches established an infamous reputation, and this unknown Louisiana outlaw simply adopted the name as a sort of pre-advertised calling card. Whatever the case may be, Leather Britches must have been an alias or a nickname, and Smith, sufficiently common for an outlaw, means nothing and easily could have been adopted. In the end, residents will agree that "he picked it up [the name] up" and that "he was on the run whoever he was." If he did cross the Sabine River because of crime, even if he brought his violent disposition along with him, he surely did not want to tote along his identity. If the outlaw had to flee his home, of course he would have chosen an alias, like Leather Britches, and as an alias, Leather Britches isn't all that bad.

Most people, even if they have an idea of his "real identity," understand that the outlaw's origins are mysterious, and remain so. The enduring mystery of the names *Leather Britches* and *Smith*, however, connect to something much larger and more relevant than a debate about identity. The names themselves label the figure as an outsider, an essential component in his raison d'être. People in the present may want to link him to an actual figure, like Myatt, but more importantly, they want to connect him to Texas, mark him as someone who does not belong. Smith and his nickname accomplish this, and more people know him by his nickname, Leather Britches Smith, than by any other name (such as Charles Smith). Labeling him as an outsider or even as an unknown, the name purposefully separates him from the community and ties him to the border. As a result, the name exists as a significant marker of identity for the people in Merryville.

Once, the subject of his name came up in an interview with a woman, a librarian by trade, whose approach to knowledge involved research. She said, "You can look up *leather britches* on the Internet also, and it's a type of leather pants and loggers would wear them because they would protect them against the woods."[15] On a separate occasion, a hunter and logger acquainted with the woods of Texas and Louisiana speculated about his name. The man said, "I figure he wore shotgun chaps, is what I think, which that was common in Texas, and over here, the woods were burned. There wasn't any need for chaps; people didn't wear them."[16] I trust his ideas. He knows the woods and knows the timber industry, and his logic seems sound. To make his case even stronger, he clarified it: "That's just pure speculation. Somebody told me one time that his pants were so greasy that they were like leather, but everybody's pants were greasy in those days. So I think that maybe he wore buckskin." Walking through the thick briar, brambles, and brush of the eastern Texas wood (now identified by the government as the Big Thicket National Preserve), a person might wade a sea of saw grass or tangles of thorns and nettles. If this person needed to navigate these sorts of woods for a living, protection for the legs would be standard-issue uniform. Burning the woods eliminates the heavy undergrowth and the corresponding need to wear leather. As these two interviewees noted, the type of pants connects the figure to place, so the nickname becomes a symbol laden with information and meaning.

These speculations seem incidental, but they touch on a relevant portion of Smith's identity. Of course, the name signals him as an outsider; it associates him with Texas—the land on the other side—and its practices. In addition, it labels him as a rough man. Dressing ready for navigating the woods, he can drift into it at a moment's notice. The name speaks to his familiarity with the forest. Wearing leather chaps on the legs becomes a symbol as potent as donning a silver star on the chest. The chaps mark the wearer as "wild" as much as the star marks the wearer as "civilized." Even though people may debate the outlaw's "real" identity, the name Leather Britches endures, and does so because it functions as a symbol. The debate about the outlaw's name indicates the passions people have about the legend and their personal variants of it, but the figure's lure merely begins with his name.

Along with his real name and his clothes, residents concern themselves with his weapons, potent symbols of his character as well. "He wore two guns and he had a shotgun, too, that he carried," a person told me. Almost everyone can picture him, each person's imagination colored by Goob Newton's famous description hanging in the air: "He'd walk into Merryville with all those guns (two .45 Colt revolvers and a .30-30 Winchester), and no one bothered him."[17] Others describe the figure as a man riding across the landscape with a rifle on his shoulder—a lean five foot ten inches, a force to be reckoned with, a man always armed, a hand deadly with a gun. Still, people counter with, "All that's bullshit. But enough people were scared of him to want to kill him." That last part is undoubtedly true. Folks feared what he was capable of. People knew the outlaw to be deadly and on the run. From where, people are not exactly sure, though they have their suspicions.

As one might expect, an outlaw's first crime, the crime that leads him on the dangerous path, functions as a crucial part of his life and portion of his legend. In the life of a good outlaw (a heroic criminal), the outlaw-hero's first choice to engage in crime usually stands as an act of retaliation.[18] As the story in any good western relates, an oppressive system looms above the figure, and its evil, greedy, lustful agents perpetrate a crime heinous enough to drive a "good" man bad. Rape, murder, considerable theft, even slander or libel can ruin this man's life enough so that no choice remains except payback—violent, bloody, relentless, as extreme as the very provocation. For the community to accept such vicious retribution, the oppressive system must drive the outlaw to a life of crime. First, if the outlaw openly chooses this life, he becomes more a killer or murderer than a heroic criminal. Second, his descent into a life of outlawry must be a social commentary on the oppressive forces at work or, at the very least, on the lack of order or goods or equality this system has created. The outlaw legend must not be a deterministic statement about the inescapable miserable lives of the poor; it cannot be proof that all is lost. Instead, the legend of the outlaw-hero must be a message of possibility for the common man.

In fact, the legends of outlaws become statements about ordinary people as much as proclamations about outlaws. Throughout most outlaw-hero legends, an ordinary man, or more precisely a common man, engages in warranted "illegal" action and by this, directs morality and exhibits true justice. In this sense, the heroic criminal—a common man driven to a life of crime—offers an alternative to an "upstanding" life of conformity, an alternative to a life of complete acceptance. His first crime also reminds listeners of the rugged individualism a frontier life required. The frontier civil and legal structure frequently included ordinary citizens acting in some sort of official or regulatory capacity. Created through this system, the frontier justice system existed as a folk justice system. As necessary as townsfolk forming a posse on occasion, the outlaw-hero must take the law into his own hands. If not, a just system here might never be established. Sometimes someone needs to live outside of the law to make the right things happen. So ingrained in the American mind-set, the idea stands as a cliché.

Like other outlaws, Leather Britches Smith's origin entails violence. About that, most agree with Granny Cat, one of the first people I interviewed about Smith. With a book in her lap, she rocked in her chair and said that he murdered his wife and fled. More bits and pieces follow from other people: "One of the things that he did, he killed his wife across the river. They tell me that he put her hands on the hot stove then killed her. Whenever you crossed the river over here, that was a long ways away . . . he carried his rifle with him all the time."[19]

Other versions I have heard about his start connect more directly to an oppressive system. In one version, a major economic setback and the greed of corrupt politicians drove him to a life of crime. During an election, politicians spent money and time liquoring up voters to loosen up their votes. "The politicians had furnished everybody all the drinks they wanted, he got his share, and he killed his wife," one person explained to me. During that time of electioneering, Leather Britches killed his wife, but the act was not completely his fault. The person went on to accuse Smith's wife of unfaithfulness and blamed his temper on drink, which the politicians irresponsibly supplied. As has happened to so many good men turned bad, women and whiskey did him in. In some versions, Leather Britches Smith's start did not really begin here; instead, his real trouble, the crime he must flee persecution from, occurred a week before the election.

Mrs. Ester Terry told me the most elaborate description of Smith's past.[20] Her work as a member of the Beauregard Parish Historical Society and her family's connections to Leather Britches supply her reports with interesting, crafted detail. I interviewed her a few times, once in front of an audience. Depending on the situation, she could vary the delivery of her narrative and the breadth and depth of her content. In front of that audience, she took a deep breath and unfolded a long story. She said, "They say back there in Fort Worth as long as he didn't have a drink, he was . . . a good man. But the minute that he started that drinking, he stopped and he went crazy." She explained that Smith, on another bender, killed a man named Cook since "Mr. Cook had stolen some of his cattle and was not punished." Once caught, Smith faced trial against an eager young attorney, Tom Connelly, wanting "to make a big name for himself." Connelly convicted Smith and won the death penalty, but by some miracle or some secret deal, Smith escaped—or was let out[21]—and headed across the Sabine. In one of Mrs. Terry's accounts, Smith's brother put the outlaw in a box and shipped him to Monroe, Louisiana.

In her narratives, several details about the outlaw's life in Louisiana before Merryville surfaced. She told me that after roaming the Louisiana woods, Smith ended up in a small lumber town and engaged in a clear-cut battle between the common man and an oppressive system. "This lumber company had a boss that was mean to the men and ugly to the men," Mrs. Terry explained. "He worked all right two days, but at the end of the second day he decided he'd just whip the boss, which he did. He whipped the boss and had to leave that place in a hurry." The story ended with Smith finding his way to Merryville, a timber town about to face its own labor struggles, a town on the Sabine River border, a town that could easily recognize and use such an outsider. Even though people still debate his actual name and past, even after hearing Mrs. Terry's enthralling version, people are quite sure about the nature of this outsider from Texas, and they are positive "his meanness followed him since it's just across the river."

Driving across the river's bridge into Texas during our trip to see the lights at Newton's courthouse, I thought of the tangible border the Sabine creates. Before I crossed the bridge, I saw a roadside historical marker near the bridge: a dense wooden sign with bold white letters, "ATAKAPA TRACE JUNCTION." The sign stood ten feet from the road. I read the information placed on the sign meant to commemorate the uniqueness of the place: "Portions of historical Atakapa trails connecting their S.E. Texas bands ('Sunset People') to the S.W. Louisiana bands ('Sunrise People')." The Atakapa believed that before time began the first man came from the sea, rising through the depths inside the shelter of an oyster shell. The arrival of Europeans must have seemed as miraculous as a giant oyster shell rising from the ocean depths. One of these Europeans was Cabeza de Vaca, a dark Spaniard who lived with the Atakapa south of the Caddo and brought with him great sickness. With the coming of de Vaca, a great many Atakapa grew sick and died until their numbers thinned. Atakapa numbers would never recover. Did a great oyster shell return and take these people back beneath the sea?

Indigenous people in the area, especially the Caddo to the north, knew the Atakapa to be an isolated people, and even though their numbers thinned rapidly from European disease after contact, the Atakapa people continued to fuel rumor and speculation. In fact, then and now people circulate sensational tales about the Atakapa's unusual reputation, including the belief that they were cannibals. Somehow, in the region, this belief not only flourishes but also seems celebrated, intensifying the region's historical and current reputation as a dangerous and rough place.[22]

To the north, Caddo territory, land that now includes Natchitoches and its surrounding area, neighbored Atakapa territory. In their origin myths, the Caddo people looked to the sky. They believed that people began with a woman who had two daughters. One day, one of these daughters became pregnant, but a monster came and devoured her. Fortunately, her sister escaped, and she managed to save a drop of blood from her pregnant sister. The surviving sister placed the drop of blood into an acorn and buried it. Two nights later, a grown man sprouted from the ground. This man, her nephew, defeated the monster and then took his grandmother and aunt into the sky. From the sky, these people ruled the world.[23]

The Caddo face—possessing high, pronounced cheekbones, a large nose, a broad mouth, and substantial ears often made even larger by the weight and space created by wearing earplugs made of white oyster shells—and the Caddo's coarse black hair further burdened a head already hefty, round, and planted flatly on the shoulders.[24] Renowned hunters and fishers, they knew the area well and often traveled with supplies, such as a knife kept on a thick strap of leather strung over the shoulder, the band falling across the chest and the small knife pocket at the strap's end hugging the hip. These people, too, saw the Sabine as a fundamental component in defining their lives.

Sturdy and stout from a diet of fish and game and colored like the silt-rich water of the Sabine, the Caddo ruled the area for many years. In leather pants and open-toed sandals, they maneuvered through the thick underbrush of the Sabine and controlled much of this portion of Louisiana. They knew the animal trails through the woods, the speed at which a man can travel the same paths, the likelihood he could meet others when taking those paths. Eventually on these paths through the woods, the Caddo met strangers who came for gold, dark fertile land, and even roads to other places rumored to hold even more gold than the strangers ever imagined finding here. The Caddo showed the strangers more of these animal trails; as a result, many European settlers came to the area. For a time after meeting these strangers, the Caddo, descendants of the ancient Sky People, continued to rule; but as stranger after stranger came to them, strange objects, strange ideas, and strange changes came as well.[25]

Even though Hernando de Soto died before he could reach the Caddo in Louisiana, his men made the first true inroads into these indigenous people, and told other Europeans how to retrace their steps. When LaSalle met the Caddo, he explained to them that he claimed all the land touched by the Mississippi River for God, King, and Country. Sick of travel, the never-ending wilderness, and, more than likely, LaSalle's haughtiness most of all, his men killed him on the other side of the Sabine. Henri de Tonti came to the Caddo people looking for LaSalle, but instead of returning LaSalle to France, he sent back only his copious journals detailing his interactions with the Caddo. The Europeans grew more intrigued. Soon, Louis Juchereau de St. Denis arrived and made quick friends with the Caddo. They taught St. Denis many secrets about surviving in the woods, and St. Denis taught them how to trade salt and livestock with white men. St. Denis and men like him began erecting structures, Fort St. Jean Baptiste aux Natchitos (established in 1714); the Caddo no doubt found these structures strange. Soon Caddo land filled with other strange men who had guns, married Caddo women, and did not leave. In response to St. Jean Baptiste aux Natchitos, in 1723 Spain erected La Presidio Nuestra Señora del Pilar de Los Adaes nearby.[26]

For some time, governance of the area's land and its people became a difficult situation. Disputes about certain borders and boundaries occurred, and tension increased. Of course, both governments wanted possession of the Sabine River Valley, and they vied for control over roads and trading rights in the woods. Navigating a neutral space between these two factions, the Caddo people—many claim under the instruction of St. Denis—began to follow their old trails and clandestinely transport fur, guns, and horses between the two outposts. Eventually, the very ground between the two became a sort of neutral ground, a buffer zone between the two militaries.[27]

Creating a buffer zone is an ancient military tactic, and in a multitude of other situations, various governments have employed the strategy. They pull out maps, sketch out a certain area, and mark it as neutral territory.[28] On different occasions, Spain tried it in the United States to set a distance between true Spanish interests and American expansion. Often American Indians—who acted as natural deterrents, almost fortifications, to stem the tide of Anglo-American growth—inhabited this land, like the eastern portions of Louisiana or the western portions of Florida. These types of barriers, however, lacked a permanency and, perhaps more importantly, persuasiveness in the minds of American settlers and the American government. Hence, they failed in stemming American expansion, even if they were (and sometimes because they were) reinforced with indigenous people.[29]

Though other sections of America, including those created by other countries, served as neutral territories throughout American history, this small area in western Louisiana, the small piece known as Louisiana's Neutral Strip, provided the most defined and most notorious buffer between America and Spain. Many reasons make this so, but these reasons begin with the land's history long before America came to be. As the Caddo experienced, this section of Louisiana Territory changed hands many times, and this interchange colored its reputation as a barrier.

When LaSalle claimed the region for France in 1682, the French government vied to control it. In typical French fashion, trappers and traders populated it, making inroads with the local people and establishing an early French presence. Spain, having its own territorial possessions near this section of Louisiana, fortified nearby claims in order to protect existing boundaries. Then, in 1754, when France allied itself with Spain and declared war on Great Britain, the ownership of the western portion of Louisiana became ripe for a shift in ownership. France's involvement in the Seven Years' War proved disastrous, for among its many lost possessions in the Peace of Paris in 1763 was "La Louisiane." As the century turned, Spain and France once again formed an alliance. When Napoleon became its head, France sought to reassert its claim to Louisiana.[30] Spain's weakening position as a world leader necessitated its transfer of Louisiana back to France, which occurred in the secret Treaty of San Ildefonso on October 1, 1800. Later, however, Napoleon's plans for Europe put France in need of money, so the country decided to sell Louisiana to Jefferson's emissaries, James Monroe and Robert R. Livingston.

As officials ironed out the details of the Louisiana Purchase, negotiating its final touches, this long history of transfers caused problems. Treaties overlapped with others, a fact due to a course of innocent mistakes and deft political maneuvers. Ambiguous boundaries spelled out in these treaties hampered a clear determination of the Louisiana Territory's exact boundaries. Officials found the boundaries of Louisiana south of Natchitoches especially problematic. The trouble with defining the boundary began long ago in the muddy waters of the 1783 Peace of Paris,[31] and when the Louisiana Purchase occurred in 1803 (signed in May and ratified in October), Louisiana's exact western boundary south of Nacogdoches in Texas and south of Natchitoches in Louisiana remained in question.[32]

Jefferson brought the full force of the American legal system to bear on the issue. Jefferson's first claim considered Louisiana ending at the Pacific . . . then the Rio Grande . . . then the Colorado . . . then at least something west of the Sabine. Spain believed it still held the Florida territories . . . or at least all of current Louisiana . . . or then at least Louisiana to the Mississippi . . . or at least to the Mermentau . . . or at the very least to the Calcasieu. The debate dragged on for years after the document was signed.[33]

As ministers pored over the tedium of official documents and as lawyers and cartographers marshaled forces to persuade each side's claim, dispute over land ownership manifested itself in the movement of emissaries and troops throughout the area. After France sold the land, loyal residents still held that the land was truly France's and they still truly French, but many residents felt no real allegiance to France. Of course, each government, American and Spanish, considered area inhabitants to be its citizens and under its control; in turn, each government wanted these inhabitants to swear allegiance to it. Some residents in the area felt little impact on their day-to-day comings and goings and thus reckoned the shifts in power irrelevant; however, the governments themselves considered ownership of this land an important matter.

Despite Spain's official position that it controlled land in Texas and

Louisiana, it sensed the loosening of its grip on Louisiana and fretted that Texas may be lost as well if precautions were not taken. In efforts to hold back the wave of white settlers and protect Texas, a territory it still considered too dear to lose, Spain began bolstering its claims: employing emissaries, building forts, and negotiating secret deals. Tensions rose. In comparison, America, eager to place its next stepping-stone west, began promoting settlement in the area by issuing grants, establishing its own forts, and making its own set of secret deals. Conflict escalated, the debate intensified, and both sides turned to military action to intensify their claims to the region. Open war seemed imminent. In fact, at one point the Sabine River acted as the only thing separating the two sides from actual conflict, the only barrier preventing war erupting between the Spanish and American forces, the first led by Lieutenant Colonel Don Simón Herrera and the other by General James Wilkinson.

When Lieutenant Colonel Don Simón Herrera planned to cross the Sabine River to fortify Spanish claims, he carried something with him and dragged something behind him.[34] Of course, he carried his rifle, his *espada ancha* or "wide sword," and his official orders. He also lugged behind him his command of 600 militiamen marching at his rear, men sent to him by Commandant General of the Interior Provinces Don Nemesio Salcedo to manage the Louisiana frontier and impose Spanish control over its rightful domain. The command of men, especially in such a number, weighs upon a man, but the pressures placed on Herrera by his superiors intensified his military burden. To that end, Herrera carried with him the concerns of New Spain. Long before Herrera was sent to the frontier, Spain became aware of America's appetite for new territory and of American explorers and frontiersmen continually making forays into the Louisiana frontier. Spain went to great lengths to maintain its claims on the area and tried desperately to find expedients to stop the influx of Americans. Various Spanish officials alerted Spanish governors in the region of the situation and encouraged necessary generals to be at the ready. Spanish towns in the territory scrambled to bolster forces, even if strengthening an armed presence meant equipping townsfolk. The viceroy of New Spain repositioned troops from the interior of New Spain to the frontier and used New Spain's forces as a bulkhead to fend off American incursion and stand against what seemed to be an impending American thrust for territorial expansion. Moreover, he placed capable leaders to command these current troops and to muster more support.

Officials of New Spain first picked Don Sebastián Rodríguez to be one of these leaders, a leader to protect what in their eyes rightfully belonged to Spain and by right should always belong to Spain. The initial stage in the process involved stationing a large Spanish force of more than 1,000 men at Nacogdoches, Texas. Then, the Spanish government ordered Rodríguez to go further than Nacogdoches, drive west of the Sabine. Patrols, pushing as far as the Arroyo Hondo, swept the frontier. Forces made camp. Military officers arrived in frontier areas claiming towns and placing residents under the dominion of Spain. In Nacogdoches, Rodríguez himself issued a proclamation that criticized the "greed and pride" of America, claimed that America had declared war, and called every settler to his duty as defender of the Spanish kingdom. This act proved to be quite costly for Rodríguez, especially after suffering a few military defeats. As one might expect, in response to these boasts American forces grew anxious, and open conflict grew dangerously close. Commandant General Salcedo berated the current governor of Texas for his trust in Rodríguez and admonished Rodríguez for his brashness and failures. In an effort to ease tensions and avoid war, Salcedo sent several apologies to America. To make his point quite clear, he court-martialed Rodríguez. To defend Spanish interests, he sent Hererra to the frontier. Herrera carried this knowledge with him as well, a heavy burden indeed.

Soon, Lieutenant Colonel Don Simón Herrera, poised on the west bank of the Sabine, confronted General James Wilkinson on the east. Both men commanded an impressive number of men, but both held reservations about entering into armed conflict. Wilkinson, burdened with command and the concerns of his nation, faced Herrera and his troops camped around Nacogdoches. When Wilkinson found himself and his troops bunkered in at Natchitoches, he, like Herrera, carried something beyond his usual gear. Wilkinson felt the pressures of manifest destiny and the weight of Jefferson's prodding and American interests. However, Wilkinson's own interests seemed to weigh more heavily on his mind than any other load he bore.

Wilkinson lugged a heavy past, one complete with a private education and tutors, with a career in medicine to take up, with the future prospect of a steady medical life, with the tedium and boredom he knew it all possessed—with a life that he knew did not suit him. For Wilkinson, proud and ambitious, medicine seemed too dull, too average, and too unlikely for the history books. Military service during the American Revolution, however, did offer the adventure and the recognition he craved.

Starting as a commissioned captain, he rose quickly to the Secretary of Continental Congress's Board of War, thanks in large part to his friendship with General Horatio Gates, its head. Sadly, that friendship soured. Rumor had it that Wilkinson spread rumors about Gates. Forced to resign, Wilkinson quickly found another position in the service. Yet again, Wilkinson resigned from that post under suspicions of improper conduct and financial irregularities. Wilkinson then decided to retire temporarily from American service, so he took a position with Spain, though he never quite delivered the service he promised (to promote Spanish interests at the mouth of the Mississippi in return for a monopoly on trade there). In 1791, Spain removed him from service.

In 1792, he returned to the American military as a brigadier general. More intrigue followed, but Wilkinson escaped real damage to his reputation and continued to regain his power.[35] In 1806, commissioned by Jefferson himself to deal with the Louisiana frontier, Wilkinson carried this past with him as he sat in Natchitoches and planned his next moves to remake the name he made for himself.[36]

Wilkinson decided that the best course of action for the Louisiana frontier (and for him as well, as it so happened) would be to prevent conflict from occurring between the forces at Natchitoches and Nacogdoches.[37] Instead, he supposed his force might be used in New Orleans. Besides, victory there would better aid his cause of making a name for himself. Wilkinson believed that rebellious forces (nearly 10,000, he would tell interested parties in foreign governments) inhabited New Orleans. Those forces planned to overthrow the government there;

then, the forces intended to conquer Vera Cruz, an important Spanish possession. Quelling this large band of rebels would mean prestige and esteem from both America and Spain. He described this very plan in a letter sent to the viceroy of New Spain. In this case, Wilkinson's shrewdness, skill, or even luck on the battlefield would not determine if his career or station in life would improve. Instead, his ability to eliminate the entire battle itself would bring greatest gain.[38]

Neither Spain nor the United States desired open conflict. Too many other concerns pressed both sides. In Herrera's eyes, the Spanish force seemed too poor to win a sweeping victory. In Wilkinson's opinion, the American force would maximize its usefulness quelling an uprising in New Orleans. With both countries unwilling to jeopardize their positions and a tad unsure of victory, they agreed the best course of action was a diplomatic one. The piney frontier was a nagging pain, relief coming only if, for the moment, the contested territory could be kept neutral, so they removed all signs of military presence and formed a commission to settle the matter.

On November 5, 1806, General James Wilkinson and Lieutenant Colonel Simón de Herrera agreed to the creation of the Neutral Strip. Instead of fighting or even meeting personally, Herrera and Wilkinson deployed two junior officers, Joseph Maria Gonzalez and Captain Edward D. Turner, to form a commission to determine the exact boundary of the strip and to execute the orders that all troops from both sides be removed. The act left the region unmanned and, for the time being, officially neutral.

In this meeting of the minds, no one drafted an official map detailing the exact boundaries of this neutral ground. No one needed to. The land had been contested for some time, and soldiers and commanders for both sides knew how far in the area one could travel before growing too nervous. The governors of Texas and Louisiana, the United States Secretary of War, Spain's Commandant General of the Interior Provinces, and especially Herrera and Wilkinson knew the entrenched nature of certain claims and the uncertainty of others; and despite the far-reaching claims of both sides, the debate boiled down to a specific area of contention. The agreed-upon neutral space existed between the Sabine and two smaller rivers, the Arroyo Hondo and Calcasieu. The

Gulf of Mexico served as the southern boundary and the thirty-second parallel of latitude as the northern. Spain extended the region twenty miles west of the Sabine River. This area comprised the official neutral ground between the United States and Spain and essentially ended the potential for war between the two countries.

Interestingly enough, the act not only created a military buffer but also a region of possibility and individuality. Residents became isolated, and since the United States and Spain for the most part left enforcing laws in the hands of the settlers, law became the responsibility of the region's inhabitants. This way of life infused the inhabitants with individual determinism. As people policed and governed themselves, they became their own means of self-definition. Often, this meant a self-image imbued with rugged individualism and a region known for lawlessness. For many, even to this day, this brief period created by the 1806 compromise would be the primary cause of the region's infamous reputation.

Even though both governments did not allow new settlements during this period, squatters and settlers—Spanish, American, French, and other groups—moved in, which forced both governments to form several expeditions to expel these unlawful tenants.[39] Outlaws seemed to make their way to the neutral ground as well. Eventually, John Quincy Adams and Louis de Onís of Spain developed a treaty. The Adams-Onís Treaty of 1819 (sometimes called the Florida Purchase Treaty of 1819) decided that ownership of the strip went to the United States. Almost without exception, the official dimensions of the region followed the current boundaries between Louisiana and Texas. To this day, these boundaries also remain in the minds of residents.[40]

The Adams-Onís Treaty, however, did little to stop the influx of squatters, capture criminals, or provide a stable military presence in order to police the region effectively. Later, Fort Jesup, established near Natchitoches by Lieutenant Colonel Zachary Taylor in 1822, would serve that purpose for a quarter of a century. In that time Fort Jesup would have many functions, including the job of clearing the region of outlaws.[41]

Ultimately, this unusual course of events that occurred on Caddo land—treaties not involving the Caddo, wars quite removed from them, and the immigration of new strangers—decided who would rule it, and it would not be the descendants of the Sky People. When new strangers called "Kaintucks" came, they cared little for Caddo rights and their territory. A few chiefs realized immediately these new people signaled the end of Caddoan rule in this wood.[42] More than the Spanish and French residents had, the Kaintucks and other Anglo settlers found it more difficult to share land with the Caddo.

Pushed by the encroaching Americans, the Caddo lived in agitation. Beset by many problems, the American agents at Natchitoches tried to keep the Caddo away from white settlements, so they moved Caddoans from Natchitoches to other areas in Louisiana. The new rulers of Texas also would not let the Caddoans in Louisiana trade with their old cultural partners, the Sunset People in Texas. There was a time when Caddo people compared their numbers to the limbs and the twigs of a great oak, but as the incidents in the neutral zone began to be governed more and more by the United States, it became clear to them that those days were falling away like autumn leaves.

Soon Chief Tarshar, whose name means "wolf" in the Caddo language, sat at a table with other Caddo chiefs standing in back of him, with many white men standing in front of him, with two white men sitting across from him, and with a treaty spread out in front of him. In 1835, nearly 500 of his people gathered that June at the Caddo Agency, not very far from their own homes. The Treaty of Cession was before him. By signing it, the Caddoans would agree to sell close to a million acres for $30,000 in goods and horses and for cash payments of $10,000 per year for the next five years. Tarshar made his mark next to his name, and the many other chiefs followed him.

Even though many Caddo people and chiefs disagreed, Tarshar responded to criticism by saying,

> My Children: For what do you mourn? Are you not starving in the midst of this land? And do you not travel far from it in quest of food? The game we live on is going farther off, and the white man is coming near to us; and is not our condition getting worse daily? Then why lament for the loss of that which yields us nothing but

misery? Let us be wise then, and get all we can for it, and not wait till the white man steals it away, little by little, and then gives us nothing.⁴³

Immediately Tarshar led his people into Texas and settled on the Brazos River. Unfortunately, all the promised money from the government never did come, and the agreement never led to the peace and prosperity Caddo people envisioned. Eventually, these people on the Brazos would be forced to move again, this time to Oklahoma. The few Caddo who remained in Louisiana, those refusing to follow Tarshar, left too. On the way to Oklahoma, many Caddoans learned this song, a melodic reminder about traveling at night to avoid Texas soldiers and other evil:

> "Redbird, redbird
> He got scared, he flew up out of the bush.
> It must be getting close to daylight."⁴⁴

As this song connects to the history and location of Caddo people, the legends of Louisiana's Neutral Strip—including its outlaw legends—connect to a place. They reflect the region's unique history and the residents' awareness of it. Residents retain ideas of what living in a neutral territory means, the nature of a place like that. A neutral ground frames the self-portraits hanging in their heads. Knowledge of their home's history helps to make sense of not only a past but also a present, a past that appears quite violent and a present that sometimes must seem bewildering. This seeking fuels an awareness of history; and awareness of history, a swelling pride in community; and pride, a desire to celebrate place. For this reason, much of the region's folklore, historical consciousness, or cultural landscape links to the place's past as a frontier and the qualities associated with that time.⁴⁵ In turn, this awareness directs even more behavior, which creates even more folklore, and the cycle perpetuates itself. In the end, a rather distinct community consciousness forms.

In Newton, a courthouse acts as center of the old town square, a town model that seems decidedly Spanish. White lights adorn the brick walls of the building. Neighboring businesses attach lights to awnings and sale windows, and luminosity envelops most of that central square. The lights in Newton do not disappoint, but my mind cannot leave the river and the legends it holds, especially the crossing of Leather Britches Smith, his trek through the Neutral Ground, and his arrival in Merryville, an arrival coinciding with the area's timber boom.

CHAPTER THREE

NO MAN'S LAND

In front of me, the area's culture stands as dense, thick, and impenetrable as the underbrush sweeping up and out of the Sabine River bottom. Perhaps I should expect nothing less from a culture of clash, a culture built on isolation, independence, freedom, and confrontation. People migrated to No Man's Land, for a time a border teeming with new enterprise, in search of all of these qualities. Though it may seem odd that people flocked to a dangerous region for freedom, No Man's Land stood as a promised land in the minds of some, as a land of few laws and great freedom. It stood as a place for striking out for a new life, starting new jobs, and settling new land. Plenty of people, though, also came in search of something a bit more ordinary—money. Travelers and residents alike searched for routes to New World treasures: lost Spanish silver, prized furs, Lafitte's gold, tracts of virgin timber, and even a waterway to the Gulf. Others came in search of the treasure of talk, and many came specifically for the legend of Leather Britches Smith.

During my own hunt for this treasure, I have heard many varying accounts of the Smith legend. Nowhere is variation more obvious in the Smith legend than in the oppositional beliefs about his basic identity. Negative opinions of him are legion, but some remember Smith in a positive way or at least have some positive comments to make about him, even though a person must listen a bit harder—or at least at the right time or to the right people—to find those stories praising or remembering his warm heart. Depending on the teller, Leather Britches might come off as a noble defender, a man who could be pushed only so far, or even a rather "normal" badman who transformed into his more violent persona only when he drank. Indeed, many tellers blame drink for his wrongdoings, but the outlaw's heart remains true. One once explained to me, "When he would get drunk he was crazy, and when he wasn't drunk, when he wasn't drinking, he was just a fine man, sweet and kind and good." Another said, "He was supposed to be a pretty good fellow as long as he didn't drink." One person added his own account, "Now, some people that lived down in there where he rode said that he was friendly to them." Most offered a more careful statement.

"Some people liked him, but most were glad to see him go" functions as a more typical comment that hints at the rift of opinion. When asked about her perceptions of the figure, one woman lamented Smith's reputation: "I have mixed emotions. So many people thought he was wonderful because he always took up for the underdog and he always fought for the little man . . . until he got that liquor. Then he was crazy. He was crazy and mean." Another person remarked, "Many women who cooked for him said that he was kind and considerate. He'd just walk in and throw them a chicken or something and tell them to cook it, and he'd go and come back later and get it."

I think the best example of hearing variation in the Smith legend occurred during a discussion with Shelley Whiddon.[1] I met Shelley the semester she was one of my students. We agreed to meet so she could tell me what she knew about Leather Britches. "I can tell you two stories because I have two different sides," she said in my office the day of the interview. To this day, one side of her family sees Leather Britches as outlaw and the other as hero. Some of Merryville's early settlers, Shelley's ancestors still form a prominent group in the town. Shelley takes pride in her family's toughness, her great-grandfather's independent spirit, and her grandfather's skill as a gunsmith.

After spending some time telling me that her father's side of the family was poor and had ties with the Industrial Workers of the World, she told me during her interview that her mother's side bought land here long ago and did not join with the Industrial Workers of the World. "The reason that my mother's side did not like him and did not listen to the good-story side of him is because he came in with the union," she said. She explained the situation: "My mother's family's side of the story is that Leather Britches was cruel, was mean, that whenever women's husbands would leave the house he would make them come and kill a chicken and cook it right in front of him while he sat there at the kitchen table until they were done."

Shelley knew that Smith was no saint, and she made a point of telling me that she wasn't a fool. Still, she was quite clear. She described Smith's interactions with workers, details she has heard from her father's side: "He came in and told all of the people that worked out in the woods what their rights were." Shelley explained the repercussions of such talk, then and now. She said, "It cost my mother's side of the family a lot of money because there were protests and there were strikes." Two sides of a family offering two variants of the story.

The duality causes one to ponder the motivations and emotions prompting such diverse reactions, and most definitely, this duality sparks many questions. I have heard many times before that some people loved Leather Britches and others hated him. Why? How did such opposite opinions form? Who felt compelled to pass this story down? Did the people who loved him want to prevent his deeds from fading into memory? Did the people who hated him want people never to forget the despicable man? Do these two depictions exist because the outlaw stands for something about the border? Does he mirror residents' self-perceptions that run deep in the currents of their minds? When these people are adrift in their psyches' black fathoms, do they use the outlaw to stay afloat? Is he a piece of flotsam that each person must climb onto so he or she will not sink in the eddying mix of settlement, family ties, history, and everyday living in order to form an idea of what living in the Sabine River Valley means?

The central division of the outlaw's status as a villain or hero, in part, derives from the weight of history and pull of individual tellers. Historical correctness acts as a significant force in the legend process, and the audience, for the most part, expects nothing less than a believable truth. So when telling the legend, the storyteller wants to get the story right. This desire to be correct or to be considered accurate by an audience—to be cautious about changes to the legend that would make it wholly untrue—contributes to the conservative nature of the legend tradition. In light of this principle, the continual retelling and the audience's reaction to each telling inform narrators which deviations are allowable. Those that are not will fade.

However, tellers also want to demonstrate individual knowledge, emphasize their special place in the community, or highlight a personal stake in the story. People's stories also convey their own worldview (their personal desires, fears, and values). These factors encourage tellers to insert themselves in their versions, and the personal details of a teller's life usually become a part of the version being told. The content of the legend, then, moves beyond the outlaw and the past; instead, the teller's present life, family, and private history occupy a place in the version. Past and present connect; individual and community intersect. All the while, each teller's desire to communicate the legend's core narrative balances each teller's desire to include additions and deviations that display individual storytelling skill and an insider's knowledge.

The same occurs in the variants of the Leather Britches legend. More than simply spoken sentences thrown away in the middle of a storytelling event, additions express beliefs and values through the details embedded in them. When people tell the legend, they reference relatives who lived during the time or participated somehow in the story. When they describe Smith's abilities, they often describe how these abilities affected family members. Detailing Smith's skill with a gun praises those skills they know their ancestors must have had. Deviating from the outlaw's actions to illustrate the grim living conditions of sawmill workers criticizes the lumber industry's greed and potentially hints at political allegiances. When they recount Smith's deeds or death, they include certain familiar components of the environment, thus honoring their environmental surroundings. Describing Smith's trip across the Sabine border emphasizes the psychological importance of the border. All the while, Smith becomes a more tangible and engaging figure as specifics of the locale act as backdrop. The Sabine River, the wilderness, the historical details—these components become emblematic of the popular cultural beliefs and border consciousness present in No Man's Land.

The legend of Leather Britches conveys the amalgamation of various borders, including geographic, ethnic, economic, and temporal.[2] For example, the residents of the Neutral Zone face not only geographic but also ethnic boundaries. The viscosity of the Cajun culture to the south borders much of the region, and the region's western boundary separates the region from the cowboy culture of Texas. By the nature of where they live, people in the Neutral Strip deal with very strong, identifiable cultures and boundaries; so in the end, the geographic borders may merely represent in a physical form the mental and cultural lines drawn in these people's psyches. The Leather Britches and other outlaw legends throughout the region embody these lines in the sand as these stories become representative of the residents' border consciousness—an awareness of a life split, liminal, marginalized, isolated. Time and time again, like one afternoon in the home of Ester Terry, I learned how the Smith legend combines with the region's lore and how the place spawns not only legend after legend but a distinct and poignant awareness of its history, culture, and isolated existence.

To meet with Ester Newton Terry, I made a right turn into the circular driveway of her home. A row of trees and a few large flowerbeds shielded the house from the road. Still, set off from the road a bit, the white house seemed inviting. My wife and I parked the car, walked up to the door, and knocked gently. The woman who cared for her—did a little cooking and tidying up around the house—opened the door. "Welcome," the woman said and began to walk us through the house. "Hello," Mrs. Terry called from another room. The woman led us through the kitchen to a sitting room at the back of the house. The woman stopped at the kitchen and gestured us through. I threw a silly wave and walked towards Mrs. Terry.

"Sit. Sit," she said, then stood from a small wooden table and walked over to meet us. The room's back wall, lined with windows, faced her back yard, and the mid-morning sun shone on the grass and through the windows. The furnishings were simple, and books were stacked everywhere—on the shelves, on a coffee table, in a basket between two recliners, piled by the table. Mrs. Terry was ninety-three, and she moved with a palpable grace as the three of us walked to the table and gathered there that afternoon to sit in the back room of her home and visit.

She was a thin woman, but she did not seem frail. Her eyes, deep-set and intense, fixed me not with fear but with a sureness, with a certainty in what she was saying so I would not miss a word. She was an assured woman, one who seemed sure of what she was saying and one that made me feel sure about listening to her. With papers spread and a plate of cookies stacked in front of her, she sat down at the table. She was still for a brief moment before she began speaking. She smiled and nodded as she spoke, moving her gaze between us, back and forth. She spoke to us in hushed tones, her voice difficult to hear, so we struggled all the more to keep up with her words and save them in our minds.

Even if my wife or Grand had not told me that this woman valued history, learning, and wisdom, I could have heard it in her voice, her choice of words, and her phrases about the importance of the Neutral Strip. Some would call Ester Terry a tradition bearer, a person endowed with a special gift for history and memory, a person burdening herself with preserving the past. She possessed a gift at recalling details and a flair for storytelling, though she referred to her brother Goob as the storyteller of the family. She reported information in a manner that made other people pleased to know it and desperate to hear it again. Proud of telling anyone, Ester Terry served the citizens of Beauregard Parish as an educator for thirty-six years, plus some. She was a teacher and a member of the school board, and when people wanted to know the weight of something in history, I surmise they often turned to her.

"This entire area existed as a neutral territory, No Man's Land, a fascinating place, full of action and sadness," she said.

Melanie asked, "What about the area? We have heard it called No Man's Land."

"Sure, No Man's Land. I suppose plenty of people came. I think a lot of it stayed here. I think some of it is still here. They got in here and nobody could get to them or touch them, and I think they all stayed. Get you some cookies and pass some. Y'all didn't eat any cookies. I'll take three. Some of it stays, I think."

I picked up a two-inch wafer cookie in my fingers. Though the plate of cookies was before me the entire time, I had not picked one up until she made it a point to remind me of them. I bit into the cookie, three layers of wafer stacked on top of each other and held together with a creamy filling. Chewing it, I thought about the mixture of the almost tasteless wafer and the potent sugary cream. The result, an unusual cookie that is not too sweet or too dry, matched Ester Terry since her stories balance the beauty of the area with its sadness.

"It wouldn't do for some of us to trace back our ancestors too far, not too far," she said.

Mrs. Ester Terry formed these very words with her lips and used them as the backdrop for her memories of Merryville, Grabow, Leather Britches Smith, and No Man's Land. No Man's Land—other people have expressed a similar awareness of the region as I sat in their homes. Family sagas and personal narratives include notorious historical locales, rugged pioneering family members, and the area's unusual pattern of settlement. Sometimes ancestors will have an intimate knowledge of infamous men. A person might say his grandmother or great uncle had coffee with Bonnie and Clyde. Another person might say that her great-grandfather came here from Texas for murder or from Arkansas for thieving. Another may explain that her family's black sheep crossed the Sabine for the Neutral Ground and went back to Texas each year to settle his grudges. Yet another might say that some distant relative settled in the area after serving the United States in the quasi-military employ of annexing Spanish land in Texas.

"I can't seem to get enough of these cookies," Ester Terry said. "Would you mind handing me another? I just love these." I picked up the plate, extended it to her. "I have so many things you would love to read. You're welcome to borrow any of this. I remember the pressures of school. Take this whole thing, this stack, and keep it as long as you like."

She waved her hand over a pile of papers on the table and then swept it over a stack of books on the floor she pulled from her shelves. She slipped one from the bottom of the stack, and the books toppled. They spilled across the floor until some lay flat and others, a tip caught on another, slanted up and down. Each one jutted up against another.

"Thank you. That's really nice of you," I said, then looked at the books spread out on the floor. I thought of the family of books laid to rest around me. Different sizes but resting side by side as they were, the books seemed to me a graveyard erected around the table. Town after town owns a story—a memorable event or unforgettable character. Legends circulate about small town after small town, outlaw after outlaw, family after family. In turn, book after book before me rested there as a memorial stone, a marker of some people's beliefs about this place. I imagined the books—two or three dozen of them with various inscriptions about explorers, outlaws, renegades, and interesting local history—to be tombstones and the row of them on the floor to be a family cemetery, a cemetery No Man's Land residents erect to the area's memory.

"This one's all about Lafitte," she said as she handed me one of the books.

Late in his career, Lafitte turned to the Neutral Zone and moved his base to this contested territory. As long as his exploits occurred in unclaimed lands and his profits came at the expense of the Spanish government, he operated with impunity from the United States. When he attacked American property, America responded with a naval force. Lafitte's crew disbanded, men settling God knows where, and Lafitte's end remained shrouded in mystery. Local belief holds that the Sabine's intricate inland waterways and the region's neutral status provided a fine final hideout for Lafitte and his crew, and in turn, people claim that banditry and privateering employed a fair share of early Sabine residents. Local legends extol the exploits of Jean Lafitte, and the promises of his treasures stretch all along the Louisiana coast and work their way inward, paddling against the current of the Sabine River. For many, Lafitte's gold remains hidden in the bayous and waterways that shoot off the Sabine. Local family sagas report ancestors who worked with Lafitte stashing treasure up and down the river, but never having the chance to dig any up before they died.

If a local buried treasure story does not involve the exploits of Lafitte, it usually involves another nefarious event. Other stories recall sunken Spanish freights or the loot of imprisoned outlaw gangs. Tales of buried treasure occur frequently in the Neutral Strip and, as in many other places, become important signposts of history and current values. They express the American notion of unlimited good[3] and the fascination about this place's settlement.

"Have you heard of Aaron Burr? This place has seen so much." She handed over another book.

This place has seen and felt a range of events and emotions. I recall her own words: "A fascinating place, full of action and sadness. . . . They got in here and nobody could get to them or touch them and I think they all stayed. . . . Some of it stays." One of the primary means of drawing inhabitants—the people who stayed—was the mid-nineteenth-century employ of filibustering expeditions.[4] The word filibuster then meant illegal attempts by political men to move into foreign territories, establish a foothold, overthrow the foreign government in the territory, and annex the land for either country or themselves. Many men, including it seems Jefferson, Madison, and Monroe, embraced the idea, considering it one cog in the machine of manifest destiny. As a result, filibustering became a political strategy along the Sabine after the Neutral Strip went into effect.

Aaron Burr advocated filibustering as a political strategy. Burr viewed the boundary dispute between Spain and the United States as a prime opportunity to ensure that his push for Texas was both successful and legitimate. As part of his secret scheme, he designed a purchase of 400,000 acres near the Ouachita River,[5] but the plan never came to fruition. Instead, he suffered charges stemming from the incident. Though at first he conspired with Burr in his filibustering efforts, General James Wilkinson foiled Burr's plan. As one of his initial steps, Burr planned to meet with General James Wilkinson;[6] instead, Wilkinson sent Major Walter Burling to Texas Governor Cordero. While miraculously not tried himself, Wilkinson testified against Aaron Burr,[7] and Burr was found guilty of treason (this charge was removed later). In a letter to Joseph Alston, Burr wrote, "General Hamilton died yesterday. The malignant federalists or tories . . . unite in endeavoring to excite public sympathy in his favor and indignation against his antagonist [Burr]. Thousands of absurd falsehoods are circulated with industry."[8] Wilkinson kept his position and post, Spain's opinion of him never higher.

The book also discusses Burr Ferry, a small town in the region. The town gained its name from Dr. Timothy Burr. Family legends abound about Burr Ferry's connection to Aaron Burr's attempt to annex Texas.[9] Facts place Dr. Burr in Louisiana roughly around 1805, and a Henry Burr, at the age of fourteen, died and was buried there in 1828. According to local legend, Dr. Burr was Aaron Burr's second cousin and a key compatriot in his filibustering plans. Dr. Timothy Burr came to Sabine River and Pearl Creek, established a community there, and operated a ferry at the location, which the family ran until 1927.[10] In western Louisiana, Dr. Burr built a replica of Aaron Burr's Richmond Hill home, and legends speculate that Aaron Burr planned on using the settlement as a launching zone into Texas.[11] A Burr family did operate a ferry in that spot for some time, but certain scholars question some of the area's lore connecting the site to Aaron Burr.[12] Not surprisingly, the Neutral Strip's image of Aaron Burr, as is the case with so many other ideas here, does not parallel ideas held by the rest of the nation.[13] Maybe it isn't all that hard to believe that in the Neutral Zone, the name Burr remains. A town still uses the name Burr Ferry; it even has an historical marker. People walk around today with the last name Burr strapped to their back, and some tell that they are descendants of Aaron Burr.

Lafitte himself had his own part in filibustering, but Lafitte did not completely side with President Monroe's emissary George Graham, nor did he completely agree with America's push to claim all of the Gulf Coast to the Rio Grande.[14] Alongside Burr and Lafitte, other likeminded men made Spain feel the pressures of Louisiana filibusters. A group of French patriots decided to make a push for Spain to provide a safe haven for Napoleon. Wealthy New Orleans citizens also pooled money to facilitate expeditions, and Monroe himself often employed filibustering for his and America's gain. Francisco Xavier Mina, using Galveston as a base, attempted to liberate Mexico from Spanish control. In 1819, José Bernardo Gutiérrez de Lara and Lieutenant Augustus W. Magee moved from Natchitoches with 150 men, rallied in Nacogdoches, and from Nacogdoches moved with a force of 300 men towards San Antonio, eventually holding that city for a time until double-crosses and greed destroyed the plan.[15] One could also cite the Riego Revolt in 1820 and the 1819 and 1821 attempts of Natchez resident Dr. James Long. All of these attempts, achieving different levels of success, ultimately failed, but these failed tries brought consequences. With each new filibustering attempt—each new promise of gaining Texas—came men and supplies. Some of these men settled and made their homes in the Neutral Strip, perhaps still endowed with a penchant for adventuring, pioneering, and individualism. In addition, this pressure intensified Texas's internal problems of revolt and rebellion, and the Neutral Strip's itchy trigger finger intensified

Another book Mrs. Terry handed to me tells the legend of the Great Land Pirate, John A. Murrell. "The Reverend Devil some call him," Ester Terry said as she passed me the book.[16] Legend has him roaming throughout No Man's Land as well. Horse thief, human smuggler, devilish preacher, scourge of the land, Murrell was famous. He ran a band of men and held a base of operations that spanned several states. Some argue about what kind of a thief Murrell really was, but in No Man's Land people seem pretty sure. Legends say Murrell even marked certain friendly homes, members of his "Mystic Clan," with yucca plants in the front yards. On a drive, a person can still see front yards dotted with yucca plants. Alongside this book, Richard Briley's *Nightriders: Inside Story of the West and Kimbrell Clan* recounts the deeds of another band of criminals—this one a group of townsfolk during the 1870s.[17] Pillars of the community—a mayor, a sheriff, many businessmen—offered unsuspecting travelers fine accommodations as they trekked through the area. However, in the middle of the night while these travelers (men, women, and children) slumbered in a ranch house owned by a local woman and man, John West or Laws Kimbrell or some other member of the "Nightriders" would waylay the travelers. The West and Kimbrell Clan stole whatever these travelers carried, killed them, and dumped the bodies in the wells of local farms. That's another tale rustling in the bushes of Louisiana's No Man's Land.

Other books detail violent events in the area's past: struggles pitting rich versus poor, people (white, black, Redbone, Cajun) versus people, newcomer versus entrenched squatter, owner versus worker. In each, to resolve certain disputes folks took up arms and started killing. These wars or fights or battles, whatever the place has come to call them, exist between one side and another and sought to settle some issue in the most effective, most expedient, and/or easiest manner available. Webster Crawford's *The Cherry Winche Country: Origins of the Redbones and the Westport Fight* (1993)[18] relives the tension existing in this culture of clash by describing how entrenched settler came to blows with encroaching newcomers in the Westport Fight.[19] Manie White Johnson's *The Colfax Riot of April, 1873* (1994) describes the Colfax Riot between blacks and whites.[20] *Schooner Sail to Starboard: Confederate Blockade-Running on the Louisiana-Texas Coast Lines* (1997) considers Confederate blockade running on the Louisiana-Texas shoreline.[21] The Conner Feud, the Grabow Riot, the revolts, and even the local shootouts between two families or simply between two men warrant books in a place like this.

Thin paper covers enclosed some of the books I carried away from Ester Terry's house. As I held the stack of books in my arms, I imagined these books, the ideas in them, stacking in people's minds, in Ester Terry's mind. The books occupied a place in the deep recesses of her psyche, created a weight she carried around with her until that weight came to bear on everything she told me that day. This knowledge burdened, if only by the ounce, every thought she possessed about this place.

After we left Mrs. Terry's home, we drove to a gas station. I took the books off the car mat and placed them in my lap. I picked up each one, looked at the title, then shuffled it to the bottom of the stack. Louis Nardini's *No Man's Land: A History of El Camino Real*; Luther Sandel's *The Free State of Sabine and Western Louisiana*; Don C. Marler's *The Neutral Zone: Backdoor to the United States*; Ralph Ramos's *Rocking Texas' Cradle*; Sam Mims's *Rio Sabinas*; Ross Phares's *Reverend Devil: Master Criminal of the Old South*; Glenn Crockett Price's *Founders and Scoundrels: History of a Town*; *The Cherry Winche Country*; *Nightriders: Inside Story of the West and Kimbrell Clan* . . . the litany of titles weighed on me, too.

Voices from the books run through my head. I go into my mind again and hear their stories. The author of one book says, "The Neutral Ground became a catch all for much of the riff-raff of Louisiana and East Texas. . . . Men from God-knows-Where flocked to this genuine no-man's land."[22] Another explains that the area "became a haven for a group of thieving, murderous men who had left more civilized places for the good of all concerned."[23] Another adds, "It was a back door to the U.S., a stepping off place for all kinds of smuggling and outlawry known to mankind."[24] Local history after local history intensifies the region's self-awareness. One states, "With the announcement of the treaty, outlaws from several states saw the area as a haven for their kind. By treaty no one could pursue them and the area was wild enough to provide a hiding place if they did."[25] Another chimes in, "One of the most lawless places that ever existed within the confines of the United States. A person's security was strapped at his hips or carried in his hands in the form of pistols, long rifles or knives."[26] Again and again, one hears the same. "Here every man was his own protector—the Bowie knife, muzzle loading rifle, and the pistol were common place," one explains.[27] "Bandits killed the men, robbed them of their horses and mules, baggage and money, crossed and recrossed the SABINE River to do their deeds of terror," another writes.[28] The voices make clear the spirit of the place, the lure of the Neutral Zone, and the historical consciousness of the residents.

These types of books—the books written by a local historian or compiled by local organizations, the books sold in local bookstores and at display tables in community museums, the books with paper covers and illustrated with local black and white photographs—thinly veil the people's impression of the area.[29] Of course, these books take different approaches to the subject. Emphasizing specific events and geographic locales, some authors choose to outline the actions of local characters, especially those whose actions mirror and promote the harsh, violent world that surrounded them. Other local works, more extensive, map the activity of the region: giving broad overviews of regional characters and legends, providing detailed descriptions of geographic nuances and occupations, and recounting important (often tragic and violent) events. Some rely on standard historical data and others on collected stories. Regardless of the approach, each author provides his or her own viewpoint of the intimate relationship locals developed with the region's rugged landscape and tumultuous history.

These local histories examining regional strife or rough times or those concerning famous badmen or treasure sites celebrate the residents' lifestyles and identities sparked and supported by the region's particularity. More importantly, they also celebrate the residents' perception of place. A certain self-awareness becomes obvious as one examines the local histories present in the region. Local authors provide a revealing insider's view of the place, especially concerning how these people view themselves. By grouping these esoteric productions together, certain recurring types of folklore become apparent. Outlaw legends flourish; buried treasure stories thrive; family sagas extolling pioneering ancestors litter history books; and personal narratives exhorting rugged individualism abound.

I hear Ester Terry's words again: "A fascinating place, full of action and sadness. . . . They got in here and nobody could get to them or touch them and I think they all stayed. . . . Some of it stays." I hear these words and think of the legends of buried treasure, the ghosts that haunt them, the families sworn to keep secrets, the people buried because they didn't. I hear these words and think of outlaw legends and local feuds. I hear these words and people's stories come to me. Again, I hear tales about No Man's Land, hear stories about remnants of Lafitte's crew staying on in some place along the Sabine after Lafitte and the rest of his crew moved on. I think of those former members of the crew making families, and whole families keeping ties with Lafitte. I repeat the details about outlaws as heroes, men as murderers, ordinary as border crossers. I hear the people's voices.

CHAPTER FOUR

SHOT A CHICKEN'S HEAD CLEAN OFF

When my wife and I heard the news, we talked softly about the good times we had with her and what we remembered most. My wife knew her far better than I did, but we both had plenty to smile and laugh about. Still, when we heard that Ocelean Fuller had died, we mostly talked about our amazement. By all accounts, Ocelean Fuller walked the Earth a remarkable woman. She slapped down dominos with the best of them. She fished up a storm. She was a better shot than a great many folks and could keep up with her brother whose reputation as a hunter spread a good ways. She paddled out at midnight to trap and kill alligators. She tended a little garden. She worked many a full-time job. She raised her boy alone after her husband died. She lived in a little house on the bank of the Sabine River nearly her whole married life, and she knew nearly every way to get along in those waters. She was tough and sweet, quiet but not timid.

The Sabine River must miss Ocelean the same way my wife and I do. So familiar to the landscape, they both seem indispensible parts of Merryville. Melanie's aunt called to tell us about the funeral arrangements. On the day of the funeral, we started the drive from Lake Charles to Bon Weir, Texas, a town just across the Sabine from Merryville. We left Lake Charles and headed north, driving up Highway 171 through Moss Bluff, past Topsy and Gillis, across Highway 190, through Longville, past the Oakdale turnoff, until we reached DeRidder. We drove by the Woodlawn Cemetery, a Dairy Queen, nurseries, and a few antique shops and flea markets. We reached the edge of downtown DeRidder and crossed the railroad tracks to hit DeRidder's center.

Like so many places in this area, DeRidder arose from the intersection between timber and railroad. The landscape, the rich game, the tall pines, and thick stands of hardwoods drew settlers long before the railroad came through the area and long before this place became a town; however, a dream changed the woods into a town. Arthur Edward Stilwell possessed that dream, a railroad man's dream to build a railroad from Kansas City to the Gulf of Mexico. The idea came to be known as the Port Arthur Route, the shortest line connecting a vast storage of exportable American meat to the open waters of the Gulf. This line, a mere extension of some of the existing lines, would promote trade, spur progress, and guarantee prosperity. Cattle, corn, coal, oats, rye, cotton: these and many more products, essentials of the American economy, could ease over land to the great engine of the ocean, the very shores of enterprise. From Kansas City to Joplin, from Joplin to Stilwell, from Stilwell to Mena, from Mena to Texarkana, from Texarkana to Shreveport, from Shreveport to DeRidder, from DeRidder to Port Arthur, and from Port Arthur to the Gulf of Mexico—the Port Arthur Route meant business.[1]

The cup of Arthur Stilwell overflowed with passion and dreams, but that cup ran short of money. In 1893, Stilwell's dream met the dry throat of a financial crisis, a crisis sweeping through the whole country. People began cursing the year, hacking and spitting as they spoke its name, The Panic of 1893. First, the money flowed a little slower and those in the know figured it best to save a little here or there. Jobs dried up. The next project waited a while, openings delayed. Bosses let people go, wages fell. With less in their pocket, if they had anything at all, people paid less, bought less. In town, no work meant buying no food. On farms, no demand meant no need to move the food. Too much rotted away and no money was to be made shipping it, so it rotted. No money meant buying no more seed, no fertilizer, no fuel, and it meant no need in planting more food. Prizes rose to squeeze out every penny. People made less and products cost more. Then workers mobilized. Coal miners, gold miners, dockworkers, stockyard workers, even railroad workers decided to strike. Demonstrations, marches, and speeches popped up around the country. Everyone sought something to wake up the fat cats, change the ebb and flow of money, get things moving again.

Gold and silver fell. The money held in the hand turned to sand, the worth of bills and coins slipping through fingers until what the fist clenched was worth no more than dirt. Businesses closed. Loans went unpaid. Banks failed. Railroads went belly up. The Northern Pacific Railway, the Union Pacific Railroad, and the Atchison, Topeka and Santa Fe Railway, Stilwell saw them all shut their doors and close down for good. Everything around America seemed to be going under. Stilwell could reach down and save something, but three other possessions would sink even faster. The hackers, the spitters, the cursers—these people cursing this year spewed truth after all, but Arthur Edward Stilwell did not go into a panic. Instead, Stilwell took a boat and held onto his dream. Stilwell's dream child would be fed by the monies of Europe. In Holland, Stilwell rekindled an acquaintance with a wealthy coffee merchant, Jan DeGoeijan. DeGoeijan proved to be an excellent salesman. His countrymen purchased the $3 million in stocks Stilwell estimated would finance the project, and from these investments, Stilwell soon had the capital he needed. When Stilwell returned with money from Holland, Germany, and England, workers started laying railroad tracks. Men drove spikes; soon lines met other lines. Local people had jobs again; towns formed. Stilwell's dream turned the scattering of people in this area into a community, and in 1903 the community solidified into DeRidder, named after DeGoeijan's niece, Ella DeRidder Janssen.

Even though throughout its history different people managed to mine the region for what it offered and even began to settle it, Stilwell's railroad opened the region to the rest of the South and the entire nation, especially those interested in timber who saw the railroad as the final cog in the machine of progress. Driving through DeRidder now, it's easy to forget the story. Turning off of Highway 171, Melanie and I left DeRidder and headed west to Merryville. The trip from DeRidder to Merryville took about twenty minutes. We turned off another highway into Merryville, went the ten miles, made the few turns, and came to the house where the family had gathered before the funeral. We visited with Ocelean's son George Fuller, my wife's uncle, beforehand and then drove across the Sabine, out to Bon Weir, Texas, for the funeral.

The church had a maroon carpet and matching maroon seat cushions in the pews. At the front of the church several microphones and amplifiers gathered around a large area where the preacher, Minister Outlaw, gave his sermon and prayed for this rarest of women. Almost in awe of this man's name, I watched as a minister named Outlaw reflected on this fiercely independent woman. He, too, seemed to recognize her special connection to this river. Eventually, we placed Ocelean in the ground, returning her to the place to which she felt such an attachment.

Like Ocelean Fuller's ancestors the Jarrell family, many families came into the area by horse and wagon. Others came by steamer or by paddleboat. Eventually, others came by train. Regardless of how they arrived, they all came to settle a landscape that many might consider wild and dangerous. Bit by bit the pinewoods became more and more settled. Bit by bit tracks of unclaimed land became subsistence farms, then general farms, then specialized farms. Bit by bit more and more families came to call this place home and make their own contribution to the region.

The settlement of the region occurred in stages and developed from a variety of sources. Some non-indigenous people remained from the time early explorers roamed the area. Some came during the area's history as a territory since Spanish and American officials encouraged settlement in the area. The governments' removal of all law drew a group of people significant to the region's identity. Not only outlaws and people on the run but also squatters viewed this land without oversight as an opportunity, something for the taking. Other settlers, the new recipients of official land grants, migrated to the area at this time too.[2] Each decade—those of the territorial period, those during the region's time as a neutral zone, and those occurring during and after the signing of the Adams-Onís Treaty—saw a growing population.

The large majority of Anglo-American settlers to the region, however, did not arrive in the Neutral Strip until the antebellum period. First hunters, then farmers, then pioneers, then timber men came. From the southern yellow pine and hardwood forests, people from Kentucky, Georgia, Alabama, and Mississippi migrated down through the trees stretching across the South. They set up camps and sometimes built a log cabin and cleared some land. Some moved on to Texas. Quite a few never left.[3]

Squatters on the land, people who hunted and trapped and maybe had a few cattle or hogs were the first to settle most of the land. Their cabins simple, their lifestyles closely mirroring the turning of the seasons, they lived independently, bartered only for what they couldn't get off the land, and usually moved on when a place's game died off or when a region grew too crowded. By 1820 or 1830, the subsistence farmer—a more permanent version of the hunter and trapper—came in wagons drawn by oxen. These farmers cleared land near a spring or natural water source, and replaced the older form of resident with a more stationary one.[4] More and more land, especially tracts nuzzling up against rivers and creeks, like Ten Mile or Six Mile or Bundick, took on the telltale spots of farming: a larger cabin, a few outbuildings, a nearby garden, a well if a river wasn't close, and some cleared land for corn, cotton, and other crops.[5]

Entrenched with cabins and crops and a daily set of chores, the subsistence farms soon grew more sedentary. Their reliance on agriculture increased. Their concern about property boundaries intensified. As people settled and drew property lines, problems crept in. Residents first worried about the people already nearby. Folks started worrying about the neighbor next door taking an extra inch. They worried about the encroaching people from neighboring parts of Louisiana, diverse geographic regions settled by diverse groups of people.[6] The Cajuns to the south, separated from the Neutral Zone by the thick pines marking the northern boundary of the Cajun prairies, began to look north to the Neutral Zone for new land.[7] Residents worried about losing land, had no desire to share limited resources, and prepared to fight to prevent encroachment.[8] Eventually, even their communications to those back home became a problem as their letters describing the life they found enticed more folks back east to follow. Then, they worried about relatives and newcomers from back home horning in on the new bounty they found.

Offering potential land ownership in the form of 160-acre and 80-acre plots after residence and improvement, the Homestead Acts of 1862 and 1866 attracted more settlers to the area than anyone could stem. Seeking a title to purchase, fertile land to raise a good cash crop, and a market to make a little money, the pioneers considered the new land available in Louisiana a boon. Pioneers, whose name implies great wagons under sail across prairie and land, changed to landholders as their mind-set changed. These settlers wanted roots and growth and diversity—agricultural and economic and social. These pioneers wanted mills and general stores and courthouses and schoolhouses. They took to raising cattle or sheep or cotton or timber, no longer simply raising it for self-consumption but harvesting the product for trade. In this region, folks made a go at sheep and cattle and cotton and timber. Timber—nothing seemed to pay out like timber. The cypress trees along the rivers were like stacks of gold, the rich hardwoods like money in the bank, and the yellow pine tracts like a steady check.

Since colonial America, lumber had been not only an economic staple but also a motivation for westward expansion. In a sense, the promise of huge tracts of virgin timber embodied the "myth of manifest destiny." In 1876, the repeal of the 1866 Homestead Act opened up lands for large companies to purchase for as little as $1.25 an acre. Soon, companies could buy an acre of pinewood for $1.25–$3.00 and hardwood for $5–$10. From this action, southern yellow pine flowed into the Midwest and the North. In a decade, almost six million acres of forest in the South were sold. Local residents remember this aspect of the region's settlement, and one ninety-year-old tells a similar story about the period's sale of cheap land: "They bought up a lot of timber, a lot of cheap land. . . . All the land from Merryville to Oakdale sold . . . back in those days."[9]

Of course, these newly available and exploitable resources invited land grabs and ushered in a new era of carpetbaggers. Many lumber companies from the North established branches in the South to acquire as many pine forests as possible as quickly as possible. Even before the turn of the century and the completion of Stillwell's railroad, companies purchased much of the cheap government timberland. The Illinois Central Railroad established a series of special runs from Chicago to Mississippi and Louisiana in order to offer transportation to a large number of land speculators. The amount of purchased land becomes evident by examining a few of the statistics at the turn of the century.[10] Henry J. Lutcher and G. Bedell Moore bought tens of thousands of acres in Louisiana alone. Nathan Bradley and C. F. Hackley owned near 200,000 acres. In 1876, a congressman bought 111,188 acres. Chicago capitalists bought 195,804 acres, and a Michigan firm made a 700,000-acre deal. A man from Grand Rapids purchased 126,238 acres, and later he would gain more than half a million. In all, forty-one groups from the North bought 1,370,332 acres, and nine groups from the South purchased 2,619,332 acres of pine timberland. However, without transportation offered by the railroad, this product could not be harvested. With the railroad—well, that was a different story.

With the railroads came mills that built spurs into the woods to move the timber. Portable sawmills became the wave of the future for the timber industry as the railroad made the region's southern yellow pine forests accessible. Business owners could bring in supplies, move around labor, and ship out the product.[11] Almost instantly, the Neutral Strip witnessed the falling away of stagnant years and the hurried growth of industry. Many large mills began to operate in surrounding towns and settlements, and many smaller mills worked between them. These mills cut an incredible amount of timber. Louisiana ranked second only to Washington in board feet cut. One historian details that by the 1910s, close to "twelve million acres of timber were cut to the ground in Louisiana."[12] In 1904, the American Lumber Co. was established in Merryville and boasted "an ultimate capacity of 135,000 feet per day."[13] With the resources of massive land deals, the use of the railroad, and the control over labor and oversight, lumber syndicates sliced gigantic swaths through forests. As expansive tracts of land were purchased, as owners built mills, as workers migrated to the area, huge profits rolled in. The income from lumber sales increased from $1,764,644 in 1880 to $17,408,513 in 1900.[14] Western Louisiana became known as the land of "green gold."

The national timber industry did create vast fortunes, but only for a select few. Not all mill owners raked in obscene amounts of money. Lumber companies with small mills produced smaller amounts of lumber. They simply made a comfortable living. Timber also meant pretty good money for others besides the mill owners. Mills offered steady work and wages for the people who landed jobs. For many ethnic groups, timber production provided massive amounts of labor and pay opportunities often better than rural, agricultural counterparts. A worker might make $376 dollars a year. Even though wages never seemed really good, especially in contemporary eyes,[15] it was reliable work and gave many families a means of having more than what they could earn from sharecropping. As these economic developments occurred locally, Louisiana became one participant in the national movement towards industrialization.

As time passed, railroads stretched across the land. Companies lined the region like pines ready for harvest: Pawnee Land and Lumber Company, Vernon Parish Lumber Company, Anderson-Post Hardwood Lumber, Kurthwood (the sawmill town that refused to die), Neame's Central Coal and Coke Company, Pickering's and Barham's W. R. Pickering Lumber Company, Stables' Gulf Land and Lumber Company, Leesville's Nona Mills Company. Since sawmills needed workers who needed lodgings, groceries, and occasional diversions, sawmill towns cropped up everywhere. Some sawmill workers had families who needed larger lodgings, more groceries, and other types of diversions; for instance, families needed churches and stores. Children needed schools, and everyone needed something to do.[16]

In 1879, people around what would become Merryville started buying up land in parcels that strung together to form a community. Called Hall City and then Merryville, the town opened a post office in 1881, and by 1906 the Jasper and Eastern Railroad, traveling from Jasper, Texas, to Oakdale, Louisiana, made a stop in Merryville. An artesian well rested near the track, so the steam locomotive could take on water. The track—banked on one side by dirt, a few wooden buildings, and a road to the mill and banked on the other side by a little less dirt, the few wooden two-story buildings of downtown, and the road to the rest of the town—cut Merryville in half.

The buildings' shingled roofs held a slope for runoff of Louisiana rain. Their sides ran with broad and narrow planks cut fresh from the nearby mill, and lumber never seemed to be in short supply. Their windows lined the walls, and each window opened. The slow Louisiana breeze moved past curtains, over beds, down stairs, out front doors. Their porches wrapped around the buildings, held columns staggered every few feet, and faced their steps to the street. Their fronts used placard signs or bold stenciled letters to announce themselves to passersby. Their yards marked themselves with painted picket fences. The fences held gates that opened to sidewalks leading to the town's five or six other buildings that weren't houses.

Any growing timber town in the region constructed itself with the same structures; the sawmill was the town's focus. The mill itself stood as a monolith in the Louisiana forest. Massive, comprised of several buildings including a large building that held gigantic saws, the mill constantly filled its parts with activity and was the workhorse of the town. Propelled by the work of a mill, the sawmill town followed the movements of the mill. In the town proper, the mill office conducted business and shuffled the papers of daily commerce. The commissary or general store shook hands and handled trade. It cashed paychecks, exchanged scrip for goods, kept the men fed and the community stocked. The post office connected the town and the mill to relatives and parent companies and principal investors. The theater or opera house offered a little entertainment—distraction for a price. The local hotel offered accommodations for a reasonable rate, and all of these limbs of the town's body radiated from the town's center, the train depot.

The depot at Merryville, still stenciled with "Hall City" at the turn of the twentieth century, had doors on all sides and windows that ran along each wall. The main entrance leading to the track was gabled. The platform overflowed with crates to stack, boxes to unpack, wagons to load, unloaded shipments to move out, and people. The men wore dark trousers, white shirts, and hats. The women, likely to be wearing hats as well, were helped on and off the cars. All sorts of people stepped on and off the train. Leather Britches Smith, though, needed no help stepping off the train, and he didn't wear black.

Goob recalled that Smith, though a small and "an easy going

fellow, the sort you wouldn't think would harm anyone in the world," carried with him something mysterious, something frightful, when he stepped from the train. Goob explained that something "told you never to cross him. He didn't fear nothing in this world."[17] The reputation of Leather Britches Smith as a tough man to be feared stays with him, evident in one of the most memorable descriptions of the outlaw. Smith made a lasting impression on the good citizens of Merryville when he came into the new town with "all those guns (two .45 Colt revolvers and a .30-30 Winchester)." What's more surprising, "no one bothered him. He'd sit on the front row of the theater with three guns. . . . He'd stop in the middle of the street at Merryville and shoot martins with the six guns from either hand. And, if that wasn't enough to impress everyone he'd then [holster the] six guns and bring down martins with every shot from his .30-30."[18] With his first footfall, Smith made a name for himself. Whether it was a name that he dragged from East Texas across the Sabine River or one he recently adopted, for a time the name Leather Britches Smith would chill the bones as it rolled from the tongues of townsfolk. That's the stuff of legends.[19]

Any legend often consists of two basic components. First, for verifiability and consistency, a legend relies on its kernel narrative: the universal information and basic plot that do not change during different storytelling events.[20] Smith's kernel legend derives from a few sources: Ralph Ramos's work in the *Beaumont Enterprise*, articles appearing over the years in the *Lake Charles American Press*, and local accounts written in the *History of Beauregard Parish Louisiana*. For the most part, these sources solidify the major events of the Smith story, giving all tellers a basic legend from which to work. Second, for contemporary utility and individual appeal, a legend contains variants: the alterations and corrections that inevitably occur as people retell their stories.[21] The flexibility allows individuals to put their unique stamps on the story.[22] These two parts, the universal and the particular, ensure that the legend remains a viable and useful form. The form connects to history, but it is not stuck in the past. The actual and real fuel it, but the psyche and deep subconscious give it its real power. The narrative can be quite basic, but it can embody many beliefs.

Regardless of the teller, Leather Britches Smith's physical attributes and renegade abilities remain at the forefront of nearly every variant. In most legends, the sheer spectacle these outlaws offer stands out far beyond anything else as these outlaws, though often common folk themselves, possess personalities, skills, and daring far beyond ordinary people. The Leather Britches Smith legend has this in spades, from his very first step into the town to his end. Unbelievably skilled with a gun, Leather Britches shot "hawks out of the sky with a rifle" and purple martins with his pistols. Mrs. Terry said her brother Goob admired Smith's skill: "Em Sapp was a United States Marshal. He was . . . the best shot . . . that's ever been in the United States Marshals. My brother wanted Leather Britches and Em Sapp to fight it out, but it didn't happen. . . . Nobody dared tried to outdraw him because he could kill anybody. And he knew it and they knew it." One man decided that Smith had to be pretty mean if people in these woods were afraid of him. This skill posed a threat to many people, and many families had to live, if not in direct fear of him, in a constant readiness, a poised anticipation.

One of his more ferocious activities involves Smith's dining rituals. One person said, "This is a tale that the old Foshees used to tell me about. They lived close to me. They're all gone now. But they were scared to death of Leather Britches."[23] Smith would roam the countryside on his horse, guns at his side. He would come upon a house. "People were scared of him, you know . . . this actually happened in Merryville," a woman said.[24] The men were away from home, working in the woods. At their home, the women and children had an unexpected guest. Smith would climb down off his horse and present himself to the woman of the house, and her children: "He'd walk up to a house," Goob Newton recalled, "shoot a chicken and pitch it to the housewife telling the lady to cook it."[25] Smith "ordered them to cook it, and then he'd sit there with that gun across his lap."[26] Informant after informant tells this story, and this episode, heard over and over again, vividly communicates an invasion of the home. Fear sits on the front porch, and prosperity loses its head. All the while, Smith's skill is apparent, his accuracy clear, and more importantly his daring and stupendous aggression obvious. As these types of stories pile on top of one another, Smith's reputation becomes cemented in the minds of Neutral

Strip residents. An isolated and rugged man by choice, Smith is half outlaw and half hero because that nature expresses the nature of the region. Eventually, Smith's gunplay would connect to the timber industry when he "would ride up on the job and shoot something" to gain "the attention of the loggers" in the woods. This activity would become the greatest danger the outlaw posed to the community and lead to his undoing . . . but his undoing would not come for some time.

Similar to their praise of the outlaw's extraordinary spiritual and physical abilities, residents make note of his mental powers.[27] Folks may not often speak of Leather Britches Smith's mental ability since his stupendous or memorable deeds do not involve wit, sarcasm, or scholarly knowledge. The situation comes off as too serious for the first two and too physical for the last, but people do remember Leather Britches for his knowledge—his knowledge of the woods, the lumber industry, and the law. One informant who knows about the woods and works in them almost every day explained, "He was evidently a good woodsman and a good shot and could live off the land."[28] In Goob Newton's account, Smith "never slept in the house at night. He'd take his sheepskin, after I finished reading and disappear in the woods. In the morning he'd return but never from the same direction."[29] Here, Goob endows Smith, a feared outlaw, with great skill and even almost superhuman or mythical powers. At the very least, Smith knew enough to keep moving and not to be an easy target. He left in the dark and did not sleep inside the house. When he disappeared into the woods at night, Leather Britches waved his diploma of practical knowledge and demonstrated his innate, outlaw cunning enabling him to avoid capture, punishment, and death. While the outlaw did know the woods and while many claim he was the only man tough and independent enough to stand up to the lumber companies "that owned everything," the power to escape and avoid capture might be the most important portion of Smith's outlaw faculties.

Several accounts relay lawmen failing or being too afraid to bring Smith to justice. Throughout the story, the official authorities could never bring in Leather Britches. Lawmen tried, but they never did or, like Em Sapp, never had the chance to face him. Another story described his escape from a Texas prison. After authorities captured

Leather Britches "near the Fort Worth area" for killing his wife and the cattle-rustling Mr. Cook, he carried out a plan to get out of prison.[30] In this story, Leather Britches enlisted the help of a compatriot and "got out of jail—this is terrible—but somehow he got out of jail and his brother boxed him up and shipped him to Shreveport." Free, Smith traveled to Merryville. In this outlandish escape, more likely than not completely fabricated, Smith's cunning and physical dexterity allowed him to remain free.

Much like Daniel Boone or Natty Bumppo, Leather Britches symbolizes a free and capable "doer" because he embraced and understood the environment surrounding him. In addition, since he escaped to the woods and used the woods to sustain himself, the forest itself exists as a symbol of freedom and possibility as much as Leather Britches does, which praises not only Smith but also the Neutral Zone and its residents by association. Throughout the legend, people subtly, often subconsciously, include details that make Leather Britches a potent symbol for the region's uniqueness. He embodies the landscape's mystery and the residents' ruggedness and tenacity.

Beyond merely being interesting, the outlaw embodies the very characteristics of rugged individualism and those necessary for a successful frontier life. His daring feats and renowned skill obviously and undeniably make him well suited for the dangerous life the frontier poses. Gun battles and brawls aside, being a steady shot often meant eating well, or sometimes eating at all. Possessing the strength and stamina to work all day and defend oneself proved to be an asset for pioneers confronting the daily obstacles of a grueling life on the frontier. Above and beyond all this, it takes some degree of fearlessness to embark on the adventure of settling the frontier. It is not surprising that Americans associate grit, skill, and pragmatism with people on the frontier and witness those traits emphasized in the figure of the rugged individualist. People on the frontier had to have their wits about them. Surviving the harsh conditions entailed knowing the environment and various trades. People had to know planting, animal husbandry, rudimentary carpentry, and tracking. They needed to possess a great deal of common sense.[31] Though incredible skill and strength were crucial to success on the frontier, the most notable of the rugged individualists usually possessed a much more important trait, a self-generated code. Life on the frontier often meant a sort of solitary existence, or at least one distanced from the entrenched legality and civility of established settlements; thus, these people generated their own laws, justice, and sense of correctness.[32] The "good outlaw" symbolizes all of these characteristics.

Unlike other traits focusing on the outlaw's inherent abilities, exterior forces—consisting of his local and common-folk supporters—facilitate Smith's freedom.[33] In the legends of Jesse James, Sam Bass, Pretty Boy Floyd, and other heroic outlaws, the local constituency offers the outlaw or gang aid. Help might be shelter for the night or a source for more ammunition. His supporters might make their homes and horses available. Some even act as permanent caretakers of secluded hideaways or as positioned informants in cities or government offices. This component not only provides tellers ample opportunity to insert themselves or family members into the legend, which intensifies the personal and familial status of the narrator, but also celebrates the community and region and validates the notion of communal interdependence and wealth.

According to some accounts, residents provided the outlaw with food and shelter, as they would if their neighbors were in a bind. One informant remembers a donated meal as a thank you to the man who fought the companies for the union.[34] Goob read the newspaper to him.[35] Others tell of their family's close friendship to Leather Britches, how relatives befriended him and even warned him about the authorities and potential traps. Some tell that Leather Britches only trusted and befriended the people he feared or saw as equally gritty and independent. (Coincidentally, often these folks he befriended are the teller's ancestors.) In another version, a local person supports Leather Britches despite his infamous reputation, despite his name that marks him as outsider:

> He slept . . . in the pressing shop there at Merryville at night. . . . They [other townspeople] said 'You better look out. You'll come back one morning and it'll all be gone. Leather Britches, that's Leather Britches Smith.' So he [Slaydon, the owner] said, 'I don't notice any-

thing about his wearing apparel that's any different than anybody else. . . . He's, as far as I'm concerned, a human being and needs a place to sleep.' And he let him sleep there every night.[36]

In the end the common people remain responsible for his success. Through having the gumption to defy the law or having the grit to warrant Smith's admiration, the ordinary people co-star in the story. In their own way, the people keep control and exert their unique brand of power. Offering shelter for Smith connects to the region's reputation for providing respite in the form of hideouts, accomplices, and free range for a variety of outlaws. The West and Kimbrell clan, the McGees, John Murrell, and many others had the support of certain families throughout Louisiana's No Man's Land.[37] Ultimately, stories of locals supporting Smith celebrate residents' power to support the figure and their own reputations for being rough, independent, and led by their own code. In the telling, these people exist as a force remaining long after the outlaw is gone. While the kernel narrative may focus on Smith, the details in the variants emphasize the abilities of the ordinary folk. In fact, these personal versions frequently put less emphasis on Smith's activities than on their relative's actions. In this way, the legend offers as much information about a teller's family saga as it does about the outlaw himself.

The stories that connect a family to Leather Britches function as markers of identity.[38] Many families reconnect themselves to the Neutral Zone, mark themselves as insiders, and even establish their place within the group through the Leather Britches legend. Knowing an outlaw, having an ancestor who was an outlaw or befriended an outlaw, migrating to the region to escape the law or flee a feud, being part of a family who is known as a tough lot—these stories connect a family's saga to the cultural landscape of the Neutral Zone.[39] Knowing this particular outlaw strengthens this sense of belonging. To make the point, people say, "We had close connections and kinfolk to Leather Britches, and he was a character that everybody should know about" or "My grandfather had coffee with him" or "He would sleep at Uncle Seab Collins's house." Ultimately, emphasizing this figure often functions as a method of emphasizing the family.

Does this mean that every family in the area has an outlaw in its bloodline? Does it mean that each family's history traces back to a fugitive or wanted man? Does it mean that Neutral Strip residents are inherently violent? Reject all laws? Have no conception of civility, family, stability, or honesty? Definitely not. These people share the same values of most Americans: security, stability, prosperity. However, the frontier engenders a physical lifestyle, one that often creates rugged bands of individuals who rely on the skills and determination of each other. Frontiers often exist without operating external social and political institutions and without entrenched civil and legal regulations. Violence and tenacity serve important functions in these sorts of border regions, for these traits often prove necessary in order to inhabit areas on the edge of civilization, areas that may be a little rougher and a little more dangerous than other places.

Perhaps social and legal systems existed, but were suspended for a time due to extreme change or some disastrous event. When existing systems of stability and support fail, aggression and tenacity become even more important for survival, as does community interdependence. A cataclysmic event of a sort did occur in Merryville, and for that matter throughout the Neutral Zone and the South. The timber boom went bust. The profits and the approach to timber harvesting could not last. Clear-cutting and a lack of concern for reforestation by several of the large companies resulted in the barrenness of these once rich lands.[40] Of course, once the land was barren and could no longer turn a profit, the great exodus of non-local lumber companies began.[41] Other events specific to the region strained the local industry even more. The mill in Longville, Louisiana (about twenty miles from Merryville) burned in 1921, and the mill in Ragley, Louisiana (about thirty miles from the town) burned in 1924. Most of the others "cut out" (used up the lumber supply) by the late 1920s and early 1930s. Though some lumber companies looked to reforestation as early as 1920, money and work in the field still fell. The land, stripped of all of its timber, caused many sawmills to close. Their jobs lost, many workers moved away, leaving empty homes and shrinking cities and settlements.[42] However, not all of these loggers who worked these mills (like the area's early mercenaries or tradesmen) moved away from the frontier; instead, many remained, sometimes residing in the most isolated and rugged areas. In addition, even though some mills closed and some of the lumber workers and their families left, the stories and histories of these people lasted and the impact of the industry on towns' identities remains firm. In this sense, timber stands as a part of the settlement pattern as well. One can see its true impact by noting the local histories dealing with the subject. Along with contributing much of Louisiana's industrial progression at the turn of the century, the industry lays the foundation for much of its cultural landscape.

These people's last names; their celebration of a funeral, like Ocelean's; their activities on the weekend; their Christmas or Easter traditions; and even their legends and family sagas connect to the past, to the economy, to the landscape. Ocelean lived on the river. Through the river, her life connected to the area's history and culture. Her family prepared her for her future through her funeral, their contemporary burial ritual passed down through generations and built upon the bonds of family. Like the funeral, the Smith legend connects to the past and prepares for the future. The legend blends the timber industry, the river, the region's role as a Neutral Strip, family sagas, and even the concerns coming with living on the frontier. In turn, history and legend—or more precisely history through legend—remains relevant in the present.

While the combination of good and bad characteristics in the outlaw-hero forms a rather odd figure, who in most circumstances has trouble fitting in since he is too dangerous for the citizenry and too law-abiding for widespread crime, the combination does effectively create a figure capable of living on the border, one ideally suited to living a frontier life, one perfectly created to symbolize life in Louisiana's No Man's Land. He stands on both sides of right and wrong. He exists as a potent symbol for a complex worldview and, as Leather Britches Smith does, addresses the most complicated parts of a life spent here.

CHAPTER FIVE

ALWAYS FOR THE UNDERDOG

"You see, Leather Britches always was for the underdog. Anywhere in the world he was, he was for the underdog," Mrs. Terry told me that day in her home. Then, she offered one of the many narratives describing Smith's mysterious past. Before he arrived in Merryville, the outlaw picked up work here and there as he made his way south from Shreveport. He came upon "a little town that had a lumber company." Smith landed a job, but witnessed "a boss that was mean to the men and ugly to the men." Leather Britches "worked all right two days," but eventually, the boss's actions crossed the line. The outlaw's tolerance reached its limit, so "at the end of the second day he decided he'd just whip the boss, which he did. He whipped the boss and had to leave that place in a hurry." Her account depicts Smith as a feared man driven by a code. Only Leather Britches could make a living outside the mill and had the skill to stay alive outside civilization. He hid in the woods and could match any union buster or detective sent in to muster up trouble. As one might expect, Leather Britches stood in opposition to the economic system established by the mills and their supporting towns. Even though some people feared him, the union men—because he was feared by the companies and wielded a type of power they must have envied or respected—saw Smith as a person who could do what they could not. Many of them believed him to be their protector.

Though rugged, tough, and even short-tempered, Smith identifies with the everyman, and as a Hollywood version of an outlaw might do, he defends the weak. Here, Smith exhibits the "good" outlaw's most basic characteristic—being a man of the people.[1] Born from common stock, the outlaw possesses a deep connection to the ordinary man, often acting on the common man's behalf. If some oppressive force looms over the common people or some unjust system exists keeping the everyday folk down, the outlaw emerges to settle the score and put the world back in order.

Of course, the heroic outlaw refuses to side with the oppressive force. He must stand on the side of the oppressed and retaliate for those who cannot. Though the outlaw may steal, his crimes spare the little man and plunder those grown rich from graft.[2] Though he may kill, his hands don't strike down those who can't defend themselves. When the oppression comes from a civil or legal source, this role of the outlaw grows even more pronounced, more terrible and terrific. Running parallel to Americans' democratic sensibility and belief in individual rights and fairness, the American outlaw retaliates for us, in place of us, as one of us, and even by us (since he often needs our homes as hideouts and our mouths to keep secrets). Consequently, his role as retaliator satisfies all the more because he connects to us, because he is us, and we are him—we are the same.

For this reason, the outlaw usually becomes inexorably tied to a cultural landscape, which encapsulates the local political, economic, social, and physical environment. Regardless of what Billy the Kid wanted, the Lincoln County War rode alongside the outlaw as one of his pals, and his legend perpetually entwines with capitalism's viciousness. Pretty Boy Floyd, even as he floors his sedan and cuts across the fields and farms of the American heartland, cannot escape the Great Depression. Pancho Villa inevitably connects to Mexico's Revolution. The bloody wounds of the Civil War color the legend of Jesse James. In all these cases, the figure's legend becomes as much about how he intersects with key political and social events as about his deeds.

Even though chance brought Leather Britches to Merryville, his fate would forever connect to the labor troubles of the time. As one person explained, "We wouldn't have any Leather Britches story if we didn't have the story of the Grabow Riot," the violent eruption of strife between union and non-union men working in the timber industry. Connected as they are, Smith and his legend extend beyond an account of a single man's life and notorious deeds. Drifting across Louisiana and roaming its pinewoods (at least he does in Mrs. Terry's version), Smith meets a dominant economic system—one with a whole set of characters, intrigues, and plot twists that become a crucial part of the outlaw's story.

One key figure in this tale is John Henry Kirby. Called the "Prince of the Pines" and the self-titled "pal" of the workers, Kirby took faith in his rise to the top through sweat and sheer determination.[3] He embraced the American potential for wealth and the power that flowed from it. Like many of his contemporaries, Kirby believed achievement was the natural result of remarkable individual effort spawned through competition. In a speech to other lumber company owners, Kirby preached to them about American industriousness: "We are a nation of laborers; that it is every man's duty to labor and to create something each day of his life. . . . I like to see men employed and I like to see them work."[4]

It's no wonder that those witnessing his speeches, shaking his hand, following his "suggestions" in meetings, or even reading his correspondences found John Henry Kirby's charisma powerful and his plan for this new future convincing. With a countenance beaming with the optimism and confidence that an unfettered belief in progress engenders, Kirby raised his chin ever so slightly when sitting for a portrait. Covered with thick black hair he smartly parted slightly off-center and swept back in a flourishing wave, his small round head peered over his right shoulder. Posing, he looked onward into the future, a future of opportunity and fortuitousness for those stout of heart and fit of muscle and mind. His small dark eyes, instead of conveying a sense of timidity or maliciousness, must have communicated to those who stared into them the confidence and determination he possessed. Perhaps his lustrous mustache—an immaculately trimmed but unstyled natural growth of thick black hair that spanned his entire upper lip—symbolized Kirby's rich faith in his prominence and fortitude, and his certainty of the wealth waiting for him in southern yellow pine.[5]

Of English and Italian descent (including from Elizabeth Longino, a grandmother whose father was an exiled Italian nobleman), Kirby—born in Tyler County, Texas, in 1860—grew up in the same southern pine region that would make him rich. A native of Peach Tree Village, Kirby attended local schools and spent a year at the Southwestern University at Georgetown, Texas. Working on his father's farm during school breaks as a child and serving as a clerk in the county tax office and then in the State Senate as he grew, Kirby gained a varied work experience, which seems to have motivated him long into his life. After college, Kirby eventually worked under Samuel Bronson Cooper and in that service acquired a sufficient knowledge of the law, enough in fact to pass the bar in 1885. Though Kirby's winning personality and indisputable keen business mind served him well, his connection to S. B. Cooper might have proven to be most profitable. In 1887, Cooper directed a group of Boston investors in need of legal service to Kirby who, in turn, convinced these investors to partner with him and purchase large tracts of pine forest for lumber production. The investments and timber business led to the Kirby Lumber Company, a corporation that in the early 1900s held $10,000,000 in capital. In 1900, Kirby completed the Gulf, Beaumont and Kansas City Railway, which drove a production line leading through the heart of Texas timberlands out to the Midwest.[6]

In no time, Kirby's timber business began to dominate the Texas pine region. The Kirby Lumber Company immediately purchased five sawmills and contracted with others. Kirby described the weakness of the East Texas lumber industry as an inadequate ability to fulfill demand. Kirby's company sought to rectify the problem. Kirby believed the only problem with growth was there wasn't enough of it, and powerful growth required control. In a publicity blurb describing the company's recent growth, one Kirby Lumber Company director boasted about the organization's business victories, "Three of our mills are in Beaumont and two in Orange. Two other mills in Orange will be forced to stop their saws and to go out of business because we now own the forest from which they would have to draw their supply of timber." Eventually, the company managed to supply all solicited trade (even business from abroad) and "through the economies of management," to reduce production costs while increasing distribution.[7] By the 1920s, Kirby Lumber Company owned 300,000 acres of pine forest, operated thirteen sawmills, and produced ten billion feet of timber. Kirby and his company would also build town after town, one even bequeathed the patronymic Kirbyville. That town, like many others, labored under the control of Kirby's timber operation.[8]

His timber operations in mill towns like Kirbyville, especially at the mill itself, offered plenty of work. The wood crews stuck to the woods and harvested timber to ship to the mill in town.[9] First, knee-deep in briars and thorns, a crew of burners lit the thick underbrush of the Louisiana piney woods. Once cleared of the brambles and growth, the large trees made neat rows and rows of timber. Next, the surveyor (also called the timber spotter or marker) divided the company's tract into sections. Lugging axes and cross-cut saws, the flatheads notched the trunk to direct the tree's fall, then stooped to cut trees as close to the ground as they could. Saws caught, their teeth caked with pine resin. Sometimes, trees fell at unplanned angles. Their tops snagged in the tops of other trees and hung there, looming over the crews. Sometimes, their trunks came crashing down on legs and arms and bodies. Even if a wood crew escaped grave injuries, a few minor ones were certain. Wounds itched, turned red, swelled. Blood flowed septic. The sun beat down. Snakes, now disturbed, grew angry and restless. Insects swarmed. No matter the discomfort or danger, though, trees still fell.

When the trunks hit ground, men in overalls crawled over them. Some men, careful not to nick knees and feet with a blade, smoothed away the branches and knots. Others, remembering the orders for the day, measured off sections of the trunk to be cut. Men worked quickly. There was money to make. The saw crews made sure to make room for the scaler to mark the log and credit the saw crew for their work. Then a man, or often a boy, stepped over brambles and cut branches to hook the crane cable to the log. In times past, skidders dragged out logs with oxen or wagons, but in a company tract with a railroad spur, a steam skidder more than likely rattled the ground and sent out a moan as it reeled in the log, which plowed over any plant, beast, and man unfortunate enough to get caught in its way. Stacked in a pile colored the yellow of dull gold, the logs waited to be loaded. A loader crane stacked and chained the company profits on railroad cars. A big Shay engine pulled all the cars to the mill pond. As the spur dug deeper into the woods—farther and farther away from the mill—the saw crews simply made camp there. Company owners explained the bad business of wasting time.

Day after day, the saws spun furiously, and the logs massed afloat in the mill pond. Knowing what it must be like to fall into the mill pond—maybe even seeing another man fight with the great wooden monsters for space and struggle for air, watching the logs' heavy stomachs roll over the drowning man's back or come together to crush the man between their great weights—the boatman was careful with his step as he prodded the logs in order to guide them to the machine that would drag them from the water onto the log deck. Blades and teeth and barbs and hooks snagged on everything. Saws moved back and forth—cutting logs into lengths, trimming them to a certain width, edging them to remove bark, planing them for smoothness and finish. The mill's machines pushed the men to their very limits of speed and strength and concentration. The men's minds never rested. Their ears suffered under the weight of the noise. Their hands guided logs perilously close to saws. Accidents happened.

Fortunately, mill towns usually came with a company drugstore, a company hospital, and a company doctor. Lucky, too, that a man wouldn't have to come up with the money; the company already deducted insurance fees from a worker's pay. The company added another deduction for hospital fees, and of course, the pay from the man's unpaid hours could cover the bill for medicine. Often, the good doctors could stop the bleeding, even if reattaching the digits and limbs proved impossible or overly burdensome. Best yet, mill towns had cemeteries, and a man earned the right for a proper burial, since the company deducted the requisite burial expenses from his pay, too. Mill towns offered many such amenities, the accoutrements of progressive industrialized living. Churches, schools, and even opera houses sprouted in these mill towns. Saloons, bawdy houses, and labor meetinghouses also grew, but companies knew that some of these activities needed curtailing from time to time, especially when they interfered with a "productive" and happy life.

John Henry Kirby saw it as his obligation not only to employ men but to improve their lives and, if need be, prevent them from making mistakes.[10] Kirby viewed himself as a father figure, a protector, not only to the workers but also to the entire American social system. Many argue this sensibility drove him to create his particular system of control, and his mind-set resulted in many of his benevolent and paternalistic activities: reducing the work day while maintaining wages, providing work for industrious men and opportunities for ambitious boys, "putting numerous children through college,"[11] pushing legislation that ensured workers would consult employees before making a consignment of their wages,[12] preventing the spread of seditious unions that weakened the foundation of American labor and industry, throwing one hell of a barbecue while speechifying against the unions,[13] and even passing out Bibles, toys, and other gifts come some special occasion. Granny Cat speaks fondly of John Henry Kirby and recalls that he treated the men fairly and even passed out oranges during Christmas.

Lumber companies had come in, built mills, constructed towns around them, filled these towns with workers and families, and brought a new way of life for locals. But this "progress" came with a price. Most workers struggled through ten- to twelve-hour workdays with little pay. Along with long hours and this sort of wage, timberwork also created mental stress for many workers.[14] Man met machine, and folk confronted mass production. Men accustomed to working agrarian hours found themselves driven by the clock. Men who changed professions with the seasons and labored according to need now worked tediously on jobs without a change and without end. Hostility to the timber barons remained in the hearts of these men, and even as men earned paychecks and "progress" ensued, they held a grudge.[15] In the backs of their minds, workers also knew that if companies began to show less profit, owners would cut wages a bit more, or might cut the jobs completely.

For this reason, a host of others sees Kirby's actions with more suspicious eyes. Some argue that Kirby's methods ran similar to those of the plantation system,[16] and lumber companies that created mill towns desired absolute control to ensure profits and stable productivity rather than to bring about true social improvements or create a brighter future. As a result, the lumber company's dominance over a worker's life became a central issue for opposing this system. Various union and socialistic papers and circulars admonished the company town. Using a former employee of Kirby as a source, one such paper, *The Rebel*, offered a description in a February 12, 1912, article:

> He [the worker] is born in a Company house; wrapped in Company swaddling clothes, rocked in a Company cradle. At sixteen he goes to work in the Company mill. At twenty-one he gets married in a Company Church. At forty, he sickens with Company malaria, lies down on a Company bed, is attended by a Company doctor who doses him with Company drugs, and then he loses his last Company breath, while the undertaker is paid by the widow in Company scrip for the Company coffin in which he is buried on Company ground.[17]

Another source quotes an employer: "I'm just like a father. I care for them while sick. I get them out of jail. I have doctors deliver their babies."[18] Other writers would go as far as drawing comparisons between the lumber company town and the feudal villages of the Middle Ages.[19] In a 1915 article for *Harper's Weekly*, George Creel (a well-known journalist, labeled a muckraker by many at the time) traveled to the South.[20] He noted the conditions in lumber towns: "Men herded in company towns, packed in company houses, forced to trade at company stores, paid in company money, voted by the company, and denied all protection of law."[21]

In his newspaper articles, Creel makes Kirbyville, Texas, the star of his show and wields his spotlight so that it burns hot on the little lumber town. Creel cites Kirby Lumber Company's use of the merchandise check, infrequent paydays, and the various deductions and penalties resulting from the combination of the two as proof of this feudal system. Creel also describes Kirbyville as a closed company town, which meant that only stores owned by the company or those sanctioned by the company could operate there. In Creel's description, a worker gets paid in July and then not again until December. In that span of time, the worker piles up rent, fees for supplies, and debt for purchased merchandise at the company store. Company stores could charge exorbitant prices, and any check spent outside of the system—which often proved difficult since people did not consider it actual money—faced discounts and reduced purchasing power. These checks as a matter of course would also incur several deductions, such as hospital fees, insurance fees, company union fees, and so on. Creel also details the hiring applications workers completed for the mills. Gaining personal information and general work experience when they were introduced, these work history forms began to ask about previous participation in unions and allowed employers to record any such behavior.

Soon, more political sources piggybacked the claims of Creel and other journalists. "Big Bill" Haywood, an outspoken participant in the Industrial Workers of the World and American labor movement, described what abuses he witnessed during a trip to lumber camps in the South. In his descriptions of Grabow, Louisiana (a camp roughly twenty-five miles east of Merryville), Haywood told of a large wooden fence encircling the camp, forced labor approximating slavery, and beaten workers. He described ragged boarding shacks unfit for human habitation and circulating paper and brass "batwings" and "cherryballs" of company scrip. He detailed the practice of lumber companies intentionally cultivating a narcotic drug habit to keep workers tied to the company and a system of camp wives that attached themselves to itinerant workers. He painted a bleak picture of families broken from the mill system.[22] Of course, Big Bill counts as a biased source (which, of course, grossly understates his position on the subject), but he does not stand alone in his assessment of the situation. Researchers for the 1912 Commission on Industrial Relations discovered similar conditions—company towns exerting complete control, usurious use of scrip, unfair deductions, and deplorable working conditions. Even locals will reach back into their memory and pull details about the men they knew who worked in the mills. As Ester Terry said, "Men that worked for these companies and . . . killed themselves [working], and that was the rule of the commissary, that you could draw your money that whole month. You didn't make anything."

Emphasizing that these words stand only as her "opinion," Gussie Townsley complained that the sawmills "worked the men to death, paid them very little money, and what little money they got they had to spend at their commissary." Mrs. Townsley called this money "fake money"—no wonder, since her family knew the worth of it. She drew from her family's history as she explained that her father sold produce: "A lot of times they didn't have the money, so that's the only way he could use what they paid him with at the commissary." Her simple comments touch on nearly every aspect of life that unions would complain about and commissions would seek to ascertain: "And they just had old houses throwed up, and you could run your hands through the cracks just about. They charged them rent. . . . They worked them sunup to sundown."

Though the industry offered more hope than slavery or indentured servitude, it created its own brand of economic hopelessness. Workers and their families had to confront small unlivable lodgings, low wages, and the reduced buying power of their wages since the "fake money" the men were paid in couldn't be spent anywhere except at the commissary, which hiked prices. Low wages and payment in scrip, not to mention men being required to purchase start-up equipment before being paid, ensured that credit at the commissary became a fact of life for many workers. This financial burden ensured a version of perpetual service a worker owed to the mill.

These notoriously horrid labor conditions existed across the country, and a movement to unionize began to confront them. The American Federation of Labor (AFL) established itself in 1886, and the more radical Industrial Workers of the World (IWW) formed in 1905. The formation of the IWW ("I Won't Work" by its opponents) and its further development took significant steps to shift some aspects of power from owner to worker. Gaining ground in the gold, silver, and lead mines of the West, the IWW provided timber workers examples of success drawn from aggressive solidarity movements. The Knights of Labor provided southern models, such as organized efforts for Louisiana sugar workers.[23] Strikes, walkouts, and the eventual formation of unions in the region soon existed as potent strategies for confronting the company town. Some of the Texas-Louisiana pine region's first responses to the timber industry's demands came in 1902 and 1904, when black mill hands in Texas struck. These men complained of days so long and conditions so poor that the companies virtually employed a system of slavery for production.²⁴ The solidarity efforts met varying degrees of success and, as one might expect, various emotional responses and levels of support. But the ripples caused from these early demonstrations would build and build until the entire region was shaken to its core.

Like the 1906 San Francisco earthquake that shattered companies' windows throughout the town and crumbled walls of homes and businesses, the panic of 1907 sent shock waves through the country's financial infrastructure. The gold standard collapsed. Cash became scarce. Stock market prices crumbled. Cracks in the current system grew obvious. Rattled, financiers and bankers flew into a panic. A few major banks dissolved, and even the southern lumber companies felt the ripples. In response to cash flow problems, an extremely low price for lumber, and other insecurities caused from the economic crisis, mill owners, such as Kirby, lengthened the working day to increase production and cut wages by as much as twenty per cent to decrease cost.²⁵ The 1907 general strike that followed, in which lumber hands across Western Louisiana formed a spontaneous walkout in order to demand higher wages and better working conditions, provided real proof of the Louisiana lumber workers' organization and solidarity. This proof only served in steeling the lumber company owners' resolve to destroy the union. As a short-term fix, Kirby and other lumber company owners promised increased wages as soon as the economic crisis ended. (Owners failed to keep this promise.)²⁶ As a long-term fix, company owners finalized the organization of the Southern Lumber Operators Association (SLOA).²⁷ The SLOA operated with the primary objective of suppressing the growing unionism in the region.

Even though the 1907 strike proved unsuccessful largely due to a lack of leadership, anyone could see the workers' interest in labor demonstration and their willingness to participate. From 1907 to 1910, a few key organizers, like Arthur Lee Emerson, moved into the area and these figures formed the leadership core of the Sabine pine region's most successful labor organization, the Brotherhood of Timber Workers (BTW). A. L. Emerson worked as a wood crew hand and a mill hand and even as a millwright in the business.²⁸ Before arriving in Louisiana, he traveled to the West, took work with companies in the Northwest and Southwest, and encountered the Lumber Workers' Union of the Bitterroot Range in Idaho and Montana. When Emerson returned to the Gulf South and compared the regions' wages and living conditions to the ones he knew, he flung himself at the problem. One informant describes the situation Emerson faced: "Emerson and Fisher[29] were good men . . . but they just decided it wasn't right, they were not going to have it any longer, they were not going to put up with it any longer."

Emerson's plan was rather simple. First, he gained employment in local mills, the first being the mill in Fullerton. Next, he threw his energies at finding like-minded workers, carefully explaining the costs and benefits of a union and enlisting men in his cause. At Fullerton, Emerson registered 85–100 names before moving to the next lumber camp in another town. Moving from camp to camp and building on the popular sentiment, Emerson quickly built a large following and developed strong ties to workers. Jay Smith, also a southern timber worker, allied with Emerson, became secretary of the local organization, and soon functioned as the union's other driving force.[30]

By late 1910, Emerson and Smith formed the first local chapter of the BTW in Carson, Louisiana (a small, now-defunct mill town about fifteen miles east of Merryville). As more and more locals formed, Emerson and other organizers decided to establish a formal meeting, constitution, and headquarters. In the summer of 1911, the first formal meeting of the BTW occurred in Alexandria, Louisiana. By the standards set by other unions throughout the country, especially those of the IWW, the constitution of the BTW advocated a moderate approach to unionizing and demonstrating.[31]

It didn't matter. As quickly as the BTW grew, fears of populism and socialism spread. During the same month of the meeting in Alexandria, Kirby gave a speech supporting the American Federation of Labor's rejection of the radical IWW. The SLOA responded in 1911 by beginning a series of mill lookouts. John Kirby, as the primary mover of the organization, offered the greatest opposition to the Brotherhood. With the SLOA and its presidency as support, Kirby first tried to discredit Emerson and Smith; then, he punished union sympathizers with blacklists and scab labor and allied himself with the less radical AFL.[32]

Owners in the SLOA decided that "infected" mills should close. Newspapers throughout the Sabine pine region ran articles documenting the standoffs and shutdowns. On July 20, 1911, the *New Orleans Times Picayune* announced that eight lumber mills would close the following Monday to fight unionism.[33] Later in the year, twenty-two would close;[34] later still, fourteen mills decided to go idle.[35] Step by step, owners intensified their efforts to curb the spread of unions. Increasingly, mill owners sought to determine the status of their employees. Armed guards (Burns and Pinkerton men) and spies landed on the mills' payrolls. These new employees discovered which employees participated in the BTW and provided armed resistance for any form of demonstration deemed unsuitable by owners.[36]

As its demands were not met, the BTW began a practice of calling large-scale meetings, marching the attendees to various mills, and conducting demonstrations in order to rally support and disrupt production. The mill owners and loyal employees tin-panned (banged metal against metal to drown out union speeches), exchanged "jeers and taunts" with union speakers,[37] and on some occasions made a conspicuous display of the mill's defenses. Mills engaged in significant efforts to maintain their control and to advertise their ability to keep workers in and protestors out. As one resident of Merryville described, "It was exciting times around here. They actually built like a fort all the way around the sawmill to keep the union out and keep their hands in."[38]

How could mill workers, trapped in what many claimed to be a form of perpetual servitude, hope for a better future? The workers felt powerless. As Mrs. Terry described the situation, the mill owners held all the cards: "But the men that owned everything had such a strong hold on the people, you had to work. . . . So they [union men] just couldn't do a thing in the world. Although, they tried. The men tried." With no leverage but their work and with the owners having everything on their side—including the hungry mouths of the workers' children and the needs of their families and scab labor willing to replace those on strike—the union men looked for a remedy. As they say, "You had to work."

No one had much of a choice, except the Leather Britches of legend. He could make a living outside the mill and had the skill to stay alive in the woods and outside civilization, too. For this reason, he could stand in opposition to the economic system established by the mill and the closed company towns. As a result, even though they may have feared him as a loose cannon or dangerous drunk, the union men viewed him as a person who could do what they could not.

In 1912, when Smith arrived in Merryville, tensions were high,[39] and when he stepped off the train, no doubt trouble was first in line to shake his hand. Smith only added to the excitement of the times, but many wonder about his exact role in the struggle and about the extent of his connections to the union. People agree that the outlaw Leather Britches entered Merryville around the same time as the union troubles escalated. However, accounts range about his actual involvement with the BTW. Some tell that Smith, an ordinary man, simply happened to be "swept up" in the union troubles.[40] Smith "came in at the same time as the union organizer came in . . . and they just naturally connected him with the union. . . . He just was running from the law, so he had to do what he had to do. I imagine probably somebody tipped him off that they might be having trouble down there." Some believe him to be an active participant in the BTW:

> But he mostly went around the logging woods to the crews that worked for the company and tried to organize them, and he'd get them to pay union dues. And they think he was just, more or less, extorting money. I don't think that he was a dedicated union man. I think that that was a way for him to make a living and hide from whatever his past was. . . . Just personally, I think he was hiding, and he was on the run and this was an opportunity to make a few dollars. He was evidently a good woodsman and a good shot and could live off the land, but I can't see him being an official of the union.

Another casts Leather Britches as a man with a noble cause, a man siding with the little man and opposing the mills: "It was real sad that he got shot that way because he was just trying to protect the working class and that's why they didn't like him, and that was coming from people that knew him, not people that just heard stories."

In many versions, Smith grows so acutely angry at this unjust system that he acts as a type of hero with social justice as his main goal.[41]

The account Ralph Ramos includes of Leather Britches saving two non-union men from death, narrated by Mrs. Willie T. Grantham, casts Smith as this type of noble figure.[42] Willie T. Grantham and Jim Whidden were two men who had not joined "the timber workers' union in which Leather Britches was active" and met the band of union workers as the group returned from a demonstration.[43] The basic story reads:

> They met midway. The union men had ropes and were intent on stringing the pair up. Grantham pleaded. He had a paralyzed arm, injured by a falling tree while working in the forest. It was difficult for a handicapped man to find work. He was willing though to pay union fees. Leather Britches sympathized and ordered the men to move on.

In his role as noble union leader, Leather Britches most clearly exhibits a self-generated noble moral code. Even though he might kill a man for crossing him, Smith would not kill an ordinary man for not following him, as long as the man did not offer much of a threat. More importantly, Leather Britches as social hero becomes a clear and direct protest of the social imbalance that existed because of the mills. One might argue, the clearer the presentation of Smith as hero, the clearer the presentation of the mills as villains.

I might add, however, that some (especially those with ties to mills and ownership) describe Smith plainly as a piece of scum. The depiction doesn't come as a real surprise. Similar to these opposing feelings concerning Smith, people's opinions split on the labor struggles.[44] Some stood all the way on the company side. Many owners and workers supporting the mill considered the union and other socialistic resistance as pernicious forces that served only in agitating the otherwise satisfied laborers. They believed most union leaders manipulated men for the union's own political gain and ignored the benefits of the industry. Plenty of workers, especially skilled laborers, earned more money in the lumber industry than they could in other occupations. In Louisiana, workers could earn $.75 to $1.50 for an eleven-hour day. Sawyers, since they possessed more skill, earned more.[45] Even though these figures seem low, Louisiana wages ranked fair among other timber states,[46] and timber money amounted to more than many poor white and black sharecroppers and tenant farmers earned and more than many subsistence farmers could steadily make.

Plenty of people look back in nostalgia at the solidarity and sense of community lumber towns created; in order to function, mill towns necessitated cohesion. Besides, George Creel and John Henry Kirby alike would argue the impossibility and futility of painting working conditions in the region with a large brush. Some mills did not use scrip or company stores that charged higher prices. Some companies issued regular and frequent checks and experienced a loyalty and reciprocal relationship between worker and owner. Mill owners and workers enjoyed this connection especially in smaller, locally owned mills throughout the region. Southern settlers had relied on harvesting timber for profit since the Civil War,[47] and even without the lumbering expertise and technology brought in from other timber regions throughout the country, locals still harvested and milled a fair amount of timber. In fact, most of the workers in these mills consisted of locals or people from surrounding communities or the Southern States.[48]

As railroads developed in the region and technology improved, some local mills grew, but maintained a relationship with communities that larger, non-local mills did not. One informant commented on this situation:

> Well, the only big mill here was American Lumber Company, and if that had been the only one here, they would've gone union because they were getting a dollar a day in the woods and a dollar and a half in the fields and the top hands, like Granddaddy, would get three or four dollars. . . . But the other mills in this country were family owned, native people who weren't paying any more but treated their people a little better.[49]

Other locals note the distinction between local mill owners and outside speculators and non-local owners. Even today, community members find it difficult to offer wholesale criticisms concerning the oppressive system of the industry since that entails indirectly criticizing local families, who might still live in the area. Mrs. Terry explains that "people never did form a union at the Galloway Mill. . . . They should've unionized old Kirby." Mrs. Terry does not offer a definitive opinion about the Galloway Mill, a local mill whose owners still live in the region.[50] Most realized the benefits and cause for a timber union while understanding the dangers and economic impossibility of radical socialism.

Many people struggled with wholeheartedly supporting the union or the mill owners. They thought some lumber companies abused and/or took advantage of the men, and plenty disliked the idea of outside companies and owners reaping great benefits at the expense of the locals—especially those Northern companies that came down to clear-cut the timber. In addition, most residents fondly recalled the local farmer's less extractive approach to harvesting timber. Others hated the idea of outsiders agitating workers and disrupting mills on behalf of political agendas. Most residents can see both sides, explaining the situation "was men against, you know just like unions are today, against the employees. They had each a side that had reasons to do it."[51] Both sides held a slice of right and wrong.

Because this sort of muddy relationship existed between the local families of mill owners and the local families of laborers, many of the local histories emphasize the role outsiders played in the event. Some emphasize John Henry Kirby's role. Some describe Emerson's actions. Though Smith may stand as a man of the people, he is not a resident of Merryville. Perhaps good reasons why exist. As an outsider, Leather Britches can oppose both locally owned and non-locally owned mills. In addition, he represents outsiders advocating unionism and serves as a convenient scapegoat. Finally, once he is rejected, which is the inevitable end for any outlaw, his actions and temperament exist outside the group. In this way, discussing and even criticizing Leather Britches serves as an effective and safe means of discussing this rather sensitive issue, so the outlaw symbolically represents the concerns and anxiety the Merryville residents faced at the time.

Connected to this historical event, Smith embodies the town's split and his legend communicates something beyond his life and deeds. As half of the residents supported the local mill owners and the other half supported the local union men—as half of the town remained loyal to the mills because for years they offered steady work and sometimes even Christmas bonuses and the other half supported the union since it promised higher wages and better hours—half of the town describes Smith as an outlaw and the other half shows him a hero.

Hero or outlaw, Leather Britches and his legend remain important to the area and its people. The story embodies the various aspects of the residents' lives; it connects to history and the past, but also provides a contemporary tool for discussing economics, work, and even outsiders. Moreover, by exemplifying a larger oral tradition of outlaw narratives, the legend links one town to others in the region. It comments on these people's lives as Americans, Southerners, Louisianans, No Man's Landers, citizens of Merryville, union or company men, and even members of a certain family—a Whiddon or Galloway or Burge or Broxton.

CHAPTER SIX

THE GRABOW WAR

When my wife, Grand, and I drove up to Mrs. Townsley's home, her dogs sniffed my car's tires and hounded my shoes and the legs of my pants. Mrs. Townsley raised up a little off her swing that sat on her front porch, a cement slab running along the front of her house. "Quit," she said. The dogs moved on. A wire fence enclosed a yard that once could have held flowers or shrubs, but some time ago those flowers and shrubs and even certain patches of grass decided that something greener and better waited somewhere else. But Gussie Townsley hadn't left. Eighty-one at the time, Mrs. Townsley began painting at sixty-one after her daughter gave her a Christmas gift of paints. "I never had a lesson in my life," Mrs. Townsley once said, "and it just come on me and wouldn't let go."

Her determination to capture the images in her head on the canvas parallels her family's determination to settle No Man's Land. She grew up as the twelfth of Annie Hickman and Soloman Loftin's fourteen children. She and her siblings remained from the line of Aaron Cherry, who received a land grant in Louisiana's Neutral Strip. One day a visiting California art dealer saw one of her paintings in her son's law firm. The dealer bought the painting on the spot. Soon Gussie Townsley would travel to Santa Barbara for her first gallery opening, and then to

Washington, D.C., to display her works. "I didn't know nobody to ask how to mix my paints or nothing," she said, "but it just wouldn't let go until I done it." Velmer Smith centers her book *The Best of Yesterday, ... Today: A History of the Sabine River and "No Man's Land"* around the life and work of Gussie Townsley. The book begins with Smith's discussion of history, before filling most of its pages with images of Townsley's paintings.

When we made it to the porch that day, Miss Gussie, as most locals know her, welcomed us inside. She began immediately discussing the past and pulling her works of art out from behind her front-room couch. In one work, soldiers—wearing dark navy shirts and sky blue trousers, their horses turned loose and rummaging through a family's greens and carrots—chase chickens through a garden patch. Occupying the canvas of *When the Yankees Came Through*, these soldiers also climb onto the family's porch and, still holding their rifles, ask the mother, her children huddled under each arm, about food and supplies. *The Neches-Belles*, another work, displays the grand majesty of one of the last steam-powered waterwheel merchant boats to navigate the Sabine River. One after another, paintings appeared from behind the sofa. An ice wagon, a country dance, a syrup mill, and a turpentine camp within other frames remind viewers of a bygone time. Then, Miss Gussie pulled out *The Grabow Riot*.

"I remember the little sawmill town quite well, going to the country commissary, selling vegetables with my pa to the people living in the town," Miss Gussie explained.[1] As I looked at the picture, I saw the story that she heard time and time again. She said, "This took place July 7, 1912, in the little sawmill town of Grabow, Louisiana. That was five years before I was born, I have heard it talked about so often as a child, in my mind's eye I was there." To the far left, the stacks of the planing mill plume smoke. Various other brown wooden buildings, and a few men wearing dark pants and hats and white shirts, fill up the background. The action in Grabow dominates the painting's right, and the Galloway Lumber office building solidly sits right of center. The white building with a four-columned porch boasts double front doors and two porch windows.

Rifle barrels with small red flames painted on their ends extend from the windows. A man peeks out the front doors; another man fires from the doorway of a wooden addition. Miss Gussie explained, "Officials at Carson called the Galloways' office in Grabow on the only telephone in the country, telling them that Emerson and his men were coming and were armed. Armed guards were ready and waiting for them." The union men, in chaos, take cover behind wagons and bushes. These men fill the bottom right of the canvas, and those hiding behind wagons return fire. "Several men were killed, others were wounded, horses were killed or wounded in a very bloody battle that lasted about ten minutes or more," she continued. Then, to the left of the office building, set back a tad from the mill office and definitely apart from both union men and company men, a wagon halts. A woman has the reins. "My uncle Bud Hickman was shot; he and his wife were coming from church. His horse was also killed," she said. The wagon's horse and a man lie sprawled on the ground. A few dabs of red convey the damage they received. Even though visually striking and incredibly detailed, Gussie Townsley's painting does not capture the entire story of the Grabow War nor the complex feelings surrounding it.

The complex feelings that some people still possess about Smith, Emerson, and Grabow had their start even before 1912. As the BTW continued to strengthen and the SLOA continued to increase its methods of control, an uneasy balance of power developed. The union gained membership, enlisted support from speakers and organizers outside the region, and disseminated information through *The Rip Saw*, *The Toiler*, and other union-friendly newspapers. The BTW movement grew in number and effectiveness. Its second annual convention from May 6–9, held in Alexandria, solidified the Brotherhood's claims and reinvigorated its approach. The convention also officially affiliated the BTW with the IWW. The organizational experience and financial support of the IWW appealed to leaders and members of the Brotherhood. The Brotherhood left the convention with clear plans and a list of demands. They sent the demands to the area's lumber companies, and when the companies summarily rejected the demands, the Brotherhood progressed with their plans for meetings and protests.

To garner and rally support, members of the "local" tried to register new faithful. Early on, they travelled to recruit wood crews; they tried to sign up workers leaving the mill or back in their homes. They took in dues; they planned public meetings and mass speaking engagements. Then, in hopes of unionizing the three most prominent local sawmills, A. L. Emerson traveled from mill to mill to mill, regaling the crowds with his best speeches and doing his darnedest to rally support for his union. The standard modus operandi became a sort of traveling union rally. Organizers at small local meetings scheduled large-scale marches and wagon rides to the surrounding mills. With their best speakers slated for the event, the union brought the meeting to the unorganized mills to address the non-union men while they worked. The skills of the speechwriter, the picketer, the carnival barker, the poet, the demagogue: these became the tools of the skilled labor organizer, the adept union-man leader.

Of course, the SLOA opposed employee membership, constructed barricades and employed guards to curtail protests at the mill, and developed organized systems of reducing the effectiveness of the BTW. The SLOA had deep pockets, firmly established lines of communication, a clear hierarchy, and "hands-on" experience with quelling union membership drives. It knew how to suppress the union message and squash rallies. Eventually, these two organizational directions erupted in their greatest and most violent expression in the form of a 1912 shootout between union members and non-union workers. Newspapers, court officials and officers of the law, and historians labeled the infamous July conflict at the Galloway Mill as the Grabow Massacre, the Grabow Riot, or the Grabow War, depending on their affiliation.[2]

On July 7, 1912, Emerson planned for H. G. Creel, a well-known union speaker, to give a speech at the Central Coal and Coke Company lumber mill in Carson, Louisiana, around six miles south of DeRidder. That day, the BTW ran into two problems. First, Creel never showed up. He claimed that men in the employ of lumber companies jumped him when he arrived in Oakdale, Louisiana. Newspapers ran with the story, and a few denounced his claim as ridiculous. The BTW, forced to cancel Creel's speech, continued with the scheduled meeting, with Emerson stepping in as speaker. Second, the BTW's reception in Carson forced him to stop his speech. Some claim that the non-union mill workers at Carson were simply uninterested; others claim the union crowd met with jeers, taunts, and even a battery of trash. Faced with this situation, Emerson and the many union sympathizers following him set out for Grabow, where organizers thought the speech would do more good.

That day, nearly two hundred supporters moved on Grabow. As Mrs. Terry described, "Where they had this Grabow Riot, they had twelve wagon loads of men that day they went there." As they traveled, no doubt leaders promised the supporters change, spoke to them of what was "right." As they walked, no doubt people described their disgust at long hours and unfair wages, described their hatred of being treated as something less than men—something no better than good dogs, something somehow less than mules or horses. As they marched, no doubt people pondered the course of the union, the repercussions of an affiliation with the IWW, the strength and lasting power of the BTW. As they talked, maybe people even sang or chanted. Some, like the spies employed by the lumber companies to infiltrate the ranks of the Brotherhood, claimed that the marchers discussed in hushed tones appropriate means of sabotage to derail a mill's progress in order to help persuade it to go union. The lumber-mill owners (and their lawyers) would later charge that these marchers even encouraged open violence and taking the mill by pistol and rifle if their demands remained unmet, but no witness, not even a spy, came forward to support that claim.

Rumors swirled that at Carson one of the union men "pulled a gun, others rapidly following his example."[3] No shots were fired at Carson, but the story spread, spread like wildfire. Grabow heard the news the same day. People say the Galloway Mill at Grabow learned of the encroaching crowd and of Emerson's intention to hold a rally there by the "only telephone line in the country." Purportedly, the men at Carson phoned those at Grabow to warn them. Some claimed that message came on horseback through the woods, reaching the mill before the march. Regardless of how they received it, the news rattled the mill at Grabow. The Galloway Mill owners claimed the rumor of fired shots at Carson prompted their nonunion men to go home and arm themselves before returning to the mill. However, many mills followed the standard practice of employing armed guards and stationing them at the mills in order to maintain control and ensure peaceful on-site demonstrations. By guard or armed millworkers, the mill prepared to defend itself. Mill bosses placed guards on alert, notified workers, and reportedly even pulled large circular saws from the mill to place in front of the company office's windows.[4]

In the reports to follow, a few key events of the day stand as indisputable. At some point, the peaceful but tense demonstration turned riotous. Close to two hundred strong, the group of men (some even claim there were about a dozen wives and children, too)[5] arrived in the late afternoon at Grabow. Near six o'clock in the evening, the heat had broken, but the day still had plenty of light left for Emerson to speak.[6] Emerson pulled his wagon up to the mill and halted in front of a crowd of roughly twenty-five non-union men. Doc Havens, a local organizer, introduced Emerson. Emerson stood on his wagon to deliver the speech he composed to replace Creel's.

As Emerson spoke, the crowd of non-union workers and bosses frequently interrupted him with taunts. Emerson continued, and his claims grew bolder. "The Brotherhood will close this mill," he said.

But the non-union men would not let that comment go unchallenged, and a member of the crowd shouted, "How?"

"We will get all the honest men into our organization," Emerson replied, "and they will quit." These words unleashed a fury. Shots rang, and the union men and non-union men squared off in a violent exchange of gunfire. However, in the melee, which side fired first remained in question.

B. F. "Happy" Harvard, a log scaler for Galloway who blamed the union men for the first shot, told his version of what happened to the papers.[7] Harvard, traveling home, noticed a crowd in front of the mill office. A union man whose name Harvard didn't know recognized Harvard from Cleveland, Texas.

"Happy, what are you doing here?" the man called out.

"I am working for the company."

"How much are they giving you?"

"$1.50 a day." When Happy announced that he was taking a wage like that, the crowd erupted.

"The son of a bitch is scabbing," one yelled.

"I'll blow his brains out," another cried. "Kill the son of a bitch." Then, people started to reach for their guns.

"He is a good boy. Don't shoot him," the man who knew Happy spoke up and made the man next to him holster his gun. Somewhere behind him a revolver discharged. Happy fell to the floor and played dead.[8]

J. C. Broxton, night watchman for the Galloway people, watched things unfold from the planing mill. He heard a revolver shot from the direction of the wagon, then saw a man fire a shotgun that had been passed from the wagon to the crowd on the ground.

Charles Gibbon, who said he was standing fifty feet from the office and twenty from the wagon, offered another version of the evening's events. He watched Galloway walk into the office, return with his gun, and fire at Emerson. "I saw no one fall," he said.[9]

"I was seated in my surrey no more than twelve feet from the wagon," George H. Gibson of DeRidder explained. "Emerson was making a speech" and someone on the gallery jeered and Emerson retorted. "McFatter and Galloway rose and entered the office. Galloway emerged and fired two shots in the wagon, after which the conflict became general." Gibson, after his horse was hit, exited the surrey and hid behind it for safety. As a result, he could offer no more of his detailed story. However, when the fight ended he came out and approached Galloway for aid for his horse. "Galloway had a gun and attempted to shoot me with it," Gibson finished.

No matter how the affair started, after the first shot, ten minutes of chaos engulfed Galloway Mill. After the initial discharging of weapons by those armed, the non-union men rushed into the company office to grab their guns. Almost everyone, including D. W. McFatter who told his version to Coroner Dr. W. L. Fisher, agreed that the first man to step from the office was A. T. Vincent. "Vincent was the first one out," McFatter said. "He fired in the direction of the wagons and this shot was followed by perhaps 20 from the office porch. I remained inside the office."[10] Armed, square in the doorway, standing ready to fire, Vincent was struck in the chest by a bullet. He died in the doorway. The men in the office spit out return fire. Unionists dropped to the ground;

those who didn't took cover—crawling and skittering to tree stumps, wagons, lumber stacks, and buildings. When they found refuge, the union men discharged their vengeance and their rifles.

In the exchange of bullets, at least eighteen men experienced wounds serious enough to seek medical aid. Countless other wounded men stumbled into the woods or inside the company offices, but some men would never make the woods. Cate Hall was one of the union crowd. His wounds to the back proved fatal. "I was sitting in my buggy about twenty feet from the wagon in which Emerson was speaking," C. O. Holley began. Holley of DeRidder traveled to Grabow in his buggy that day. "I heard a shot fired, and a few seconds later it was followed by another," Holley said. The sound told him the shots came from the direction of the lumber company's plant. "After the first shot my horse turned and ran away," he said. Then, Holley jumped from his buggy and sprinted down the road. With Cate Hall outdistancing him by thirty feet, Holley looked right towards the gallery. He saw Galloway on the gallery and saw him fire. "I turned and saw Hall fall and turn over. I kept on running," he said.

Bud Hickman and his wife, whose home stood near the mill, rode in their wagon back from town. The day must have been a pleasant enough Sunday until they found themselves in the crossfire. Hickman and his wife scrambled from the buggy and sheltered behind the general store. Soon, Hickman saw his horse take a fatal bullet to the neck. Bullets ripped his abandoned vehicle. For the moment, though, he and his wife hid safely. Then, some Galloway men crossed into a mill residence and fired on a group of unionists. Hickman again found himself caught in crossfire. Hickman decided to do something, and eventually ended up near the door of the residence. Then, as Hickman "faced toward the house to ask the men in it to desist," a Galloway man stepped through a doorway, took deliberate aim, and fired as Hickman took cover. The shot glanced off Hickman's ribs. He and his wife both saw the man who fired.

In all, three men died on-site from the shooting; another man died later in a sanitarium because of his wounds. The final count of the wounded would reach near forty. However, some dispute this number collected by the sheriff and coroner. "Nobody will ever know [how many men were killed that day]. The men, of course, didn't want anybody to know. They say that they buried six men that were shooting at the union workers or union organizers."[11] In fact, part of the debate rests with Leather Britches. "Leather Britches was sitting off in the distance and he took down six of them," Mrs. Terry claimed. "They know he got six right there, and they buried them that night out there in the dark, dug holes, didn't let anybody know," she continued. "They said there wasn't anybody killed that belonged to . . . the good people, and the scabs, they called the people who were . . . trying to keep the mill going, lost a lot of men, but they wouldn't tell anybody," she finished.[12]

As one might expect, details about the day vary, and certain key details stand as important points of argument. No one disputed the extreme nature of the violence at Grabow that day, and no one disputed that both sides fired their weapons at the other. The two sides, however, split with regards to how the firing started. In the days that followed, blame for the start of the fight shifted from side to side, and this single issue of who fired the first shot may be the most heated bit of local talk following the event. Even the subsequent legal proceedings considered this a crucial point.

Dave Burge's older cousins, Alfred and Bob Burge, hid behind wagons during the gunfire that day, and Coroner Fisher scrawled the names of Dave Burge's close friends, Cate Hall and Uriah Martin, on death certificates because of the affair. Decades later when Ralph Ramos interviewed people in the area, he stumbled upon Dave Burge. When Ramos interviewed him, Burge recounted what he knew about the events of Grabow.[13] Nearly eighty and a retired preacher by the time Ramos spoke to him, Burge didn't remember the name of the union organizer, but he did remember that Leather Britches Smith played a large part in the trouble. "As for Leather Britches's part in the actions, Burge [said] he heard that it was Leather Britches's shot which killed Goleman," Ramos writes. In the interview, Burge said, "I wouldn't be surprised if it wasn't for that reason Leather Britches was ambushed and killed at Merryville. Everyone was mad about the way Leather Britches was killed. They should have given him a chance."[14] Even though the Smith legend and Grabow do not dominate the Ramos book, in 1912 the violent turn of events at Grabow engulfed the interests of not only the local towns of DeRidder, Merryville, and Lake Charles, but also the entire lumber community throughout Louisiana and the South.

In fact, news of the violent eruption spread quickly. Nearby farmers claimed that the ten minutes of shooting at Grabow reached its end by 7:00 p.m. By 8:30, residents of Lake Charles had heard of the event. Worry and concern and excitement wandered up and down Lake Charles's Ryan Street. News reached Sheriff Henry Reid of Imperial Calcasieu Parish at roughly the same time. Reid and Coroner Fisher caught the 10:15 on the Kansas City Southern. Catching the first train to DeRidder after the fight occurred, Sheriff Reid stepped off the train shortly after midnight. Reid and local deputies W. A. Martin and Del Charlan proceeded to arrest ten men involved in the event and placed the mill property under guard. Their quick response eased local tensions about further violent outbreaks. In his report, Reid wrote that three men were found dead: Decatur "Cate" Hall, Uriah "Roy" Martin, and A. T. Vincent. Bud Hickman, Ed Brown, and Philip Fazeral (a.k.a. Farro or Faro) stood as the badly wounded.

Reid and deputies planned on making a thorough search of the surrounding area at sunrise to try to round up the wounded men who had fled into the woods. After fleeing Grabow, Emerson reached DeRidder and reported what had occurred. He also contacted Louisiana Governor Luther Egbert Hall and asked him to send troops to the area as quickly as possible. Though no troops would arrive before Reid, the next morning state militia Company K of Lake Charles and Company M of Leesville arrived in DeRidder for what would turn out to be an uneventful stay, even though many locals and company officials feared more violence.

During this July 8 trip, Sheriff Reid and the local deputies arrested ten men, eight being wounded, to answer to the charges of murder, inciting a riot, and even highway robbery. Paul Galloway, John Galloway, and A. L. Emerson numbered among the ten. None of the ten received serious wounds, Emerson no wounds at all. The ten men, Sheriff Reid, and his deputies traveled to the Lake Charles jail. Reid locked the men he arrested in cells. On the same day, Coroner Fisher's inquest returned. Through the testimony of several witnesses, Fisher held John Galloway responsible for the death of Cate Hall. Fisher could not gather sufficient evidence to place responsibility for the other deaths. The public wanted justice, and District Judge Winston Overton of Lake Charles demanded that deputies bring in all involved parties. Deputies arrested both Bob and Alfred Burge for their role in Grabow and on a charge of highway robbery, but on a list of wanted names, Smith's led the roster of persons of interest. Every few days, deputies came in with arrested men. On July 10, officers arrested six more men. Six more men came in the morning of July 12. Day by day, papers detailed the arrests of certain men and praised Sheriff Reid's efforts to keep the peace. In fact, eventually the mood calmed to the point that Governor Hall recalled the militia from Grabow and DeRidder.

Faced with such extreme violence, Overton acted quickly. He immediately called the grand jury to meet on July 15; and only a little more than a week having passed since the occurrence of Grabow, interested people and witnesses filled the courthouse to hear the grand jury charge. At that time, Overton charged the jury with its duty: "Gentlemen of the grand jury: I have found it necessary to call you together again."[15] Overton filled the room with his voice. "Many arrests have been made and the jail is now full. I have therefore deemed it necessary to call you together, the public interests manifestly requiring it." Indeed concern had spread across Louisiana and in certain segments of the country. Such a violent protest made many people, especially the residents of mill towns and the owners of mills, quite uneasy. Overton continued, "I now submit to you especially for your consideration and careful investigation whether any violations of law have grown out of what are commonly referred to as the troubles between labor and capital in the northern portion of our parish."

In his charge, Overton advised the members of the grand jury about their course of action, emphasizing certain points of the law and the jury members' obligations: "Wherever you find a violation of the law, and who the violator is, to return a true bill for such violation." Overton also explained the nature of conspiracies, the role of the attorney, and the importance of the case; then, Overton made an additional comment concerning the labor/capital relationship: "I further charge you that men in seeking employment have a right not to hire themselves save on such conditions as are satisfactory to them, and that employers in hiring men have the same right. This is fundamental, and the rights of each must be respected." Overton seemed careful to stress this crucial relationship, the trust and respect that both sides owed, but he saved his most forceful comment for his last as he added a key point to the end of this charge. He said, "But I also charge you that neither have the right to use violence or other unlawful means to attain their ends, nor to interfere unlawfully with those in the employ of another or of themselves." Eight days after the shots were fired, the grand jury began its official investigation. On the same day, Constable Gus Martin brought into jail six other prisoners charged with murder in connection with Grabow and with highway robbery, which later was ruled unconnected to the Grabow incident. Smith did not number among them, but the wheels of justice sped along the tracks.

With equal speed and decisiveness, news spread to members of the SLOA. "Dear Sir, Probably as a result of the incendiary speeches that have been recently made in this territory by Haywood, Hall, Emerson, and others, serious trouble occurred at Graybow [sic] at the plant of the Galloway Lumber Company last evening," began the letter that M. L. Alexander, manager of the SLOA in Alexandria, Louisiana, composed the following day. Though Alexander possessed only meager details of the event, he hastily sent the letter to C. D. Johnson, the current SLOA president. To construct its appropriate responses, the SLOA relied on constant and immediate updates during this time. In this first letter, Alexander highlights the events of Grabow and lists the several previously scheduled speeches and the corresponding town's responsiveness: "At DeRidder there was a large audience though not especially enthusiastic. At Merryville the crowd was quite large and much enthusiasm displayed." Creel's activities, Haywood's speeches, Emerson's marches—all were discussed as Alexander stressed the seriousness of Grabow, but Alexander carefully reassured Johnson. He ended with "the situation is critical at the present time, but it is being watched closely, and will be handled with discretion." Alexander also added a scrawled note in the bottom margin: "Emerson in jail at DeRidder without benefit of Bail."

Alexander wrote Johnson again on July 9, explaining that he was traveling to Lake Charles for a conference concerning the riot. He seemed hopeful as the wheels of justice turned, but he also warned Johnson of the various IWW leaders arriving in Merryville and Lake Charles and the "socialistic" feelings welling up in the surrounding areas. On July 19, the grand jury traveled en masse to Grabow in order to develop a clear sense of the layout of the mill. In a letter on July 20, Alexander appeared confident that the "large mass of evidence" would be "sufficiently strong to bring indictments against Emerson and the leaders in the trouble."

Though early that morning Judge Overton had urged the final report's fastidious and quick completion, when he inquired about it again at 5:30 in the afternoon, the jury returned the news that it would not be ready even by its promised time of completion, 7:30. Spectators and legal officers waited until 8:15 for the sound of feet descending the stairs and the clamor of the jury's entrance in the courtroom in order to read its report. At 8:30, July 22, the grand jury finalized its report and stood ready to deliver it. Foreman Moss led the jury back into the room and remained standing. Citing the late hour, Moss handed over a stack of folded papers in lieu of an official report. Judge Overton began by first reading aloud the names of the men who were exonerated on the charges of murder: Paul Galloway, John Galloway, V. D. Spraull, H. E. Turner, James Broxton, and R. G. Green. All six non-union men arrested were released. No charge remained on any non-union man. The jury issued true bills for sixty-five participants. The twenty-three already in custody heard the warrants for their arrests read to them, and the court issued warrants for the remaining men.

Ultimately, several cases would be filed in relation to Grabow. Case 6021 charged the accused that on the "7th day of July 1912 did feloniously, willfully, and of his malice afterthought kill and murder A. J. Vincent." Case 6022 read the same for the murder of Decatur Hall, and 6023 for Uriah Martin. Case 6024's charge stood as "shooting at with intent to kill." For cases 6021–6024, the same sixty-five men stood accused.[16] Cases 2025 and 2026 charged Charles Smith, Henry Simpson, Alf Burge, Bob Burge, John Hilton, and Bud Stacey with highway robbery and assault on James Whiddon and W. T. Grantham, a deputy. Case 6027 charged Philip Fazeral, who remained in St. Patrick's Hospital, with carrying "concealed in and about his person a dangerous weapon, towit, a pistol." Eventually, almost all sixty-five were arrested. Charles Smith was not one of them.

The court's speed and the SLOA's dissemination of information and tactical maneuvering were only matched by the endeavors of the BTW and the IWW, the BTW's powerful affiliate. As Emerson and other men waited in prison, the legal defense organized. The BTW hired several prominent defense attorneys. For the union men in jail, "Big Bill" Haywood also established the defense fund, for which he and Covington Hall, the poet and propagandist of the BTW, solicited contributions. In order to garner sympathy and quickly generate money, organizers scheduled rallies in other cities. One rally occurred in Lafayette, Louisiana, as early as July 9, and Big Bill also planned a mass meeting to be held in New Orleans. In addition, Haywood circulated complaints of Emerson's treatment and rebuttals to the several fallacious stories the SLOA released to the press.[17]

Even though the typical worker might support an effort to improve working conditions, the BTW faced the huge task of quelling people's fears and reconciling the common person to the violent acts. Many people, especially those outside the timber industry, held a firm image of the character and devices of a union group, especially one associated with the IWW. Labor's opposing force, capital, had successfully cast these forces as agitators, populists, and socialists, and people feared the connotations these words conveyed. Circulars acted as another persuasive tool for both groups, casting the other side as aggressive, malicious, contentious. Hall began a steady assault on the people's sympathies by submitting articles in several union papers. "Brothers, Comrades, Fellow-workers," he called out to his listeners. "Thugs concealed in the office of the Galloway Lumber Company fired upon our people with rifles and pumpguns loaded with buckshot," he wrote.[18] *The Toiler* and *The Rebel* published many of Hall's descriptive pieces meant to inspire passion, engender public support, and humanize the union men and the entire effort: "That our boys were neither looking nor expecting any such trouble is borne witness to by the fact that many of them had taken along their women and children, and that none of the last were killed by the trust's gunmen is a miracle."[19] In another circular, Hall waxed poetic about the "20 long months we [the BTW] have fought this mighty and merciless combination of capital, this vicious combine of grafters and gunmen, and because they have not been able to whip us back into their mills and slave pens they have planned the massacre of Grabow."[20]

Emerson himself began to respond to circulating newspaper articles, pamphlets, and town talk, and in one instance, his response won the sympathies of the Lake Charles citizenry. Although the trial's early progression seemed to be moving along rapidly, in mid-trial a forced vacation delayed the entire process. The annual summer recess meant the court would not reconvene until middle or late September. At the earliest, the Grabow trial would not be able to get underway until early October. Arrests, however, continued throughout the summer, and the men waited. On July 29, Sheriff Reid stuffed the fifty-fifth man inside the Lake Charles jail. The day before, the ladies of DeRidder served dinner to the men in prison over concerns of malnutrition and depression. Unease about the conditions mounted. Eventually, the Louisiana State Board of Health, led by Dr. Oscar Dowling, accused Calcasieu Parish of forcing these fifty-five men to live in unsanitary conditions and ordered that the men be moved to the courthouse's basement. It is here where Emerson spoke out. Even though Emerson acknowledged the conditions, he defended the jail, citing that the building was never designed to hold such a number, and praised the new conditions offered by the basement. By August, the court slated jury service to begin October 7. The prisoners endured the wait, but it took its toll on the Brotherhood. Caring for the men, funding the defense, and sustaining the families of the men in prison proved too costly, and the expense would forever cripple the BTW.

Before the trial began on October 7, a few significant events transpired. First, Philip Fazeral (Farro) died in the sanitarium. Second, the defense made a motion to quash the bills of indictment based on jurisdiction, but it failed. In addition, the prosecution filed for severance, realizing the difficulty in dealing with the large number of men. It was granted. Third, the state also hired detectives employed by the Burns Detective Agency. These detectives had the responsibility of collecting the "bulk of such evidence as will be presented by the state."[21]

As the trial date neared, excitement and curiosity built, and emotions ran high. The press reported a growing sentiment for the men in jail and a growing uneasiness about the methods of the detectives. It also promised an unusual trial, one that might prove to be the most significant in the history of the area. At the last moment, the defense asked for a postponement to seek the Louisiana Supreme Court about altering the severance of some fifty men to eight, one of which was Emerson. "We have got 'Gum Shoe' Burns and thirty-nine detectives looking for evidence. We are only asking for justice," complained Judge E. G. Hunter, a noted lawyer serving as the defense's leading attorney.[22] Congressman Arsène Pujo, for the prosecution, argued otherwise. Postponement was refused.

When the trial began at eleven in the morning, the courtroom overflowed. Day after day the courtroom filled as the jury was selected. Covington Hall, manager Kinney of the Burns Detective agency, Congressmen Pujo for the prosecution, Judge Hunter for the defense, Emerson, the Galloways, the jury, other interested attorneys, the prisoners, their families, curious citizens, and Judge Overton—they all regarded the progress. Even though Judge Hunter complained of illegal proceedings by a Burns detective concerning the jury list, he filed no formal charge, and by October 10, the quest for a jury reached a conclusion.

The burning heat of July had changed to the bright skies of October and three months and fours days had sloughed off the calendar by the time the Grabow trial began. The men sat first in the cramped jail and then in the courtroom basement as the days and weeks dragged on. The court called the list of ninety potential jurors; then, Judge Overton directed that the roll of witnesses be called. Eighty-two men and women, standing two deep and the entire width of the courtroom, lined up as an army of witnesses for the prosecution. They heard their instructions, and then the deputies escorted them from the room. Next, Judge Hunter, as instructed, manned the courtroom with his sixty-seven witnesses. They heard their instructions, and the deputies escorted them from the room. After they left, an eerie feeling emanated from the deserted room.

Coroner Fisher first took the stand and mapped the locations of the bodies he identified and their specific wounds: The body of A. T.

Vincent, found on the porch of the Galloway office building, had one shot through the neck, one in the left chest, two in the groin—one a No. 4 buckshot. The body of Cate Hall had a wound in the back. After a short recess, B. F. Harvard took the stand. Harvard repeated the story he had given Coroner Fisher some three months earlier, placing the blame with the union men. Attorney Bell's first cross-examination of Harvard left the witness haggard, but did little to damage his testimony. However, Judge Hunter's second cross introduced an interesting question. "Had you been drinking on the day of the so said riot?"

"No, sir, I was sober, and hadn't drunk anything that day except some cider."

"What kind of cider was that; was it 'squirrel' cider?" At that point, the courtroom learned the details of squirrel cider. The potent form of liquor earned its name from intoxicants' habit of climbing trees and performing other sorts of stunts. Harvard struggled to respond about the type, but maintained the effects of the brew were not harsh. Judge Hunter hammered this point home. Hunter argued that the Galloway men were drunk and anticipating a fight. Eventually, Hunter came to his last point with Harvard and questioned him about his actual title with the Galloway mill.

"Guard," Harvard replied.

"What were you, that is, what was your title?"

"Guard," Harvard said again, and seemed a tad confused.

"Well, weren't you what they call a 'gunman'?"

District Attorney Moore objected. Judge Hunter rephrased the question, and at the end of the examination, the crowd learned Harvard drifted from mill to mill as companies needed him, and had only worked at Grabow for a very short time.

Witness after witness stood in their good courtroom shoes, walked to the front of the room, and took the stand. Both sides saw the need to establish some pre-conceived threat. The prosecution sought to prove that before the union men marched to Grabow they planned on shutting the mill down by force, and the defense, that before the union men arrived the Galloway men planned on stopping the demonstration by force. The prosecution depicted the unionists as anarchists and conspirators against the Galloway mill. The union side showed Emerson and the unionists as men who called for change through peaceful means. The prosecution claimed the mill owners armed themselves for protection against an angry mob; the defense argued the union men took up arms out of a fear that violence might be done to them.

To their ends, both sides questioned W. A. Martin, the first deputy on the scene, about Emerson's works in DeRidder and Galloway's knowledge of the speech. When questioned by Pujo, Martin said, "On Sunday morning before I left town, Emerson walked up the street with me and said, 'Old man Gus is liable to have some of us before night.'" Judge Hunter cross-examined, and Martin explained that Emerson didn't tell him they were in danger of being attacked and couldn't remember many other details. Even when Pujo re-directed him, Martin said, "I don't recall Galloway calling on me for protection that Sunday before the fight began." In the end, the deputy failed to give enough information to show either side planned on a violent exchange that day. One by one, other witnesses climbed the stand to deliver their accounts. Congressman Pujo even called James Estes, a deputy sheriff, in an attempt to prove a conspiracy and to prove that Emerson advocated violence at his earlier speeches. The testimony given by Estes, however, did little to prove a conspiracy to commit violence existed, and the witness stepped down from the stand.

Ed Ezell was married with five children, forty-one, worked as log cutter, and one day took an oath with the Brotherhood. The court accepted this oath that all BTW men recited, and the BTW handbook containing the oath, into evidence:

> I do hereby swear to my God and fellow man. That I will hold forever sacred the vow that I am about to take. And I will hold forever secret the signs, gifts, tokens and passwords. I will never wrong a brother by giving his name to any one not belonging to the order. And I will never wrong a brother by taking his place from which he has walked off for more money or better conditions. But will stand by him and protect him as long as he is in the right as long as life lasts. So help me God.[23]

Perhaps the faithfulness pledged in the oath and the fervency the words conveyed made some in the courtroom uncomfortable. Perhaps to them the tone seemed too seditious, too radical. Undoubtedly, others must have felt the oath reassuring. For them, the oath existed as a sign of solidarity and as proof of members of the Brotherhood's loyalty to each other and care for the workingman. However, most probably realized either side could twist the oath's words to mean what it wanted them to mean, knew there wasn't much proof or incident buried in that book entered into evidence.

Like those of Deputy Estes and Ed Ezell, many witness testimonies proved uneventful, but when Bud Hickman took the stand and told his version the crowd would fall silent.

Bud Hickman occupied an unusual place in the trial. Not a member of the Brotherhood and never an employee of Galloway, Hickman positioned himself as an impartial witness. His now well-known story to Coroner Fisher reached the public the day after Grabow occurred. "On my way from Carson I passed about one hundred and fifty men," Hickman said. "Mr. Emerson was riding with a crowd of men on a wagon. I passed ahead of the crowd. I saw men with shotguns. Don't know who the men were who carried them." Hickman's version changed little; however, two new details emerged, and one stunned the crowd. When describing his wounds in the breast and ribs, he said, "I was looking at Ezell when he shot me. Uriah Martin was about twelve feet in front of me in a line with Ezell. Ezell killed Martin. Martin ran past me about twenty feet when he fell to the ground and died." Hickman ended his testimony, saying "Ezell used No. 8 buckshot."

When Attorney Bell cross-examined Hickman, he asked how a shot would strike Hickman in the upper part of the body and Martin in the stomach, particularly when Hickman was standing at a higher point than Martin. Bell continued, "Did you know when you were shot that Ezell's children had been shot in the fray?" Bell presented Ezell as suffering from mental agony and using his gun only after his children had been hurt. The courtroom fell strangely quiet as Hickman pointed out Ezell and it remained so as Bell described Ezell's sorrow and anguish, but Hickman would make another sensational comment during his testimony, one that would point to who started the shooting.

Hickman was on the gallery when an older man walked up. Hickman said, "The older man said to one of the boys, 'What are you doing here?'

'Working,' the boy said.

'Scabbing, I reckon,' said the man. Then a row started along the east end of the gallery."

Then Hickman would make a statement that would lay the foundation for the Smith legend. "A man named Smith—they call him Leather Breeches—told the union boys to 'line up,'" Hickman said. "I knew that meant shooting."

Even though the courtroom fell silent when Hickman delivered his testimony, the details themselves did not cement the case against the union men. The defense effectively countered. As the prosecution called each witness to the stand, one after another gave testimony aligning with his or her deposition, but Shirley Buxton changed all that. His testimony would do more to shock those in attendance and upset the prosecution's case than any other. Buxton told the courtroom, "I heard Emerson speak, heard him say 'We'll shut you down.' Another man said, 'You'll pay hell. How will you do it?' Emerson replied, 'By organizing the good honest men.'"

So far nothing of Buxton's account appeared all that surprising, even when he added, "We'll shut you down even if we have to do it with this." Buxton could not see what "this" meant, but at the time, Buxton assumed, as did the entire courtroom during his testimony, that "this" referred to a gun. Since Buxton took the stand for the prosecution, even these words did not appear sensational.

Thirty, a round man, Buxton worked as a laborer at the Galloway mill and possessed knowledge that he desired sharing. "I was at the mill office when John Galloway said 'By God, they shan't speak. Don't let us let them do it,'" Buxton explained. But Buxton also testified that after Galloway uttered those words, Buxton reminded Galloway that the road was "public and they had a right to speak." Buxton then told how "Mr. Martin Galloway replied, 'He is right. Those who don't want to hear them speak should go home.'" Again, this testimony did not surprise the court. However, during the cross-examination Buxton did offer a bit of testimony that flabbergasted the courtroom.

Buxton began the cross-examination by reviewing a map, created the first day of testimony and used as an exhibit ever since. Buxton placed himself 360 feet from the scene during the fight, and when asked to describe the events leading up to the gunfire, Buxton said, "Vincent said that afternoon that he would love to shoot 'every union son of a bitch.' He had been drinking. The boys had all been drinking what they call Mexican hot." With these few words, Buxton severely hindered the prosecution. "They were all pretty well organized," he continued. "They had been drinking from 2 to 6 o'clock. Green was the drunkest of the lot." The room exploded with gasps and mutterings and denouncements.

"Order in the court," Overton barked.

Then, the defense brought in George Green for Buxton to identify, which he did. "John, Jim, and Paul Galloway and Green had guns when I reached the office," Buxton said. "I was sober that day if I ever was in my life. About 4 o'clock I saw Harvard and the other boys hail Wimberly, the commissary man and ask him to open up. Wimberly said, 'I think I sold you boys enough of that stuff.'"

The details of Buxton's testimony mounted. The men at the mill had guns and had been drinking to the point that the commissary did not want to sell any more liquor—squirrel cider or otherwise—but Buxton held a few more tasty bits of information. Buxton finished, "Martin Galloway said, 'Hell, no; pour it into them till the union men come up.'" Furious, District Attorney Moore re-directed and other men gave testimony that day to rebut Buxton, but nothing could undo what Buxton had done.

As days passed and the court gathered more information, attorneys for the state developed its theory of a conspiracy in the Grabow case. The prosecution meant for evidence to demonstrate Emerson's and the union men's willful intent to march on Grabow and commit acts of violence. Witnesses testified describing isolated incidents, and the state attempted to weld these accounts together. The prosecutors turned to the highway robbery of Deputy Sheriff Grantham and James Whiddon, one of the charges hanging over Smith's head, but the court ruled the event not relevant to the Grabow trouble. The state also brought in two detectives, Detective Mabry and Detective Harrell, who had been operating as spies and infiltrated the Brotherhood of Timber Workers.

Mabry attended the Brotherhood's annual convention in Alexandria and heard Haywood, Hall, and other leaders speak. Harrell went along with Emerson's crowd to Grabow, and even though both detectives testified that men in the Brotherhood advocated protest and even industrial sabotage, neither recalled any instance of a man threatening violence or promising physical harm.

After the prosecution finished with its witnesses and the defense opened its testimony, witness after witness claimed that the first shot came from the mill office. The defense's evidence matched the prosecution's, and while attorneys for the state mainly pulled men and people experienced in the industry to the stand, the defense pulled many women and children, witnesses who seemed beyond reproach. After five days and calling only about twenty witnesses, the defense concluded. Both sides delivered closing arguments. In his final statement, Judge Hunter claimed that "these billionaire lumber kings have determined to crush out the union and employed the blacklist pledge, Law and Order leagues, with their armed gunmen, to do so. They thought they could prevent the organization of working men by intimidating them, and in the Grabow case they thought they saw a chance to accomplish their purpose."

At 4:45 on November 8, all fifty-eight defendants heard that they had been acquitted of murder. Those charged with highway robbery were acquitted some time later. The men were set free, and the Grabow case came to an end.

Even though after the trial ended people remained concerned about future violence, nothing would match the intensity of the Grabow War. "The Grabow Riot was a fascinating story," Mrs. Terry told me. Years later, her words echoed the feelings of the time. "There was a lot of action and sadness to it. We had at least three people die there . . . didn't do much good."[24] That afternoon when we talked, I waited a bit after she said this statement. It stuck with me. A few moments later I asked for an explanation about Grabow not helping anything. She paused for a second and spoke, "Nothing came of it." She stammered, "It was just useless." She paused for a second. "Lost lives—we lost a young boy—lost lives, caused disruption in our community, and everybody was upset in the parish, and they had been hurt and scared to death. It caused pain, pain to too many people, and nothing came out of it," she said. I thought she was finished, but after another moment she concluded, "It didn't do any kind of good."

"Without the Grabow War, we wouldn't have Leather Britches Smith," Mrs. Terry once told me, but I find this statement hard to believe, or at least I do not want to believe it. Did Smith need Grabow? Even worse, if Grabow meant nothing, where does that leave Smith? I suppose these questions are impossible for me to answer, but the fact that I am still digging exists as some proof of Smith's legacy and Grabow's importance. I would hope Smith is an interesting enough figure without Grabow, but that thought is probably delusional. He crossed the dark water of the Sabine, showed incredible prowess with a gun, and terrorized the town, but when he became a hero and villain because of his connection to the union he was unforgettable. Through the years, Grabow has become a symbolic fight between union men and non-union men and, at least for locals, real proof of the lengths that outsiders like the BTW and the SLOA will go to for control of this place and its people.

Years later, in the articles Ramos wrote and in the excerpts from the *History of Beauregard Parish Louisiana*, Smith's role at Grabow deepened. In some accounts, not only did the outlaw go with the men to Grabow and not only did he fire the first shot, but the outlaw also acted in nearly heroic fashion. When shots rang out and the horse with the wagon ran, the union men lay in the open. Unprotected, none of them had a gun, except Leather Britches. He alone returned fire, explained T. H. Peyton during an interview with Ralph Ramos. "Harry Simpson stood his ground with Leather Britches. He loaded while Smith poured his fire into the mill," Peyton said. "He was apparently trying to cut down the supporting posts because it wasn't long before the roof started to sag." Then, Peyton finished his interview with what one assumes to be his final and most direct statement on the matter. Peyton said, "We knew he was dangerous, but he was our hero."

Though Mrs. Townsley's painting depicts the gun battle at Grabow, Leather Britches Smith is nowhere on the canvas, not that I can tell, nor is he mentioned. This isn't surprising. We know people debate

Smith's role in the Grabow War. Some doubt that Leather Britches Smith ever attended any union rally much less this one in particular. Others, on the other hand, state quite plainly that he was there. When I ask Mrs. Terry if Smith was at the Grabow War, she explained, "He was there. It happened to be that that's where he stayed." As Mrs. Terry explained, Grabow was "down near a house where he [Smith] lived in the woods. But he roamed up and down the tracks." During a conversation when both Mrs. Terry and Mrs. Townsley were present, Mrs. Terry said, "He was there all the time." She felt certain that Smith not only roamed the area but also accompanied the union men to Grabow. Still, Mrs. Townsley quickly added, "That Emerson was the one that led this [Grabow War]."

The long-standing animosity that existed between labor and capital erupted in the fight at Grabow, touching nearly every family in the area. Then, the Grabow War was the unexpected endgame of both sides' tactics, leaving residents reeling in fear, confusion, anxiety, and polarizing opinions.[25] Today, the shootout stands in the memory of residents even if they can't quite articulate its cultural significance, and Leather Britches Smith, even cast as an outlaw, exists as a symbol. Metaphorically, Smith might always roam free. Literally, although the jury indicted Smith on six charges and warrants had been issued for his arrest, he was one of three men never arrested and brought to the jail. For a time, he remained free, but unlike the men in prison, he would not have a chance to earn his freedom. Moreover, unlike the other two men who were never arrested, Smith would not have the chance to be anything more than what he was on September 25, 1912—the date of his ambush and death.

CHAPTER SEVEN

THEY DIDN'T GIVE THE MAN A CHANCE

I suppose some might call the situation ironic. It was December 1997, a few days after Christmas, and I was planning my first real interview about Leather Britches Smith. Up to that point, I had heard only a few brief conversations and some talk around the dinner table, but I hadn't discussed Smith with a person outside my wife's family. My thoughts turned to the conversation planned for the next day. I was slated for interviewing Mrs. Catherine Stark, Granny Cat. Granny Cat had a reputation for knowing a good bit of historical information, and I envisioned hearing details about the outlaw's real name, his exploits, and other facts about his life. I wondered if she would describe Smith roaming through the woods and his connection to the union. I wondered if she knew about the Grabow War and about Smith's role in the fight. I speculated what she might say about how this river, these trees, the landscape itself exists as integral parts of the story. Despite all my speculations about how her story would reveal the juiciest and rarest tidbits about the outlaw's infamous life, Granny Cat's story centered, ironically, on the outlaw's death.

I suppose I should not have been too surprised about Catherine Stark's account. An outlaw's death comprises a crucial part of the story, and I suspect many people consider how that sort of man meets his end as the most interesting portion of any outlaw legend.[1] Perhaps, the times that the outlaw cheats death accumulate to make that final encounter so captivating.

The famous outlaws developed their infamous reputations in part for their ability to escape capture.[2] Pretty Boy Floyd broke roadblocks, Jesse James avoided one posse after another, and Billy the Kid survived shootout after shootout. Ordinary forces of the law seemed insufficient, inappropriate for these heroic criminals, and this experience is quite typical of outlaw-heroes. It makes sense. Nothing common should ruin the dramatic high point of an outlaw-hero's capture. If the oppressor captured the heroic criminal by the typical means of the law, these details would reduce the "good outlaw's" lure and power. Invariably, these outlaws—who seem almost immortal and like trickster figures in the process—cannot be captured in the customary fashion. Instead, the people must purge themselves of this poison, a painful but necessary act.

The outlaw-hero must enter, exist, and exit by the actions of the people, not by the actions of some outside force, especially agents of the oppressive system. Just as no town, region, or civilization can do without the outlaw figure's momentary existence at some point in its history, it cannot endure his perpetual existence. The outlaw is too wild and chaotic for that. Instead, the civilizing entity must possess the power to remove these sorts of figures when necessary. Exerting this control over the outlaw's capture and death also typifies the frontier sensibility and the folk system of justice that developed in these frontier regions. The people of the frontier needed to govern and police themselves. The common people, especially those on the frontier, must direct their own fate, but bringing an outlaw to justice is not all that easy. A defiant doer, an outlaw exists beyond the ordinary; therefore, to bring about his end, the extraordinary often becomes necessary. The outlaw is notorious for a reason. Since the law can't capture him through conventional means and the common folk may also have trouble bringing him to justice, the outlaw often comes to an end through trickery or treachery. As a result, in several legends, and in the Leather Britches story, people capture the outlaw because of a compatriot's betrayal.[3]

Leather Britches lived beyond the ordinary. In the Smith legend,

"No one dared to try to outdraw him," no one dared to oppose him, and no one could stop him. People thought only Em Sapp, that noted U.S. Deputy Marshal of Beaumont, could match him in a gunfight, but Sapp never got a chance. During the span of time between Grabow and Smith's death, other local authorities seemed helpless, completely unable to nab the outlaw. The sheriff's deputies who arrested the many men charged with murder and highway robbery after the incident at Grabow were not able to apprehend Charles Smith. Sleeping in the woods and never in the same spot, Leather Britches avoided capture for two months. Smith's own abilities and knowledge of the woods ensured his freedom. There, he became a legend.

Even though witnesses testified about Smith's role at the fight, people knew the matter remained unsettled because Smith never saw the inside of the courthouse and never had the chance to testify. While some wanted Leather Britches to come in so they could hear his side of the story or so he could defend his good name, many others wanted him brought in for other reasons. Some scared townsfolk called for his arrest. The mill owners feared a man with his nefarious nature—and seditious ideas—still on the lam. The law wanted to bring him in, but deputies, too, knew Smith's reputation. No one wanted a one-on-one fight with Leather Britches, so a few key people organized an ambush to get rid of him. One woman I spoke to put it directly, "They shot him. They ambushed him, about six of them."

The story of the ambush begins with a place. First, the authorities needed to know where Smith would be and when he would be there. Deputy Del Charlan searched for the outlaw for six weeks; then, the deputy finally learned Smith's location. "Then, they called it Pump House Branch; now they call it Leather Britches Branch," Robert Carmen told me. "A logging train went out there, and this pump house is where the train got water. It was a steam engine. And Leather Britches took over the little shack that was there and started living in it." Smith rode the train and would get off there when the train stopped to take water, so the posse staged the ambush at that location. Deputy Charlan and a few men would wait for Smith near the pump house, and when the outlaw showed, the force would end the Leather Britches saga.

Next, the members of the posse needed choosing. The posse organizers selected men for their hunting ability or for their faithfulness to local mills or for their desire to end the problems plaguing the town. Killing Smith may have been a necessity, but having the job does not seem to have garnered the sort of attention one might expect. "I know who killed Leather Britches, but I'm not going to tell. I'm not at liberty to tell," a man once announced during a discussion panel at a local library. "He was an outstanding . . . he was a prominent citizen of Beauregard Parish that killed Leather Britches."[4] As I talked to people I found that the subject of Smith's death is a sensitive one, and many people hesitated to mention the names of the three men who went along with Deputy Charlan, despite the fact that these men were deputized. "Some of these others that we know about that did this killing of Leather Britches don't want to talk about it," Mrs. Terry told me. "They wouldn't tell it; they wouldn't talk. And so that's why not many knew about it for so long." For privacy, respect, community loyalty, or perhaps the desire to make a good story, naming those who shot Leather Britches proves uneasy for some, even though several newspaper articles include the men's names.

Three men accompanied Deputy Charlan to Smith's suspected location. According to varied accounts, the events of the actual ambush occurred in one of a few ways. Some say the men surprised Smith asleep under a log truck and never gave him a chance to pull his guns or escape into the woods. Charlan's version differed. In his version that appeared in the paper, the group saw Leather Britches coming down the track around 8:45 a.m. When Smith came within about hundred feet, Charlan called for Smith to surrender. When Smith answered by shouldering his rifle, Charlan fired his automatic shotgun loaded with buckshot and killed Smith instantly. Charlan stacked Smith's two six shooters and his Krag-Jorgensen rifle on top of the body and took a photograph. (This photograph, however, never made it in the paper and even though people are sure it exists somewhere, they haven't been able to find this picture or any of the photographs rumored to have been taken when Smith's body was displayed in town—yet another way Smith lives on).

On Wednesday September 25, 1912, the *Lake Charles American Press* titillated the community with its release of a front-page article entitled

"Chas. Smith Killed by Del Charlan."[5] "Threats he had made, and his general reputation, led authorities to believe that Smith would meet death rather than arrest," the newspaper reported. Sheriff Reid waited back in Lake Charles for Charlan to come in, and Coroner W. L. Fisher deputized J. M. Cox of DeRidder so that Cox could conduct an inquest immediately. By the time Charlan told his story to the paper, he said he felt regret about the necessity of shooting him down and regret about a man who chose to commit such notorious deeds and develop such an infamous reputation.[6]

For the next few days, several articles about Smith followed. Thursday evening's front page pumped the story with even more life as it turned to Beaumont authorities. That morning authorities from Beaumont informed Sheriff Reid that "Charles 'Leather Breeches' Smith, under his real name Ben Myatt, perpetrated two murders in Corsicana, Texas." There, he killed his own wife and another man before adopting the name "Leather Britches" Smith and crossing the border into Louisiana. To fuel the fire, the newspaper posted at the center of the front page that a reward of $2,000 sat on Myatt's head. Since everyone was certain Smith and Myatt were one and the same, Charlan figured to be a rich man and Lake Charles, the proud owner of a soon-to-be-famous resident lawman. That night Del Charlan also arrived in Lake Charles, bringing with him Smith's personal effects: a .38 Winchester rifle, a Krag-Jorgensen rifle, two .45 Colt revolvers, two knives, twenty-eight rounds of ammunition, and $36.90 in money.

The article also said that Smith ran forty steps after being shot. He tried to raise his rifle, but too weak to do so, he pulled a revolver. He collapsed without being able to fire it. That same Thursday, Emerson released a statement to the newspaper explaining that Smith was not a leader of the BTW, as the paper reported the day before, and that he did not know the deceased. On the surface, as the newspaper speculated, Smith's life ended in the manner everyone expected—a deputy finally brought him to justice and the brutal, deadly outlaw met his end violently. However, the Smith legend extends far beyond the newspaper articles and far beyond the expected.

First, some ill feelings surrounding the ambush lingered in town. "They felt they were right, or they wouldn't have done it," one informant said. Many people might resent that the men ambushed Smith, but few resent the people who did it. Fear is reason enough for that. Among others, Mrs. Terry explained to me that these newly formed deputies "were good men. They were trying to protect their own families, trying to protect their own families. They were deathly afraid of him. Everybody was deathly afraid of him." Even years later, when Ramos discovered the fifteen-year-old daughter of Grantham, she told Ramos, "Most people were glad to see Leather Britches dead. He had all the farm people terrified. Those were terrible times. . . . Country folks couldn't do anything but what Leather Britches told them to do."[7] Still, the deputies all held firm reputations for being tough and able to handle a gun, so fear doesn't seem to be exactly the right word. On October 2, 1912, the last grand jury of Imperial Calcasieu Parish (the last because Imperial Calcasieu split into five smaller parishes) ruled that Deputy Del Charlan, Ike Meadows, Paul McMillan, and James Broxton killed Smith because he resisted arrest and exercised every precaution before they took his life.[8]

Second, people began to wonder how lawmen finally pinpointed the location of Leather Britches's hideout. To locate the outlaw's hideout, an insider must have come forth. In this part of the story, a betrayer lurks. Some say that the betrayal resulted from the crew of the train that kept the outlaw supplied, talking to the authorities. "One day he told the train crew that he was getting low on shells, to bring him some shells back the next day," one person told me. "At night they [Charlan and the men] rode out there, and at daylight, they were waiting for him when he came out of that shack, and they shot him down." In Mrs. Terry's version, betrayal occurred as the result of a union man, who may have even earned a reward for helping them: "He [Smith] was getting ready to leave the country, and they [the union men] told him that they'd made up a pot for him and for him to go down there and get it, and these men were waiting for him to waylay him that morning, and so they did."

Shelley Whiddon's version describes the ultimate betrayal. In her account, Leather Britches turned on himself. "He was supposed to have some money in the shed or something and he was going to get it and was finally going to get out of town," she told me. Repeating the story she heard from her grandfather, she continued, "They [her great-grandfather and another friend] said, 'Don't go to the shed today. Just don't go. Just leave it. Don't worry about it, and you can get it later. Don't go there.'" Then, Shelley described what happened next: "Leather Britches said, 'I'm tired of running. I'm tired of hiding. People are going to do what they want to do.' And they shot him in the back walking away."

In other versions, people warned Smith of the ambush before it happened. Written in 1972, "The Last Violent Days of Leather Britches" recounts what Ramos learned from Joe Meadows of Merryville, the son of "Little" Ike Meadows, who was a member of the posse. In this version, Ike Meadows learned a few days before the ambush that Smith was at the home of John Foshee, a local man in whose home he used to hide out. "He [Smith] was seated at the end of the dining table bench, right next to the door, when Meadows called out he was unarmed, wanted to palaver and stepped through the door," Ramos reported. As soon as Meadows came in, Smith "grabbed up his rifle" and fled into the night. Meadows called out to the outlaw. "I told him they would kill him surely if he didn't give himself up. I tried to assure him that on my honor I'd guard him with my life until he could get a fair trial."[9] Joe, remembering what his father had told him, also claimed Ike Meadow's shot killed Smith.[10]

Regardless of the exact course of events and whether or not a betrayer aided the posse in its plans, the ultimate outcome remains the same. Deputy Charlan and three other townsfolk ambushed Leather Britches and killed him. Parallel to the death of many other "good outlaws," Smith meets his end, and the unconventional manner in which he does heightens this legend's effect. In fact, for many the way the deputies killed Smith cements his reputation. As Robert Carmen pointed out to me, "The fact that they killed him and the way that they killed him tells me that first of all he was a bad man, a rough man, and somebody to be feared, and second he was hurting them some kind of way. It wasn't that he wasn't doing any good."

When interviewed by Ramos, Goob Newton finished his account connecting the way Leather Britches died to his legacy: "He didn't fear nothing in the whole world, and we all had wanted to see him in a fair fight, not killed in an ambush." During his research trips, Ramos also encountered Arch Slaydon, a Merryville barber. Eighteen when the men ambushed Leather Britches at Merryville, Slaydon claimed to have known Leather Britches. He told Ramos, "The dirty dogs didn't give the man a chance."[11] People suspect that Smith's actions at Grabow forced people to retaliate, and for many the ambush symbolized another oppressive act, proof of the lumber companies' unfair advantage. That members of the community ambushed Smith illustrates at least two other points about the residents of No Man's Land: (1) the toughness and resilience of the community members to handle problems themselves and (2) the workings of the folk system of justice that governs the area.

Superficially, this extreme act of violence might seem to be the product of a lawless community, one with no sense of justice. However, any folk system of justice involves a certain amount of violence. Guided by a system, violence, even murder, can be quite acceptable, and the violent events of a legend can be a method of instructing residents about this system.[12] In this case, the degree of violence balances the violence of Smith. The community reacts in an expected and necessary manner to deal with the deadly behavior and chaotic events marking Smith's life. By supplying Smith, warning him, betraying him, and even killing him, the common folk wield the power and direct their own destiny. The common folk remain in control and decide to cleanse the town of this dangerous element. On the surface, the sheriff's deputy (the authority that serves as a representative of the oppressive system) seems to control whether Leather Britches will be killed or remain free, but the folk who give him the information make all the difference.[13] Even if one of its members performed the questionable act of betraying Smith, the role of the folk does not diminish.

Typical of the outlaw legend, much more of the story remains after the figure dies, so the legend of Leather Britches does not end with his death. "Where the big crowd came in that I saw when I was three years old . . . they were all waiting," Mrs. Terry said to the crowd seated at the library. That night she wanted to raise their anticipation. "I can remember just as well as anything. We lived right where the museum is today. That was our home. Right there is an alley going from our house down to a street of Merryville, a main street. That was absolutely covered with people," she said. She sparked the crowd's interest and then asked other people on the panel to tell what they knew. After a half an hour of history about Smith's past, an audience member asked, "What happened when you were three years old? Did you see Leather Britches?" Mrs. Terry answered, "Well, I saw all of the people, and that's the end of the story. I'll finish that when we get to the end." The crowd laughed, and waited.

During another interviewing session, one man explained that "Goob said that they were so afraid of him that after they shot him down, he crawled back into that shack, and they came back into town and hired a black man to go out there and see if he was dead, and he was."[14] Once they were sure the outlaw was dead, they retrieved Smith's body and loaded it on the Merryville train, which brought the body to town. Similar to the way crowds amassed to see the body of Jesse James or the bullet-ridden carcasses of Bonnie Parker and Clyde Barrow, Smith's funeral received a large amount of attention.[15] Even though residents did not arrange a grand funeral, they turned out in droves to view the outlaw's body. Goob Newton remembered that people built a special crib or box for the body and stacked it with ice. "Everybody in town was there, everybody in Merryville was there. We were scared to death. Everybody was deathly afraid," Mrs. Terry said. She continued her story that night in the library: "They brought him in on a special wagon and put him up against a post there in Merryville, tied him up there, and stood him there for two hours. Everybody in the country by that time had heard, and they came to see, and that's what the people were doing in Merryville that day." When the men brought the body into town, "they put his body out so people could see it."

Stories like this one point to three main reasons people turned out to see the body. First, people wanted personally to see that he was dead. They wanted real proof that he was gone. Second, people who supported him wanted to mourn his death. Third, and this seems to be the most important reason, people came out to see the body because they wanted to participate in the event. Smith may have been ambushed and betrayed, he may have been daring and incredibly skilled with a gun, he may have been dangerous, heroic, or even pious, but most people attended his "funeral" because he involved the townspeople and demanded attention. He became a part of history; he became legendary. He became a part of residents' lives and a part of the community's permanent consciousness.

The story, though, continues even further. "They wanted for one thing to preserve his body because the Texas Rangers wanted to come look at it and check it to see if it was the same person, the same man, so they took it down," Mrs. Terry told me. On Sept. 27, two days after Wednesday's article about Smith's killing, the *Lake Charles American Press* ran another article about Leather Britches. "Desperado Not Yet Identified" left the readers of the *Press* in suspense. Sheriff Rushing, the Texas lawman who knew Ben Myatt and described good ol' Ben down to the scar under his left eye, planned on arriving in Lake Charles on the No. 10 Southern Pacific. The whole town was abuzz. Everyone expected that once Sheriff Rushing saw the five-foot ten-inch frame, the 145 pounds of man, the light scraggly mustache, and, of course, the scar under the left eye that all collected on the body of Leather Britches Smith, he would pronounce the dead man to be the escaped convict from Corsicana—he would pronounce the dead man to be Ben Myatt.

But any outlaw worth his salt manages to stir things up even after his death.[16] Rumors may swirl about the figure being alive somehow, and people may continue to talk. Folks whisper that the man still roams the wild. They stress that officers never found the body or that someone or some thing disturbed the grave in the days following the death. Like his previous dynamic escape, the outlaw here, too, avoids imprisonment in the ground. For the Leather Britches legend, this emerges in two ways. First, questions surrounded the actual identity of the outlaw. For example, to everyone's surprise Sheriff Rushing did not visit Lake Charles, after all. Instead, he traveled directly to Merryville, and once there—surprising everyone even more—declared that Smith was not Ben Myatt, the criminal he had chased for years. The October 4 weekly issue of the *Lake Charles American Press* placed "Texas Officer Views Remains" on its front page. The article described the pivotal piece of information that identified the man. Rushing said that Smith's eyes did not match Myatt's. Local authorities, confused, considered the practices of the Texas lawman dubious, and many still wonder about the real reasons motivating Sherriff Rushing. Even in my present-day interviews, Mrs. Terry said, "Whether they didn't want to just get into it anymore, they said, 'Oh, no. That's not the man.'"

The debate about the actual identity didn't stop there. Some people even claim that the Leather Britches in Louisiana borrowed a Texas criminal's name and that two Leather Britches actually existed. "Whenever they came down and looked at him they said, 'This is not Leather Britches.' This was another guy," Shelley Whiddon stressed to me. In fact, she doubted any real connection between Charles Smith in Merryville and the notorious Leather Britches in Texas. She said, "He's not really the true Leather Britches. . . . He's who they made into Leather Britches. Well, the other guy just happened to have the same nickname and have the reputation to do really bad things, and so they just fed off that." In her version, the outlaw stands as a ploy, a tool of the lumber companies to malign the union. "I'm saying that the stories that were told were told so that they would have a right to kill him, so that it would quit costing them money," she explained.

Second, people often claim that Smith was never actually killed. Even during the trial, a month after Smith had been ambushed, testimony raised doubts about Smith's death. A painter and paperhanger, William E. Gahlman, who went with the union men to Grabow, testified at the trial that he didn't see any guns in that crowd. When being examined by the defense, Gahlman produced two letters from friends of the defense. Both letters warned about a detective spy, Ed Whitten, in their midst, but the second half of the first letter mentions Smith. "Lether Briches aint dead," the letter read.[17] "I seen him las nite he says he was erbout Whitten and him and that felly Harrel is dubs [not to be trusted]. Regardless of what Gahlman claimed, however, authorities in Merryville had a body to bury. At the time, the newspaper articles made a point about no person stepping up to bury the man, but someone must have decided to bury him because many accounts (and quite varied ones I would add) detail his burial.

At fairs, high school events, and dance recitals when I ask a group of kids or young adults about Smith or when I talk to someone who knows about Leather Britches but claims not to know much history about him, they often supply various descriptions of where he is buried or how or why. First, people disagree about how the people placed his body in the coffin. During the lecture at the Beauregard Parish Library, I heard such a story. A woman in her early forties said, "From the time I've been a little girl, I always heard that he was buried facedown with his hands handcuffed behind his back. Is that true?" A few members of the crowd nodded and stated their own similar experiences. In their versions, many people explained that Leather Britches Smith did not receive a Christian burial. Mr. Carmen said, "Goob told me one time that they buried him facedown, north-south. In case he scratched out, he'd go to China." My wife once told me, "They buried him that way because that's where he was going. That's what I was told when I was a little girl."[18] One of my college students rather casually said, "I don't know anything about Leather Britches really except that he's buried in the cemetery by the school and that he's buried facedown. I think because that's where he was going."[19]

I don't find stories about the unusual burial practices Smith's body incurred all that surprising. For many people, the cemetery communicates principles of faith; in fact, for some, the area provides a resting place for the spirit until the end-time.[20] For example, some Protestants face the bodies of the deceased with feet towards the east. In effect, the deceased remain positioned for the Second Coming since for these Protestants their belief in this case relies on a literal interpretation of the Bible. Smith's burial and comments about it, then, become meaningful expressions of cultural beliefs. If the outlaw's body does suffer from inverted or strange burial rituals, his status is rather clear. By burying him facedown, the community would have made a statement about its view of Leather Britches as one who failed to adhere to cultural expectations.[21] The death and burial of the outlaw stand as the community's final judgment about the figure and warns community members not to behave as he did.[22] Of course, there's no proof he was buried facedown, but no one is digging up the body for evidence. Besides, even if people wanted to, they would have a hard time finding the grave. People's versions, after all, also differ on the placement of the grave itself, the second point of contention about the outlaw's burial.

When I visited with Granny Cat during our first meeting, I heard about Smith's grave. Granny Cat spoke plainly and matter-of-factly about this event so significant and meaningful to her, yet so complex and mysterious to me that I remember that day vividly. I pulled the car into the shell driveway, killed the engine, and hurried to get Grand's door on the other side. She had it opened and pulled herself out of the front seat by the time I walked around the car. I did make it to the door in time for her to use my arm as a brace. She grabbed onto it and hoisted herself up. We walked up to the trailer where Granny Cat lived with her daughter, Sukie, and we knocked on the door. Someone had built a porch onto the front of the trailer and attached latticework skirting so that the house resembled a manufactured home. Sukie opened the door and brought us inside. Granny Cat, sitting in a recliner in the front room, stood as we filed in and made a step or two towards the door before Grand met her with a hug. Melanie did the same. I shook her hand and found a seat on the couch. Grand sat in the other recliner across the room, and Sukie pulled a chair from the kitchen to the neutral ground existing as a small, but powerful expanse between the two rooms. There, Sukie sat on a stool standing half on front room carpet and half on kitchen linoleum. A big striped sienna cat jumped into her lap.

They began the conversation not with the past but with the present. Both shared what they had heard about a close friend whose husband or child recently died. As they threw out names, I couldn't discern who had died; in fact, sitting there, I struggled to keep up with anything they swapped between them, two old clan chieftesses weighing what comes and goes as they barter, and understanding the worth of every ounce. For the first time, I was trying to tape-record stories of Leather Britches, and I was already lost. I didn't know any of the names and couldn't ever quite tell if the conversation about Leather Britches had started or not. I didn't know when to start the recorder, and part of me thought I shouldn't even be listening to this private conversation. Stories flew around and my head spun. I could hear the words they spoke and understood the sentences, but the talk held no weight and my stomach couldn't connect the words to the meanings they held for these people. Family histories unfurled; their trees twisted in my mind. Place names spread out before me, unknown and unrecognizable. Bits of the story spilled out all over the place, but I could not seem to piece any of it back together. I spent the first ten minutes of the visit dizzy. Finally, Granny Cat looked at me. "I love history. I put it down in this book," she said. With that, she helped me realize the interview had started, and I pushed "record."

She pulled out an oversized book, hard bound in black leather. She showed me the title pressed into the leather in white type: *History of Beauregard Parish Louisiana*. "I've written several of these stories in here." She flipped through the pages, finding the short pieces on Stark family history that end with the byline "Catherine Fuller Stark" in bold type. "One time, the largest mill in the United States was here." She flipped some more. "He was over in east Texas and that's where a lot of his meanness was done and, of course, it just followed him across because it's just across the river." She left him as suddenly as she brought him up. "I just used to sit and listen." Then, she began to tell me how she had recently changed, willing now to unlock her mind and talk and even write down what she had seen and heard. "When we hear guns shooting and people hollering and bells ringing, we knew exactly what it was. It was fire," she said.

In what follows, Granny Cat relived the great 1908 fire she watched as a young girl, standing in the street. All their men at work, the women and young boys fought the flames. She gazed in awe as a teacher's home burned to the ground. She saw the two-story hotel ablaze, the church go. She followed the fire as it jumped the road and took another home and another and another, and she worried as it swept towards her own home. Then she was holding buckets, taking them from one person near her and then passing them to another. Rotating her body back and forth, she passed buckets and watched people pull quilts, pictures, and furniture from nearby houses not yet in flames. The schoolboys wet quilts and draped them on roofs, on the sides of houses. The DeRidder fire truck arrived; then, the men finally returned from the woods and their jobs. Together, they stopped the spread of flames. "The August storm and this fire. Took everything. Two things that happened in Merryville. They ranked something else as second, but I'd put that fire second."

That story ending, she searched for the article that detailed the history of Merryville and the list of the town's great tragedies. "Ah, Sugarfoot." She continued to search, looking up now and then, a steady stream of words pouring from her the whole time: drops of history, family names, Christmas mornings, Easter services, sheriffs, lumber companies, John Henry Kirby as the kindest mill owner around, her tricks on her little sister, her now-deceased husband Leonard's first words to her, "Get over here, you crazy girl." Then, she found it and read the words aloud: "Here it is. 'The greatest tragedies were the August 16, 1918, hurricane that destroyed all the virgin pine timber and the first union strike in the United States.' I guess it was . . . but that was men against men and each side had a reason to do it, but this other, all them houses burned up, there wasn't no need for that." The book forced her hand and in the end, Granny Cat conceded the importance of Leather Britches and the strike at the Grabow Mill.

Then, her talk finally drifted to the outlaw. She explained that her family was too busy having fun to talk too much about him, but that she did know some and the some she knew centered on the outlaw's death and burial.

"They put his body out so people could see it."

"Where's his grave?" The people in the room threw out questions to draw out more of the story. "Which cemetery?"

"The one right here. In the little fenced-in part, inside, that's the Newton part, and all their people are there, but Goob put a little tombstone by the side for Leather Britches, but that's not where he is."

The people in the room waited silently. I wondered if she could read the cloud of confusion that covered my face. "I see," I said.

"He's over by that north fence because that's where that baby is."

At that moment, I could not completely understand what she meant, and I was unsure if the other people in the room could either. Interrupting her, someone in the room asked for clarification. "So he's not in the cemetery?"

"He is. Just inside the north fence. They put him as close to the fence as they could get him."

Melanie asked, "Why did they do that?"

"Well, there was enough people that wanted him buried there. It all depended on the people who were there."

"So some people didn't like him?" Melanie asked.

Granny Cat answered, "A few liked him, but might near everybody else, the whole population, was glad to see him go."

Immediately, I plotted out the cemetery in my head. I had seen it from the road and had once walked its rows, but I did not see the tombstone. Driving back to Grandmother's home after the meeting with Granny Cat, the cemetery remained stuck in my head. First, I imagined myself standing in the middle of it, trying to get my bearing. I plotted the arrangement of stones that I could recall in my mind. In my head, I spun my body to the north, but I couldn't remember a fence there. For the life of me, I had no idea what the discussion of the baby meant. Stuck at a stop sign, I turned to Grand and Melanie and asked if they understood the reference, but they didn't either. I planned on visiting the cemetery before I drove back home.

Highway 110 borders the Merryville Cemetery's west side, the side that holds the entrance. Trees, mostly longleaf pine that are reminders of the town's long history with the lumber industry, form the cemetery's back, but they are cut when the cemetery needs to expand. The south boundary is a chain-link fence that separates the cemetery from the high school. An old gully, thick brush, and trees marking the cemetery's north boundary offer a stark contrast to the well-kept cemetery grounds.[23] The only cemetery bearing the name of the town, a cultural landmark of sorts, the cemetery seems typical of many North Louisiana Protestant cemeteries.[24] The cemetery contains many belowground burials, a feet-to-east burial arrangement, head and foot markers, and no central cross or crucifix. Family groupings section off much of the cemetery, and coping surrounds many of these burial sections. In fact, the Merryville Cemetery appears much like an urban cemetery as several markers indicate union affiliation and the entrance is gated. Maybe these hint at its date of construction. The town built the cemetery during its timber boom. At the time, newspapers praised the city for its growth and its promise of a secure and prosperous economic future. The Smith marker rests near the section holding the Newton family—relatives of Goob Newton and Ester Newton Terry.

Though rather simple, the gravestone of Leather Britches Smith serves as a brief, though tangible, historical record. The two-feet-high-by-one-foot-wide square tombstone communicates its contents through crude letters scratched out by some tool before the stone's cement dried:

SMITH, LEATHER BRITCHES SLAIN–1912

The small gravestone marking Smith's grave mirrors his status. This most ordinary of all markers reminds us that he was of and for the common person.[25] It does not carry denominational symbols, such as statues, reliquaries, or crosses. "Smith, Leather Britches" does not betray the mystery surrounding him, but still places him by his surname. Void of any sort of gravestone motif, the marker seems meant more to record that the outlaw lived rather than to pass judgment on his life. However, "Slain—1912" obviously communicates one side of the story surrounding his death and definitely marks the year of upheaval and strife. The plastic flowers that decorate his grave perhaps don't offer grand sentiment, but they prove that people still care for and about the man. Furthermore, how Smith's marker fits in with the design of the cemetery, which includes the types and placements of gravestones, vegetation, and the cemetery's layout of paths, reveals some of the community's values.[26] Most of the markers in the cemetery are either older, large stones that tower above the surface or thin, sleek modern markers that rest level to the ground. Smith's marker does not fit this pattern. The gravestone is definitely not modern, but it cowers under the markers surrounding it, especially the grand stones in the Newton section closest to his stone.[27]

The marker seems perfect for the figure, and even its placement in the cemetery seems revealing. The cemetery's front is old; the back, new. People erected the marker in an older portion of the cemetery, a section filled with family names—some important to the area's settlement and some alive when Grabow occurred. Smith's markers rests next to one of the families who view him positively, or at least appreciate his importance. The marker rests near the fenced-in rectangle marked off for the Newton family, but remains excluded from the family section by that small fence. Located in the portion of the cemetery with plots organized around families, Leather Britches conspicuously sleeps alone.

But Granny Cat told me the stone did not mark the actual burial site. Could the stone be inauthentic as well? Granny Cat isn't the only person to question the authenticity of the grave and burial site. Many people in their accounts argue about the Smith grave not being where some people say it is. One perfect example occurred after I finished giving a public lecture in Lake Charles, Louisiana. The first large public lecture in Lake Charles on the subject for some time (probably at least ten years) and part of a larger series of publicized cultural events, the lecture drew a large crowd. People drove in from towns north of Lake Charles, and they filled the large meeting room. The latecomers stood in the back and sat on the floor up front, and the organizers even turned away a few people because the room could not hold any more.

At first, I was excited that so many turned out to hear what I had to say about Leather Britches. After I finished the lecture, I realized that people turned out for a very different reason—to correct me, or at least to make sure I got most of the story right. I pulled from both printed sources and the interviews I conducted. I told the entire legend: what I heard about how Smith came into the area, what happened at the Grabow War, Smith's ambush, and the debate about how and where he was buried. I showed a few slides, one of which was an image of Smith's marker. At the end of the lecture, the moderator asked for questions. Nervous, I knew it was a tradition I couldn't avoid, and I wondered what the audience might ask.

Immediately, one man stood and, instead of asking a question, made a remark concerning the outlaw's grave. He said, "Leather Britches is not there. He's next to the gully running outside the boundaries of the cemetery." His uncle once told him this story and showed him the old, crumbled grave marker that had since been washed away by the erosion of the gully's sides. This man felt compelled to explain this to me.

Though this debate may seem inconsequential in a random version of the Smith legend, the teller's opinion about the location of Smith's burial betrays that teller's opinion about the outlaw's role as criminal or do-gooder. If the body rests near a local family or a union supporter, Leather Britches lies as a defender. If the body of Leather Britches Smith did not cross the cemetery's fence because people wouldn't allow it, there's no doubt about his role as an outlaw. Burying him outside the area established for normal community members (even if it is inside the cemetery but on its very edge) and placing him with no hope for the Second Coming (facedown or in a north-south position), the people could make no stronger comment about his status in the community.[28]

The debate about the grave exists for good reason. In the mid-1960s, a group of people, Goob Newton included as a hand of the Beauregard Parish Historical Society erected the simple marker on a plot the Newton family owned. Despite appearing unconnected to the historical legend, the newly erected marker comprises an important component of the legend. In spite of the marker's potential lack of authenticity, the gravestone remains culturally communicative. The motivations and choices behind its creation express recent values and beliefs from an important segment of the community, one concerned about the promotion of local history. Whether it supports the sympathizers' view of him or supplies the opposition ammunition for rebuttal, the marker acts as a constant narrative device. Sometimes it functions as a simple starting point of the legend, and sometimes as a point of contention.

In my experience collecting the legend, many people began their version by referencing the marker. Often, this first step framed their discussions, offering them a concrete starting point and triggering the memory with a vivid image. In this sense, the "fake" marker ensured the legend's veracity. In addition, describing the placement of the marker, the teller placed the listener on equal footing. Once listeners indicated that they understood the marker's location, tellers continued their story with the knowledge that a point of connection existed. Starting with the death and burial also began the story at a dramatic highpoint. Finally, I noticed that the marker served as a fieldwork device to initiate conversation with people. When faced with a quiet person or an interviewing session at a standstill, I often asked if the person knew about Smith's marker. Almost without exception, informants began talking about the marker itself, then about whether the outlaw deserved the death he received, and finally about their own family's involvement in the legend.

The gravestone provided many people with a narrative device that helped them begin talking and, perhaps more importantly, provided them a safe, non-threatening opportunity to pass judgment on the figure and express beliefs about a sensitive or controversial subject, the Grabow War. The final articles written by Ramos pose the essential question: "Was Smith a hero or outlaw, benefactor or murderer?"[29] To answer it, the articles describe the headstone that marks Smith's grave. Ramos writes that beside "that tiny headstone is a pot of artificial flowers," and raises the questions of "Who placed the headstone?" and "Who leaves the flowers?"[30] Mrs. Terry stated frequently that "everyone should know about" the outlaw and the history of the area. As proof of her own dedication to the story, she maintained the grave of Leather Britches up until her move in 2003. She admitted to refreshing the flowers whenever she visited her father's grave. During the library talk, one person in the audience asked Mrs. Terry, "And your family just felt a need to take care of the grave because he had nobody?" In response, Mrs. Terry said, "Because he had nobody else." Her care for the grave tried to balance the outlaw's solitary nature and, by it, her opinion of the outlaw was clear. Maybe the individuals who placed the marker presented only a certain side of the story and made biased judgments about the outlaw's life, but more important, they stressed the area's history, the uniqueness of the place's culture.[31] Far from acting alone, the outlaw's grave works in conjunction with the rest of the culture's pronouncements about the figure.

Leather Britches undoubtedly lives on in Merryville. He remains an important part of many people's lives through the stories, the songs, and the arguments about him. People argue about his grave. They pursue the mysteries surrounding his death and burial. They claim to have know some secrets about him. They tell their memories of his deeds and explain the parts their relatives played in the events. Some even claim to be his descendants. Though the outlaw legend celebrates the deeds of the figure himself, the telling of the legend celebrates the deeds of townsfolk, and their values and beliefs even more. On the frontier, a certain compromise between individual ability and communal support ensures survival. The outlaw-hero embodies this balance. For the sake of the community, the independent outlaw-hero acts outside the laws instituted by some outside oppressive system; for the sake of the community, townsfolk put him down. Ultimately, the legend becomes a cultural resource. The outlaw's life serves as a history lesson; his death, a moral one. Smith's body may rest below the earth, but his actions rise above it, for they roam in the memories, family stories, and routine conversations of the people here. He can be their best teaching tool, their most tangible tie to the past, and their most valuable piece of cultural heritage.

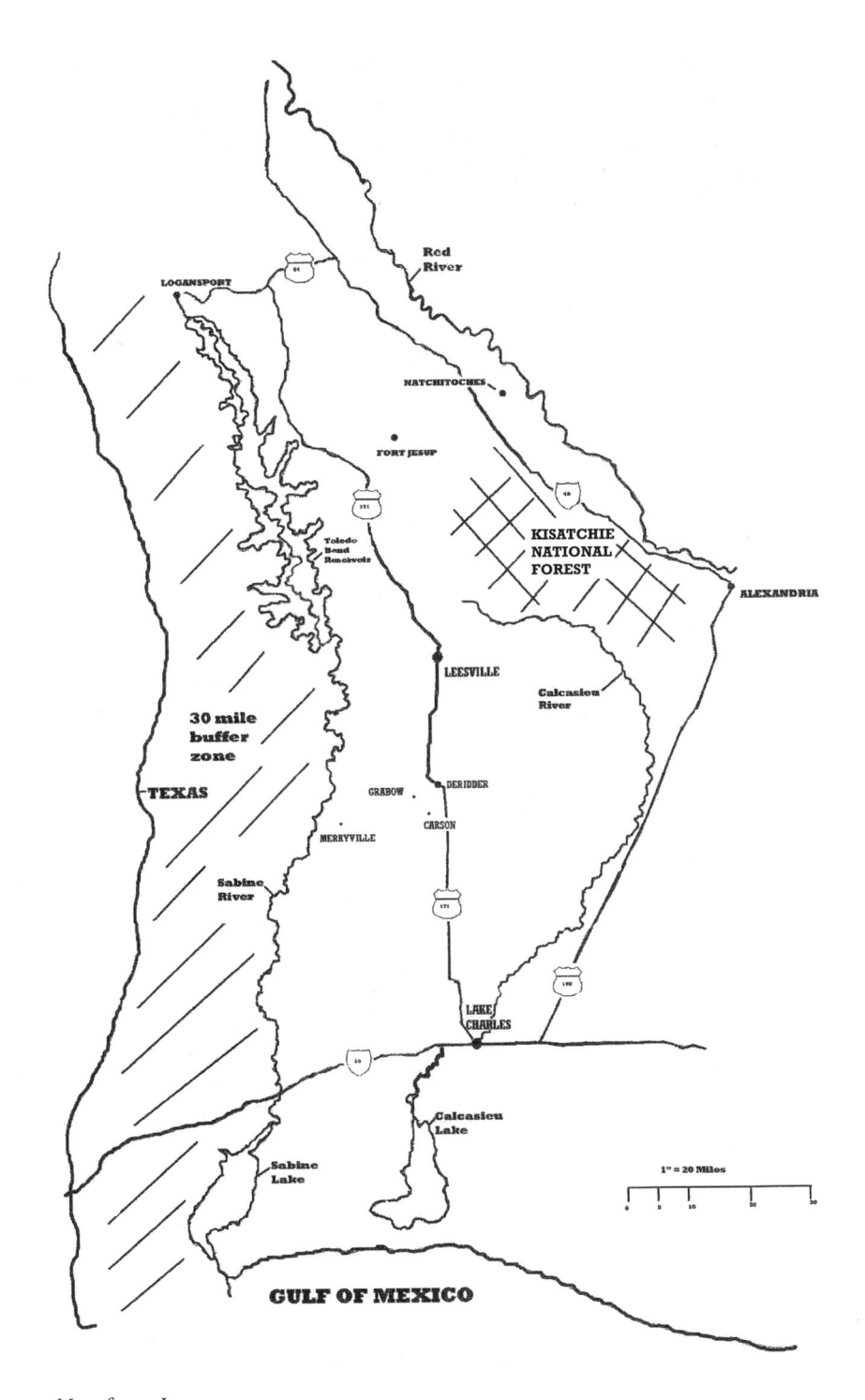

Map of area ILLUSTRATION BY AUTHOR

Louisiana longleaf pine Courtesy McNeese State University Archives

Carson logging camp COURTESY MCNEESE STATE UNIVERSITY ARCHIVES

Felling trees near Lake Charles

COURTESY MCNEESE STATE UNIVERSITY

Typical wood crew   COURTESY MCNEESE STATE UNIVERSITY ARCHIVES

John Henry Kirby speaking in DeRidder   COURTESY MCNEESE STATE UNIVERSITY ARCHIVES

Company office for mill at Carson   COURTESY MCNEESE STATE UNIVERSITY ARCHIVES

Co. K First Infantry   COURTESY MCNEESE STATE UNIVERSITY ARCHIVES

Union prisoners in Lake Charles Jail   COURTESY MCNEESE STATE UNIVERSITY ARCHIVES

Portrait of Judge Overton

COURTESY MCNEESE STATE UNIVERSITY ARCHIVES

Union prisoners at the big dinner COURTESY MCNEESE STATE UNIVERSITY ARCHIVES

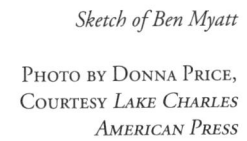

Sketch of Ben Myatt

PHOTO BY DONNA PRICE,
COURTESY *LAKE CHARLES
AMERICAN PRESS*

Leather Britches's tombstone PHOTO BY AUTHOR

Leather Britches's tombstone with flowers PHOTO BY AUTHOR

Burks House PHOTO BY AUTHOR

Outlaw parade for Merryville Heritage Festival PHOTO BY AUTHOR

Amarillo Slim, member of No Man's Land Gang PHOTO BY AUTHOR

Pioneering couple, members of No Man's Land Gang   Photo by author

Reverend Devil, member of No Man's Land Gang Photo by author

Beginning of a shootout skit at Merryville Heritage Festival   PHOTO BY AUTHOR

Reverend Devil during a skit PHOTO BY AUTHOR

"Gang Wardens" parade float PHOTO BY AUTHOR

Wanted poster PHOTO BY AUTHOR

CHAPTER EIGHT

THE OUTLAW APPLIED

Weeks, months, years, and even decades following the Grabow trial, the story still makes the papers. Months after the trial, rumors of a potential strike in a Merryville mill circulated. Tensions rose, but the fears proved to be unfounded. A year later, Charles Cline, a man arrested during the Grabow Trial, found himself arrested again. This time Cline turned out to be the leader of a band of arms smugglers whose band dealt guns and ammunition across the Mexican border. After his capture, Cline led officers to the smugglers' current camp, and another great gunfight ensued. Cline also produced several documents proving IWW's interests in Zapata's Mexico.[1]

From around 1930, every ten or twenty years, the *Lake Charles American Press*, the *Beaumont Enterprise*, the *DeRidder Daily News*, or some other local paper runs a story about Smith and Grabow. Usually, a news reporter, such as Ralph Ramos, or even a folklorist, adds a few fresh details or a scrap of news. Sometimes the work, like the work of Ramos, delves a bit deeper or stretches a little broader than past discussions. Sometimes an article looks at the closed mills or the weeds currently taking over Grabow, warning readers about the past fading away and urging them to work to preserve it. Each time, those in the know reinvigorate their own ideas, and those unaware learn a bit about the story. Each time, Leather Britches rides again.

When the library gathered Ester Terry, Gussie Townsley, Frank Hennigan, and me around a table to address a crowd of people, the Grabow War and Leather Britches Smith returned to the forefront. This event offered an opportunity for both teller and audience to share and revitalize the past, if only in a small way. Open to the public, this environment also extended a teller's typical audience beyond family members and close friends. The event displayed people's storytelling skills and knowledge; it validated each teller's status in the community. When Mrs. Terry told her version at the panel, she captivated the crowd, keeping them on the edge of their seats. She demonstrated her own knowledge of the past and her skill as a narrator. In a sense, not only did she celebrate the area's past and stress the importance of the outlaw figure, but she also employed the figure as a cultural resource for her own ends. At the end of her version, she explained, "We had close connections and kinfolk to Leather Britches, and he was a character that everybody should know about." Almost a hundred years later, people do still know about him. In fact, Smith, like other outlaws in other towns throughout No Man's Land, functions as an important cultural resource for all of Merryville. People know about him, and they use him when they need him—summer, winter, spring, or fall.

The end of January 2005—a cold front crawled its way to Lake Charles, and the brisk air livened people's steps. The city, poised to experience the annual Southwest District Livestock Show and Rodeo, readied itself. Schools planned field trips, and hotels prepared every room they could. With the livestock show and rodeo a week away, the city sensed the closeness of the event, especially as its herald came to town.

Every year, the Western Heritage Days celebration starts a week before the rodeo. Beginning on the Saturday a week before the rodeo weekend, Western Heritage Days, a kickoff event, labors to generate interest in the rodeo and attract new fans, especially newcomers. During the event, throughout the city of Lake Charles, residents witness events hearkening back to the Old West, which easily could be the Old Southwest or even Old Texas or, for that matter, even Old Southwest

Louisiana since these events primarily deal with a crowd interacting with livestock or watching a reenactment of a gunfight. After all, a long tradition of cattle and cowboy culture stretches through the history of Southwest Louisiana; the Lake Charles university even uses the cowboy as its mascot.

Quite unexpectedly on a Saturday, my wife witnessed this opening event one year. She drove into a Wal-Mart parking lot, found a space, and parked. She unloaded our two little girls (four and two at the time), buckled them in a shopping cart, and made her way to the door. With their own children in shopping carts or standing at their sides, a crowd of people gathered near the entrance. My wife wandered up in the middle of the show, so Rhonda "Madam" Wood, a fortysomething woman dressed in a purple saloon can-can dress, already had been moved from the lap of Craig "Pine Knot Luther Hayes" Cooksey. Already, she had stood directly in front of him, and already she had been shoved aside so "Pine Knot Luther" could pull his pistol on Calvin "Captain Sam McCord" Farrell. My wife arrived right as the other gang members joined in. After ten minutes and a cloud of smoke, the battle between the Up the Creek Gang and the No Man's Land Gang ended. Then, smiling parents and excited children meandered through Wal-Mart's food center entrance to buy milk, bananas, washing detergent, and light bulbs. My wife and children must have shopped that day with the gunfight echoing in their minds because my daughters told me about it as soon as they stepped through the door. To excite a crowd and build interest in the rodeo, each year organizers stage gunfights like these and other similar demonstrations at Wal-Mart, Lowe's, or local restaurants, preferably one like Logan's Steakhouse and Grill, where the shootout in the parking lot matches the décor inside. Entertaining for sure, but do they make pronouncements about history and heritage at the same time?

A driver through Louisiana's Neutral Strip can navigate the highways to find loads of festivals—similar to Western Heritage Days—that celebrate tough and rugged lifestyles, the pioneering spirit, and even the region's reputation as a rough place. In April, the black smoke of cannons, the booms of the fake explosions, and the spray of dirt and water shot in the air by pyrotechnics engulf the visitors to the Battle of Pleasant Hill Reenactment. In May, tourists can step through the original opera house or company store of Fisher Lumber Company during Fisher Sawmill Days and witness a mock shootout. At Lake Charles Contraband Days they can watch Jean Lafitte storm the Gulf Coast and militiamen fire cannons. The militiamen always lose, Lafitte and his fleet of ships land, and the town's mayor walks the plank into the lake. The Zwolle Loggers and Forestry Festival in June displays logging competitions and appropriate antiques. The Zwolle Tamale Fiesta in October heaps plates full of tamales to celebrate the unique combination of American Indian and Spanish culture developing from the area's time as a Neutral Zone. In November, Florien, Louisiana, holds its Free State of the Sabine Festival. Festivalgoers see shootouts at an Old West saloon and hear buried treasure tales concerning the lost loot of the outlaw Hiram Midkiff, who traveled the area with his band of fellow bandits.

After witnessing shootout after shootout, a person might ponder the purpose of these festivals. After seeing T-shirts of Hiram Midkiff or Jean Lafitte, a person might question the merit of events celebrating outlaws and brigands. After hearing about outlaw after outlaw, a person might wonder if people end up celebrating someone or some place for all the wrong reasons; but people participating in these festivals make this effort in order to celebrate the past more than an individual outlaw or a notorious gun battle. Besides, the outlaw legend usually celebrates the ordinary folk rather than the outlaw. Versions of the Smith legend focus on the community more than the person and emphasize the landscape, history, and a way of life above everything else. As time passes and the region encounters a world that appears to be more global and diverse, residents turn to local traditions for feelings of identity, for messages about behavior and values, and for stressing the uniqueness of the place. As times change, people still will find the need to talk about the haves versus the have-nots or capital versus labor. They will want to warn of a life gone wrong and praise the power of the ordinary person. They will desire to reconnect to a significant time in Merryville's history, and they will yearn to understand and appreciate their home's rich, identifiable cultural landscape.

As heritage tourism and historical preservation develop in the region, the frontier mentality and the rugged gunman shine as unforgettable pieces of the past. On a continual basis, local historical societies and promoters and marketers of the region need outlaws and similar figures to understand, symbolize, and market themselves. As a result, Smith and figures like him become the focus of roadside markers, local festivals, and educational forays outside the classroom. These rough-and-tumble figures, these epitomes of masculinity, are cultural landmarks. Of course, they don't tell the whole story, but they act as an intriguing start; they tantalize and fascinate, and they may be enough to pique people so they will want to learn more and, more important for the economy, want to visit.

It's not a new idea. Residents have always possessed a pride in the area's history and culture, and communitywide celebrations of the region stretch far into the past. Organized efforts to celebrate No Man's Land's unique culture go back long before now. In the early 1900s, people held rowdy Fourth of July celebrations that included men on horseback conducting mock shootouts. In its current incarnation, Florien's Free State of the Sabine Festival stretches at least twenty-five years into the past. Merryville's local historical society has functioned for more than thirty years as a mechanism for promoting local culture. Founded in 1968, the Beauregard Historical Society formed in part to mark an anniversary celebration of "progress in Beauregard Parish."[2] The Society endeavored to record and to celebrate the unique culture of the region, and at its founding, its primary mission focused on compiling a record of parish history between 1818 and 1968.[3]

In 1818, the "first" settlers made their way into the area that eventually would become part of Beauregard Parish. They established the small town known as Sugartown. The year 1968 marked the sesquicentennial of the parish settlement, and residents all over Beauregard wanted to mark the occasion. Towns throughout the parish planned activities, newspapers ran articles, and historical societies ran at full speed. As one of its first activities, the newly formed Beauregard Historical Society organized a community celebration that included a parade, a pageant, a fair, school programs, and other activities. The pageant, performed on one night, consisted of various historical skits. Along with presenting the pageant, the society compiled a pageant program for the celebration.[4] Distributed to attendees of the sesquicentennial celebration and members of the community, the booklet, along with offering brief historical sketches, outlined the list of skits slated for the big doings.

Titled *Chapters in History*, the pageant pamphlet briefly covers the history of the three largest towns in Beauregard Parish with sections titled "Merryville," "DeRidder," and "Queen of the Frontier—Sugartown." The pamphlet also discusses the history of other definitive components of life in the region: economics, religious life, and basic social systems. For instance, "Early Sawmills," "Old Time Religion," and "Readin', 'Ritin', and 'Rithmetic" try to capture life as it was in the past. Void of any cultural analysis, most of the sections in the pamphlet simply describe significant events in history. They list the names and dates of early industrial or educational endeavors and describe certain accomplishments of noteworthy individuals. Other sections focus on specific incidents; for example, "The Grabow Incident" provides a limited account of the events leading up to, during, and immediately following the "incident." One or two sections do attempt to provide a cultural overview or at least encourage the development of cultural pride. Perhaps, most interesting, the pamphlet's first section is a brief history of the area written by the society's Honorary President, Louisiana Governor Sam Jones.

He writes, "We have another identity that is even more significant. We came from 'a long narrow slice of Louisiana' . . . generally known as the 'neutral strip.'" He relates the area's settlement, formation as a parish, and role as a No Man's Land. For Jones, the place owns "the richest variety of resources to be found in America." He ends with praise and hope for tomorrow: "We are learning that we have recreational facilities which, alone, will give us a score of income sufficient to sustain an economy double anything we have known in the past." He writes, "We are restoring our traditional and historical attractions that will soon bring not hundreds, but thousands of tourists and sportsmen to our section," and then points to the past as a promise for the future. Sam Jones believed in the economic windfall cultural revitalization and tourism offered, or promised to offer, and he advocated employing the folklife in the region not only as an economic tool but also as a psychological one. Floods of interested tourists would only prove what residents knew already and felt a deep sense of pride about—the uniqueness and worth of this area's culture and history.

The sesquicentennial pageant, the star of the whole affair, proved to be a demonstration of that pride. An early example of the region's emergent self-awareness, the pageant provides an indication of what pageant organizers viewed as the most important, most interesting, and most culturally specific aspects that deserved highlighting.

The weather must have only recently started to turn cooler, and the light from the football stadium field must have illuminated the dark Louisiana sky. Headlights must have burned as the cars pulled into the fair grounds. The cars must have nuzzled close together to find a place in the crowded parking lot of tall weeds and dirt tracks. People must have worriedly searched for seats in the stands. Friends must have saved places for other friends, and relatives must have embraced when they finally found each other in the stadium. They must have nodded and said "how do" to the people sitting next to them and smiled at the idea of what was to come. People must have chatted, nervous with anticipation, or thumbed through the pageant's booklet that they held in their hands. Plumb in the middle of the booklet, a two-page spread unfurled before their eyes. The schedule of the night's events must have peered back at them. It must have stared into their eyes and seen those eyes glow with patriotism and community spirit.

Today, these pages provide an early look at the region's blossoming cultural identity. Then, the two pages in the middle of the pamphlet must have fixed the audience's attention as they outlined the celebration that night. The top of the first of these two pages ceremoniously announced the evening's event:

BEAUREGARD PARISH FAIR ASSOCIATION
presents
THE SESQUICENTENNIAL CELEBRATION PAGEANT
OF BEAUREGARD PARISH
TUESDAY, SEPTEMBER 24, 1968, 8:00 P.M.
FAIR GROUNDS
Pageant Director, Mrs. George LeRay

The evening began with "Presentation of Beauregard Parish Fair Royalty" and then moved to a variety of skits or reenactments depicting key moments in history. The first skit of the evening, "Indian Encampment," opened the show, and to do so, reached back to the very start of the region. The pamphlet listed sub-headings under each skit. Under "Indian Encampment" came "Tribal habits and customs," "Spanish explorer wanders into camp," and "Dance of braves and cannibalistic rites." Each part of the skit had its time in the spotlight and regaled the audience with the "authentic" and mysterious behavior of the first people to roam the area. The skit concerning cannibalistic rites connected to the popular legend of the Atakapa, obviously a favorite of local historians even then. The night roared on until "Finale—Beauregard Parish Today" ended the show, standing as the audience's last stop of this marvelous trip from the past to the future. With "Train arrives with executives of new industry and equipment," "Band, mayor, and townsfolk welcome," and "Re-entry of entire cast and patriotic song America" as its sub-headings, the final skit assuredly left the audience feeling proud and hopeful, messages of progress and cultural pride ringing in their ears.

Besides these skits serving as bookends, the evening held many more entertainments. "Coming of First Settlers to Sugartown" and "Huey P. Long Political Rally" reminded people of those key moments when their community "really changed," as the program explained. They detailed those times when the place experienced major civic developments, when the ordinary folk settled land, and the little man gained real opportunity for education. People watched skits of economic developments. They heard the buzz of saws during "Birth of the Sawmill Towns" and the shouts of oilers in "Drilling of Wildcat Oilwell." Soon, faith gained a voice as a preacher held a "Brush Arbor Preaching at Old Campgrounds"; then, the badman made his claim. "Hanging of Outlaw in No Man's Land" titillated the crowd. Men and women saw the notorious past in vivid detail. "Grabow riot incident" and "Leather Breeches Smith Legend" stood alongside the rest of the performances in a prominent and conspicuous display to the audience. People must have loved the show.

Even though the pageant sparked interest in local history and the historical society must have deemed the project a success, interest in the Beauregard Parish Historical Society waned soon after the performance. Next, the society experienced a lack of leadership. In three short years, the society receded to a state of dormancy. Eventually, in 1981, a group of citizens organized again to make a town building, a local jail interestingly enough, part of the National Register of Historic Places. This activity rekindled interest in the historical society, and residents reformed the society that same year. During this reactivation meeting, the society changed its name from the Beauregard Parish Historical Society to Beauregard Historical Society and set forth new goals. Of course, these goals included collecting and preserving historical artifacts and generating public interest in parish history, with a special focus on the young people in the parish. The society also endeavored to collect oral histories in order to compile and publish an extensive book on Beauregard Parish history.

The compilation titled *History of Beauregard Parish Louisiana* became the largest project the group pursued. The book aimed to increase public awareness of the "history of the parish" and help the public appreciate "how important it is to preserve this cultural history, its records, and artifacts."[5] With a length of four hundred and forty pages and written by individual residents from the parish, the tome contains various personal accounts on a host of civic and historical subjects. Topics range from brief histories of families, churches, schools, local organizations, and even cemeteries to longer descriptive reports of historical events, reminiscences about the past, and articles from old newspapers. The book sums up the history of DeRidder in two pages and Merryville in one, but the various accounts of the Grabow Riot and Leather Britches Smith run five pages. Everyone had to own a copy. Currently, the book not only stands as an artifact of the area's growing cultural awareness but also still sits on bookshelves in many houses.

Even though the Beauregard Historical Society's projects, like the book, included the town of Merryville, eventually citizens of Merryville desired preservation work more focused on their own town. Thus, a few key Merryville residents formed the Merryville Historical Society in 1976. Like the Beauregard Historical Society, a larger community event and a national trend spurred the formation of Merryville's society. In response to the national bicentennial celebration, the Merryville Historical Society sponsored a citywide July 4 celebration and a contest for local schoolchildren to name it. A young girl, the winner, came up with the name Heritage Days, and the celebration became an annual event. Appropriately, organizers scheduled Ester Newton Terry as the speaker for the group's inaugural meeting; in fact, records show her as being the first person to pay dues. During its first decade, the Merryville Historical Society established the main goal of building a museum to house "memorabilia pertinent to the Merryville area."[6] In 1981, the organization purchased four downtown lots and placed a donated log cabin, built in 1883, in the middle of them. Quickly, they began restoration on the building. Around 1987, the society constructed a second building, its exterior built to resemble a log cabin. The community eagerly waited "for the new building to be built so they [could] give their old family heirlooms to it."[7]

For the first ten years, Merryville held annual July 4 celebrations and the Heritage Days on museum grounds. Currently located off Louisiana Highway 110 in the middle of downtown Merryville, the museum grounds consist of two buildings: the museum building itself and the 1883 log cabin known as the Burks House, which is on the National Register of Historic Places. The rectangular building that acts as the museum displays a variety of historical artifacts. Books ranging from specific histories to scrapbooks to high school yearbooks rest in bookshelves that form a small library. Keepsakes and mementos donated by community members adorn the walls and fill the display cases. Great saws, turpentine devices, pictures of gigantic log stacks, and other sawmill implements share the space with rifles and saddles and wagons. In this way, since its inception the museum has functioned as a beacon of cultural heritage and community pride.

In the early 1990s, in conjunction with the Heritage Days celebration, the Merryville Historical Society added a historical Civil War reenactment, billed as the Battle of Bearhead Creek—the name of a nearby creek where no battle actually took place. Inspiration for the event came from legends of area "jayhawkers" who attacked Confederate and Union forces for weapons and loot. Sponsored by the Merryville

Museum and hosted by the Twenty-sixth Louisiana Infantry, Semmes Battery, First Louisiana Light Infantry and the Sons of the Confederacy, the reenactment's events occurred primarily on the grounds of the Merryville Museum but extended to cover some of the town.

The reenactment began with a parade, and throughout the day, various mock skirmishes and skits, such as the hanging of a deserter, popped up on city streets. A period dance held on Saturday evening and a worship service Sunday morning rounded out the festival activities. Even though the museum remained open during Saturday and Sunday and the museum board directed the event, the reenactors, many of whom were not local residents, seemed to have directed much of the day's activities; thus, outsiders not only attended the festival and contributed to its atmosphere but also controlled the tone of the events. During the 2000 reenactment, locals decided they wanted more control over the activities. While the events of the 2000 reenactment unfurled around them, museum board members devised a change. At some point during the weekend, organizers canceled the next year's reenactment and created a living history festival as a replacement.[8]

In 2001, the inaugural Merryville Living History Heritage Festival began.[9] Even though this new festival resulted from the community rejecting the Civil War reenactment, emerging tourism concerns and the state government more than likely encouraged the new focus of the festival. Much like the sesquicentennial pageant, the development of the living history festival aligned with trends in state and local government. First, at the state level Louisiana began an effort to broaden its tourism industry. Noticing the increasing value of heritage tourism and knowing that every town possesses an abundance of this natural resource, the Louisiana Department of Culture, Recreation, and Tourism encouraged agencies at the local level to collect and present various aspects of their heritage to stimulate growth in historic and cultural tourism. In 1993, Secretary of the Department of Culture, Recreation, and Tourism Phillip Jones said, "Tourism is bringing in cash and leaving it here."[10] Jones understood that Louisiana depended upon heritage tourism to attract visitors, so he argued that Louisiana must adopt an aggressive approach to show potential tourists that "history may be boring elsewhere but not in Louisiana."[11]

Second, in 2003 Louisiana employed a marketing blitz aimed at heritage tourism in order to generate interest and participation in celebrating the Bicentennial of the Louisiana Purchase. In 2002, Merryville High School and Merryville Historical Society and Museum received a total of $11,000 from the Louisiana Division of the Arts in grant monies to support the festival and its focus on this unique historical aspect of the Louisiana Purchase. Seen as its greatest cultural resource, the area's history as part of No Man's Land became an interesting item to sell. Organizers rescheduled the event from the end of February to the middle of April to avoid conflict with Mardi Gras festivities held in parishes south and east of Beauregard Parish, and with a new Civil War reenactment renamed the Battle of Hickory Creek and now held in the nearby town of DeRidder. Billed as "celebrating the unique heritage of 'No Man's Land' and America with skits, entertainment, demonstrations and attractions reminiscent of the late 1800s and early 1900s," the festival spanned three days.[12]

Even though the events vary from year to year, the typical festival schedule falls this way. On Friday, the festival opens for schoolchildren.[13] The day's events include lectures on local history; historical demonstrations concerning making lye soap, basketry, and saddles; and exposure to the various artifacts housed in the museum. On Friday evening, the Merryville Historical Beauty Pageant for grades K-12 begins at six o'clock and ends roughly around nine o'clock.[14] The activities on Saturday begin with a parade that usually runs thirty to forty-five minutes, and opening ceremonies follow the parade.[15] The opening ceremonies conclude with the entrance of a local group of residents who pose as an Old West outlaw gang, the No Man's Land Gang. The gang enters town and symbolically takes over Merryville. By noon Saturday, the festival is in full swing, and the grounds swell with people. On the weekend of the festival, cars line nearby streets and the festival parking lots. Vendor tents, concession trailers, and booths sponsored by local organizations fill the alleyway and grounds.

For the 2005 festival, my family made it into town just in time for the parade. When I pulled up with my wife and kids, I struggled to find a parking spot. By the time I parked the car, my girls were already excited. The festival began with a bang, literally. Around ten thirty that Saturday morning, the No Man's Land Gang (some members of the museum board dressed as outlaws and armed with guns that shot blank cartridges) came into town in a symbolic show of power. We watched as one man discharged his shotgun cradled in his hip, and then reloaded. Another in a mustache and long trench coat yelled at the crowd and fired his pistol in the air. Among the gang, one woman dressed as a madam hiked up one side of her ruffled skirt and flirted with the crowd. In any other situation, these people would not engage in this type of behavior, nor would they embrace roles as murderers, thieves, and criminals. But during the festival, it's allowed. Acts of reversal are common in festivals; they're expected. As a result, the very people committed to celebrating the community can take on roles of those who would attack it.[16] What's more, they can adopt the outlaw, the gunman, and even the madam because they connect to the area's notable history and celebrate the fiercely independent nature of many of the residents. An added bonus, since they occur during the festival, people can dispose of them when the festivities finish. The crowd gets it.

The parade that opens the festival symbolically revives the area's notorious past and ushers in a brief period of celebratory time. Participants dressed as rough characters wield pistols and shotguns and march down the main streets. In a sense, many residents take on the characteristics of Leather Britches. Normal systems of government temporarily adjourned and rules of conduct inverted—the outlaw gains control; the community becomes a place of lawlessness. Symbolically taking the law into their own hands, as they did when they formed the Smith posse, makeshift sheriff deputies ceremoniously jail normal citizens for unfounded crimes; then, other community members bail them out as a show of community support.

After the parade, we crossed the street to the festival. We paid the small entrance fee and walked west down the small alley to the festival. After my two girls saw the fun jumps to their left, they begged me for tickets, but I managed to convince them that the real action waited up ahead. Before we hit the vendor booths lining the right side of the alley, we turned right and stood facing the museum. Roland Burks's log cabin, the historical structure that was moved to museum grounds, hung over our left shoulders. A man ahead of us made arrowheads by shaping some other stones. His finished products rested on a folding table. At another table outside the museum, a woman sat ready to tell stories. Children's drawings of No Man's Land and pioneering days decorated the exterior wall of the museum. The soft sounds of a flute wafted from the American Indian paid to demonstrate it. The smell of food drifted through the air.

As we walked around Burks House, I pointed out its details to my daughters, but they seemed more interested in the men dressed in cowboy hats, western shirts, and leather vests and squaring off against each other. The men wore gun belts and facial hair; wrapped bandanas around their necks, faces, or arms; and posed for pictures between skits. We had missed the music performance held the night before, and we couldn't make the Sunday morning worship service. Late Sunday afternoon, children will receive awards and the lucky raffle winners will hear their names called. At five o'clock, townsfolk will run The No Man's Land Gang out of town, which will mark the festival's end.

Knowing we had only Saturday, we made the most of it. We meandered through the festival and savored what the event had to offer. My wife immediately reconnected with people she had grown up with or who knew her family. I perused the antique weapons, bullwhips, lye soap demonstrations, and listened to stories dished out by museum members, local volunteers, and hired traditional artists.[17] Outside the museum, my girls heard stories about the "old days." Inside the museum, we all inspected the old farm tools and sawmill implements displayed on the floor or on the tops of tables. Photos of logging crews, of gigantic stacks of harvested timber, and of towns during the lumber boom hung on the wall. We wondered at these objects and images, and we praised the skilled craftsmen who made them, the hardy stock that put them to use, and the area's history flowing from their connection. Later that day on the music stage, a hired cowboy balladeer created an "Old West" feel. Gospel music emphasized religion's stabilizing role in the area's settlement and its lasting importance. Local Cajun or Louisiana bands proved that the place has real talent. Most important, at the festival people had fun. They reminisced and talked with another; they had shared a past.

In fact, a great deal of ritualized sharing occurred. In addition to the food served by vendors and artifacts displayed by the museum, several local organizations set up booths at the festival to sell food and crafts and to earn a small profit. The Methodist church served up its chicken and dumplings, and I knew to try some of the winning chili from the cook-off. Tables of homemade Mayhaw preserves and snickerdoodles in little plastic baggies allowed us to take a bit of the local goods home with us. We knew that local booths developed reputations for certain recipes or crafts, and people looked forward to these products each year. More to the point, the 4-H or high school band or some other organization gets a little money. Typically, the people from one booth will buy a little something from neighbors at another, and those people will end up at the first booth picking up something to take home. Just as Smith relied on locals for support or pioneers relied on neighbors for aid, festival attendees rely on community members for specialized food and crafts—food beyond corn dogs and funnel cakes and crafts beyond inflatable toys or plastic kitsch.

Though these booths and the historical demonstrations attract visitors and keep them entertained, the highlight of the festival seems to be the mock gun battles—visceral celebrations of No Man's Land. Each year, when the clock strikes a certain hour, the crowd shifts its way to the roped-off portion of the grounds. The ropes mark off a fair amount of grass, a stage, and other pieces of a set, like a small wooden jail or a wagon. The sheriff, wearing a leather vest, a badge and a holster and gun, checks his blanks. Preparing for the skit, the men and women dressed in costumes make jokes and smile in the background. The skits vary from performance to performance, but they all share humor and a little gunplay.

That day, Santana Jack, a man in black boots, a black hat, and brown leather vest, brought a lockbox to center stage and propped his right foot on it. The first of many outlaws stepped up to claim the prize, and soon the grass in front of the stage swarmed with hats and boots and pistols. The festival sheriff now faced six or seven outlaws hellbent on stealing the goods. Quickly, he devised a plan. Projecting his words so the festival crowd could hear, the sheriff bragged that he was a good shot, the best, too good to waste time with of a bunch of riffraff and second-rate gunslingers. To a man, the gunmen fell for it, delighting the audience with yells about who was the meanest and the toughest. They argued about outdrawing any man and facing down any challenge. Then, the sheriff slyly pulled a deck of cards from his back pocket, and each outlaw drew a card as the sheriff explained the rules.

The outlaws holding the lowest two cards would face off. The winner drew against the man with the next highest card. The loser, well, the loser did his best flop for the ground and stayed dead, which meant lying quiet and still for the rest of the skit. The winner of the last face-off got his chance with the sheriff. Hilariously, one by one they fell. The Reverend Devil, a man dressed as the notorious land pirate Murrell, drew a three of hearts; defeated Amarillo Slim who drew a seven; and then died by the hands of Booger, who had drawn a nine. As the last two outlaws stepped off the distance, the sheriff slowly moved into position. After taking a series of slow backward steps, he steadied his feet behind one of the duelists. In order for the skit's joke to work, the man the sheriff stands behind must win the duel. When he did, the sheriff, gun already drawn, quickly shot him in the back. The crowd clapped and cheered, so we could barely hear his final speech to Bayou Belle, the dancing girl who watched the entire fight. The lockbox saved, the crowd entertained, the smoke from the guns still hanging in the air, the outlaws took their bows and returned to mingling with the crowd and posing for photographs. In the same high dramatic fashion as Smith's life and legend, lawlessness takes center stage, then exits—then, perhaps after a dramatic pause, steps to the fore again.

Every year, the festival ends in exactly that manner; law is restored. Around five o'clock Sunday afternoon, the No Man's Land Gang is run out of town. The event signals the festival's end and the return of everyday life. Law once again rules, the outlaw expunged. With the festival, residents reaffirmed their own heritage and praised the rugged individualism and fierce independence that have become hallmarks of their identity. Examined piece by piece, the festival unveils deep social values and concerns.[18] It safely emphasizes ruggedness, celebrates the area's complex cultural identity derived from an awareness of the area's violent past, proceeds from a contemporary desire to be economically prosperous, and derives from an overriding human impulse for community connectedness. Plus, my family and many others had some fun and spent a little money. In this sense, the festival acts as the latest and in some sense the largest expression of cultural awareness. It stands alongside the legend, the gravestone, and the museum as symbolic statements about the region's cultural landscape.

When residents search for a sense of identity and belonging, repeatedly they seek out the cultural resources of No Man's Land and Leather Britches. Beyond using the legend at a dinner table or at the local truck-stop café to share with close friends, people employ the legend in tourism brochures, at the local museum, during the spring festival, or even in the cemetery with the makeshift grave marker that operates like a sort of historical marker. These activities stress the legend's continual validity and value and the important and unique history surrounding it. The debate surrounding the marker's authenticity engenders continual discussion. To supply and manage the museum, residents actively donate time, money, and museum pieces. In a display of local pride and community awareness, residents during the festival pitch in and volunteer to create a festival particular to their town.

By attending various events and participating in a range of programs sponsored by local historical societies, residents learn about the past, offer their own recollections about it, and even actively participate in recreating it. In turn, they become informed and aware of the place's history and culture. Eventually, they even begin to develop a sense of themselves based on this knowledge. Ultimately, they may organize, sponsor, and patronize these events and thereby solidify their preconceived ideas of community identity. In other words, a few events make pronouncements about what it means to be from No Man's Land. People embrace these ideas and consider them a source of pride. Then, they create more events that express this identity. As a result, seemingly negative or regrettable moments in the past—for example Leather Britches Smith terrorizing the town and the tension of the Grabow War—become important parts of resident's regional identity.

By developing historical societies to collect local histories and to promote culture, by creating museums to display artifacts, and by sponsoring local festivals, residents of Louisiana's Neutral Strip use cultural heritage to promote tourism and to define themselves. Merryville's identity as a place in No Man's Land and Smith's outlaw legend become marketing tools to entice visitors and generate local interest. As a result, the community extends the legend's usefulness from recording a single historical moment to serving as a renewable cultural resource.

My wife stands as a perfect example. At one time in her life, she was a fierce softball player. She played centerfield for the 1990 1A State quarterfinalists Merryville Panthers. She has played since she was small, and even after she graduated from high school, she played in local co-ed ragball tournaments with her friends. Ragball offers a little recreation, but many people compete as hard as they can. DeRidder holds a city league, as do many towns in the Neutral Strip. In addition, churches, Rotary Clubs, youth groups, or even friends of families in need will organize these tournaments to attract teams from surrounding communities—sometimes communities some distance away—to raise money for a cause. My wife's team competed against teams from Merryville, DeRidder, DeQuincy, Ragley, Singer, and other surrounding communities. She has told me that they were good and she has the T-shirts to prove it. She doesn't play much anymore, but sometimes she still wears the T-shirts. In fact, she gave me a shirt with the team name on it.

The shirt is maroon and the lettering is white, Merryville High School colors. The words "Young Guns" and the image of two pistols with crossed barrels are printed in white across the shirt's front. "Young Guns," borrowed from the popular movie about Billy the Kid, comments about the strength of her team's throwing arms and, of course, connects to a region known for outlaws. Even though usually it's another person who mainly reads the front of a shirt a person is wearing, the T-shirts really communicate more about the self-perception of the person wearing it. Even though the simple shirts do not mark the burial site of Merryville's most famous outlaw, do not record the area's most significant historical events, and do not stage an elaborately structured celebration that subconsciously stresses the area's cultural landscape and community values, they are statements of identity.

In 2009, the Merryville Historical Society took on another project after the James R. Whitely family donated the Merryville Jail to the group. As this book is being written, the group wants to restore the old Merryville Jail, the jail that once held the body of Leather Britches Smith as it sat on ice. Plans are in the works to move the building to the grounds of the Merryville Museum. Made of eight-inch-thick reinforced concrete, its original bars and doors gone, the old jail remains as something of worth. At the 2009 festival, organizers also plan on including skits about Leather Britches Smith to generate interest in the jail project. Undoubtedly, someone will dress up like the figure, wield two guns, shoot the head off a chicken, and wait to be ambushed. The outlaw again becomes a tourist attraction, a cultural resource.

This happens throughout No Man's Land. A land of runaways and bandits, a place where only the strong could survive, an area of hardy folk exists as a tourist destination. Like other towns in Louisiana's Sabine Valley, Merryville embraces its outlaw legend not because its citizens applaud infamous deeds or yearn for a life of violence, but because the outlaw embodies the people's ruggedness and frontier spirit. He condenses the place's history into a span, simultaneously connecting to the river, the landscape, lumber, Grabow, and the struggle to make a life.

APPENDIX A

The information for this manuscript comes from a variety of sources. In addition to the many articles and books cited throughout the work, the manuscript builds on interviews, field notes, and archival material. The work also draws from the many local sources that collect various people's accounts of the Smith legend and the Grabow War.

Long before the official work for this book began, I had heard various stories and details about life in No Man's Land and several accounts of Leather Britches Smith's life and deeds. Some of the more general observations about the region's culture draw from these experiences. In 1999, I focused my efforts on the Smith legend and its connection to the Grabow War. I interviewed many people, often relying on taking notes rather than recording the conversations.

No attempt was made to select consultants based on gender, age, or status in the community. Instead, through the course of the conversations and informal meetings, I realized that for the Leather Britches legend many people turned to a few key persons in the area. The nature of this research dictated a focus on those persons known to possess the deepest knowledge of the time. Moreover, hesitancy by many to slander a family's name on tape or to have their conversations about such events recorded on tape necessitated an approach focused on key members of the community. These people had garnered enough community status (either by age, behavior, or association with key sources) to speak honestly and with a degree of immunity. I interviewed and recorded these key community members several times.

The bulk of the interviews, recorded and not, were with members of the Merryville and DeRidder communities. These people often had ties to the timber industry or ancestors involved in the events, and most of them have a long family line running through the area's history. I also conducted numerous follow-up calls and conversations with various people to clarify any confusing points. In addition to personal interviews, a few public discussion sessions occurred. One at a local library collected four people known to possess a deep knowledge of the area and of the Smith legend. These four community scholars shared their knowledge of the events; then, the audience responded with comments, asked further questions, and added or argued details. I led the second of these discussions, presenting the material I had collected up to that point. Again, the audience responded. People in the area have also read several versions of this book, made suggestions, and have directed its ultimate form and contents.

Details presented in the book include material collected from interviews, field notes, local historical or archival sources, newspapers, letters, and court records, in addition to more general academic sources. The specific descriptions in the book come from personal observations or from sources. All of the quotations in the book come from tape recordings or, in the case of the Grabow trial, from newspaper reports or court records that quote individuals. I have tried to cite all of them.

APPENDIX B

If we consider the oral lore we share, we see that folklore operates at our most basic levels. Items of folklore exist, circulate, and remain because they serve a specific function: they occupy a role in our lives, perform a service for our family or community, and express and fulfill our individual needs and desires. They entertain, educate, warn, advise, and validate us.[1] Jokes tap into our greatest anxieties. Fairy tales teach us how villains scheme and how heroes act. The urban legend about the promiscuous cheerleader serves as a powerful warning. A funny story makes us laugh and teaches how to behave. A ghost story scares us and relates the history of an area. That folklore often functions in multiple ways is a testament to its power. Its power means that people and communities often develop items of folklore to confront multifaceted problems.

The outlaw legend, especially those involving "Robin Hood" figures, serves as a good example. The good outlaw stands as a concrete, though complex, image of rebellion and social justice, of right beyond the law, and of the existence of higher laws. Even though these outlaws commit criminal acts, they often serve a higher good by counteracting social wrongs.[2] Connecting to the principle of unlimited good, the outlaw breaks class structures, redistributes wealth, and acts as a social climber. The promise of a better future is his, even though he breaks the rules to gain it and will, without a doubt, quickly lose it. But his loss is no matter to us. By robbing the rich to give to the poor, the outlaw actively promises a hopeful future to us all, the American entitlement of a better tomorrow.

In the outlaw legend, class-consciousness and issues of ethnicity, only two of many potential issues hidden in the legend, lurk beneath the surface details of the story. If the outlaw uses his guns to rob only certain folk, this detail also could indicate the outlaw arms himself with a political agenda. Geography and regional history, as another example, may direct the superficial events of plot. Living in a frontier region engendering a rough and dangerous life, people may create or emphasize outlaws—the ultimate border-crossers—in order to deal with the isolation and frustrations this way of life brings. Since boundaries and borders seem inexorably tied to America's past and settlement patterns, the outlaw figure litters the pages of American history and literature.[3]

In the past, newspapers, dime novels, and even more sophisticated literary works titillated the public with tales of outlaws who crossed some line someone told them they couldn't cross. Popular national legends—like those of Jesse James, Billy the Kid, or Pretty Boy Floyd—not only entertained Americans, but also spoke to people who felt angry and betrayed by an oppressive system neglecting the lower classes but who also felt the American system offered a hint of hope.

Even today, the "good outlaw," the Robin Hood figure, seems perfectly suited for conveying American opportunity.[4] Essentially, the heroic outlaw symbolizes community power and individual determinism; in other words, the symbol communicates core American ideas. Today, television and movies ensure the popularity of the "good outlaw" legend. The West undoubtedly provides the nation with most of its national outlaw legends, and the West, like it or not, still stands as emblematic of the American experience.

Some basic need for and some basic appeal of the character seem undeniable. The Robin Hood figure possesses a long academic tradition and appears in the lore of England, France, Spain, Italy, Russia, Japan, and many other countries.[5] In Europe and the Americas, noble robbers retaliate against oppressive economic systems, navigating in negative space between the haves and the have-nots. Also important, Jesse

James, Billy the Kid, Sam Bass, Pretty Boy Floyd, and even Pancho Villa share elements that are noticeably similar.[6]

Legends resemble each other, and plot lines run parallel. For example, the legend construction of Leather Britches Smith as outlaw and hero parallels these other well-known American figures. Basic core components of Smith's life and deeds align with those in famous outlaw-hero. Like arguments arising in the telling of the Jesse James, Billy the Kid, or Pancho Villa legends, arguments arise about the exact origin of the outlaw in the telling of the Smith legend.[7] People debate how someone drove the heroic criminal to a life of crime and how the authorities finally managed to bring him to justice. People shape stories from what they have heard and read.[8] Even though a person may never have heard or read about a local outlaw, that person may have nonetheless heard another Robin Hood legend. These well-known outlaw legends establish expectations, and people may borrow the structure of these stories and apply them to a different legend. However, this borrowing does not mean parts of the story are false nor does it mean that all of these legends appear the same.

While certain general traits and basic components seem universal, many details remain specific to a locale. In the story, the particulars of a natural landscape may facilitate the outlaw's escape or the outlaw's crime may connect to a historical event. In this way, anytime people tell the legend, they describe the place and history surrounding it. As much as Jesse James, Pretty Boy Floyd, and other popular "good outlaw" legends transcend region and geographic boundaries, they also remind us of our own local examples. Different outlaw legends have developed across the country to represent specific cultures. Pirate, gunman, gangster, union buster, union organizer, fugitive, guerrilla, and even hacker comprise the spectrum of outlaw characters.[9] Each type populates a different region based on that region's history, terrain, settlement patterns, and other distinctive traits.

While the structures of these stories may share similarities, their specifics still can display remarkable differences, and in any local version of an outlaw legend, particular details reflect place, economy, and historical moment. In addition, each individual variant of a local legend usually incorporates the teller's personal values, family history, and so on. In this way, the framework addresses universal concerns and the specifics capture local issues. When I hear the Leather Britches Smith legend in Merryville and other similar stories circulating in Louisiana's Neutral Strip, I experience this phenomenon.

NOTES

Preface

1. Richard Dorson, *American Folklore* (Chicago: U of Chicago P, 1959).

2. Richard Dorson, "American Cultural Myths," in *American Folklore* (Chicago: U of Chicago P, 1959), 57.

3. Beverly Stoeltje, "Making the Frontier Myth: Folklore Process in a Modern Nation," *Western Folklore* 46 (1987): 251.

4. Mody Boatright, "The Myth of Frontier Individualism," in *Mody Boatright, Folklorist: A Collection of Essays* (Austin: U of Texas P, 1973), 13–38.

5. I would like to thank the McNeese State University Archives. Many historical records are courtesy of the library, and their availability is due in large part to the work of Kathie Bordelon, Pati Threatt, and Tammie Pettis.

6. Much of Merryville's and Beauregard Parish's history can be found in *History of Beauregard Parish* (compiled by Beauregard Parish Historical Society, Dallas: Curtis Media Corporation, 1986).

Introduction

1. Merryville's lore of Keener Cagle is varied and extensive. "Red Flash," rising from meager beginnings, is renowned not only for his athletic prowess but also for his popularity, charm, good looks, and innate intelligence. As they do when telling the Leather Britches Smith legend, many people specify information that is known only to them or will correct or add to published versions of the legend. *History of Beauregard Parish Louisiana* provided me the best source for general information on Keener Cagle. See Reba Lafargue, "Cagle, Christian Keener," in *History of Beauregard Parish Louisiana*, compiled by Beauregard Parish Historical Society (Dallas: Curtis Media Corporation, 1986), 212.

2. The club did not put up a Community Christmas Tree in 2000.

3. Merryville is approximately sixty miles away from Lake Charles. As most regional papers approach news coverage, *Lake Charles American Press* covers the business of cities outside the city of Lake Charles, including those towns in adjacent parishes to the north, south, and east.

4. Tensey Pricer, "Lady Panthers: Pride of Merryville, Girls Basketball Team Gives Town Plenty to Cheer About," *Lake Charles American Press,* Feb. 6, 2000, C8.

5. Clair Brown's *Wildflowers of Louisiana and Adjoining States* (Baton Rouge: Louisiana

State UP, 1972) provides informative descriptions of individual flowers and explanatory overviews of the botanical regions. The work does contain several color photographs.

6. In "Regionalization: A Rhetorical Strategy" (*Journal of the Folklore Institute* 13:105–20), Suzi Jones explains that folklore "can be made meaningful by the inclusion of local environmental detail, but the local environment can be imbued with meaning by the mythological traditions of a culture" (115).

CHAPTER 1

1. Joe Gray Taylor, "The Territorial Period," in *Louisiana: A History*, ed. Bennett H. Wall, 2nd ed., (Arlington Heights, IL: Forum Press, 1984), 91–109.

2. I have heard several people say, "Oh, that's just folklore. It's ridiculous," or "But this is true. This actually happened. This isn't folklore." Indeed, many people see folklore as meaning unreliable information. They have this idea that folklore isn't true, that it's easily dismissed, that it's old wives' tales and backward thinking. The other idea is that while folklore might be true or at least was true at some point, it is only those ancient stories grandfathers and great-aunts tell us as children. For them, folklore is old, and the older the better.

Even folklorists, those people who make a living out of collecting and studying folklore, emphasize its traditional aspects and its "unofficial" nature, since it is disseminated by "ordinary" people in everyday situations. With this academic background, people's perception of folklore meaning old or untrue isn't really shocking. However, "traditional" does not keep folklore stuck in the past, and "folk" does not confine it to uneducated or uninformed people or reduce its reliability or effectiveness.

3. Unfortunately, Goob died before I started researching this topic. This description comes from what people have told me about him and from an article on Goob and its accompanying picture that appeared in *Rocking Texas' Cradle* (Beaumont, TX: The Enterprise Company, 1974).

4. In addition to his work on frontier individualism, Mody Boatright compiled a significant amount of work on family sagas. His "The Family Saga as a Form of Folklore" (in *Mody Boatright, Folklorist: A Collection of Essays*, Austin: U of Texas P, 1973, 124–44) explains that a *family saga* is a cluster of tales and motifs which do not form a factual, connected family history but a repeated recollection of memorable events and characters in the family history that become representative of social values and worldview.

5. Ralph Ramos, "Preface," *Rocking Texas' Cradle*, (Beaumont, TX: The Enterprise Company, 1974), xvii–xxi.

6. In the book, Ramos groups smaller individual accounts into larger sections. "Pioneering People," "Two Preacher Men," "Hunters," and "Two Old Salts" are only a few. Each section contains several accounts of individuals speaking about the past. Though rich in historical details, reminiscences, and information about "the old ways," the book includes very little of the author's analysis. In the book, Ramos feels content simply to present the stories he collected. In this book, Ramos also gives away his fears that these stories are fading and the "old ways" will be lost forever when the "old folks" die. Any reader can sense his worry that progress will pare away the virtues of the past and whittle down the frontier spirit until nothing remains. Despite the reporter's fear that these stories would die, those he interviewed told stories to their children who in turn told stories to theirs. The lore survived.

7. Ramos, Preface, *Rocking Texas' Cradle*, viii.

8. In addition to Ramos's brief work on Smith, a few other scant sources, like the Beauregard Parish Historical Society's historical report, cover Leather Britches. Even though a few other articles containing information about different subjects mention the outlaw in *History of Beauregard Parish Louisiana* (compiled by Beauregard Parish Historical Society, Dallas: Curtis Media Corporation, 1986), the article titled "Leather Britches Smith" deals with him

specifically. I also find it interesting that this article, unlike most of the articles in the book, is not attributed to an author.

In a way, the number of these sources worried me, especially the prominence of Ralph Ramos's work. Herbert Halpert's "Definition and Variation in Folk Legend," appearing in *American Folk Legend: A Symposium* (Berkeley and Los Angeles: U of California P, 1971), deals with the prevalence of variation in folklore, especially in legends, and warns that any time only one version of a legend exists or is heard unchanging through many informants, one should expect a dominant informant or the influence of print. I feared that I would find a legend, once active and dynamic, now fixed in the pages of a book and simply recited by people. If this situation did exist, the problem would be that the legend no longer would vary through individual perspective, no longer offer a person the opportunity to express individual concerns. I found that people consistently deviated from the printed versions of the legend.

9. Ralph Ramos. "Leather Britches: Hero and Benefactor? Or Murderer?," "Tale of Horror Recalled"; "Leather Britches: Hero or Killer"; and "Legend of Leather Britches Untold," *Beaumont Enterprise Journal*, Aug.–Sept. 1972. All of these articles are located in a vertical file in the Beauregard Parish Library.

10. Catherine Stark is known to many as Granny Cat because her family helped settle the area long ago, because she's related to a great many people, and because she holds a personal stake in Merryville and how it is doing. Catherine Stark will often speak of the generosity of many local mill owners and the interesting history of the town.

11. In all of the transcribed portions the ellipses, unless mentioned otherwise, indicate where I have intentionally left out words in order to condense the material. I have tried not to alter the meaning of the account.

12. What varies from one informant to the next is often as revealing or important as the kernel narrative, and what changes in those stories more often than not connects to an individual's own desires and values. The legend must function as an accurate record of the past, yet it must be flexible enough to be told and retold again and again. As individuals alter specific aspects of the legend, they signal important messages about themselves and their families. First, they mark an individual's ability to tell a story or to remember details. They also emphasize personal knowledge of the region or outlaw. Next, they note a family's social status or its long-standing position in the community, and they stress the importance of a family's history to the community or its role in the area's settlement. Finally, they highlight current values of the community.

13. Sam Pruitt, "Leather Britches," *Something Old—Something New*, Warner Robins, GA: Pruitt Productions, n.d.

CHAPTER 2

1. For this work, Clair Brown's helpful and informative *Louisiana Trees and Shrubs*. (Rpt. of Louisiana Forestry Commission, Bulletin no. 1, 1945, Baton Rouge: Claitor's Publishing Division, 1972) proved to be the best among the many books on Louisiana's flora. Along with black and white photographs (even though the lack of color is a bit discouraging), the book contains a variety of clear information on the subject, including a brief introduction, a map of the tree regions of Louisiana, some notes on identification and classification, and solid descriptions of each plant.

2. U.S. Committee on Public Works, "Letter from the Secretary of the Army Transmitting a Letter from the Chief of Engineers," *Sabine River and Tributaries, Texas and Louisiana* (Washington: U.S. Government Printing Office, 1970), 88–89.

3. Standing as a clear demarcation, the Sabine River defines the region as much as it defines the outlaw. It stands as a key marker of Louisiana's Neutral Strip and has long served as an environmental border. From the times of the Caddo Nation to the present-day Louisiana/Texas

culture, the water has played its natural role, simultaneously providing a thoroughfare serving the region's hunters, explorers, traders, loggers, etc., while providing a defining line keeping the region separate. For a discussion, see Clarence H. Webb and Hiram F. Gregory, *The Caddo Indians of Louisiana*. 2nd ed. (Louisiana Archaeological Survey and Antiquities Commission Anthropological Study no. 2, 1978, Baton Rouge: State Printing, 1990), 18.

4. In "Compromised Narratives along the Border: The Mason-Dixon Line, Resistance, and Hegemony," in *Border Theory: The Limits of Cultural Politics* (Minneapolis: U of Minnesota P, 1997), Castronovo points out that national borders "disturb the nation, but in a strategic turnabout, the nation also employs the border to imagine the limits beyond which it might expand, to scout horizon for future settlement, to prepare the first line of attack" (196).

5. The river itself, like many other borders, exhibits two sides of its personality. Even though frequently acting as a line of separation, the river exists as a line of connectivity. Due to its depth and width and its opening into the Sabine Lake that in turn opens into the Gulf of Mexico, the Sabine has been connector to the outside world through transportation. However, due to its unpredictable nature and dangerous crossings, the Sabine also offers three hundred miles of separation, a means of isolation for residents, and a cultural defining line.

6. Living on a frontier, a border, or a boundary line—such as the Sabine—engenders a unique mental state in people. In "Compromised Narratives along the Border," Castronovo considers the stories that develop from someone being conscious of a life led on a border, being marginalized, being in limbo. In fact, the way people on this line define themselves and the stories they tell become irrevocably tied to their consciousness of living on the border." Proverbial lines drawn in the sand, borders exist as dynamic locales, places clarifying significant aspects of our lives. In "Border Secrets," an introduction to *Border Theory* (Minneapolis: U of Minnesota P, 1997), Scott Michaelson and David E. Johnson explain Renato Rosaldo's view of a borderland as a "place of politically exciting hybridity, intellectual creativity, and moral possibility . . . the privileged locus of hope for a better world" (3).

7. Most of us exist in some sort of border zone, whether physical, mental, or cultural. For an interesting discussion on this topic, see Scott Michaelson and David E. Johnson, *Border Theory: The Limits of Cultural Politics* (Minneapolis, U of Minnesota P, 1997). Others have discussed this concept. In *Culture and Truth* (Boston: Beacon, 1989), Renato Rosaldo reminds us that "more often than we usually care to think, our everyday lives are crisscrossed by border zones" and consequently these zones function as "sites of creative cultural production" (207–208).

8. Of course, borders limit us. They tell us what or where we can't be; they provide a clearly defined line of who we are, where we belong. But borders simultaneously mark the lines we can cross to be different, where we can go to expand, explore, rebel. This mind-set developing from the existence of a border becomes a psychological negotiation of identity. However, the negotiation does not rely only on the separation or isolation that most think of when considering boundaries; instead, the interactions with other groups often reaffirm identity. In his introduction to *Ethnic Groups and Boundaries* (Boston: Little, 1969), Fredrik Barth claims, "If a group maintains its identity when members interact with others, this entails criteria for determining membership and ways of signaling membership and exclusion" (15).

9. When groups interact with others, challenges to identity emerge. During these challenges, people assert identity most vigorously. After all, definitions of "the same" derive from knowledge of "the other." To cross a border, face the "other," and choose to return to the "same" is the most dramatic statement about connectedness.

10. James Clifford once noted, "Culture is contested, temporal, and emergent" (qtd. in Alejandro Lugo, "Reflections on Border Theory, Culture, and the Nation," in *Border Theory: The Limits of Cultural Politics*, eds. Scott Michaelson and David E. Johnson (Minneapolis: U of Minnesota P, 1997). In other words, culture must be considered not only in terms of its structure, but also in terms of how the structure is challenged or changed. A few sources seem crucial to Lugo's discussion concerning this interplay: Perry Anderson, "Components of

the National Culture," *New Left Review* 38 (1968): 50–62; Gloria Anzaldúa, *Borderlands/La Frontera: The New Mestiza* (San Francisco: Aunt Lute, 1987); James Clifford, "Introduction: Partial Truths," in *Writing Culture: The Poetics and Politics of Ethnography*, eds. James Clifford and George E. Marcus, (Berkeley: U of California P, 1986), 1–26; Michel Foucault, *The History of Sexuality: An Introduction*, vol. 1, trans. Alan Sheridan-Smith (New York: Random, 1978); and Stuart Hall, "Gramsci's Relevance for the Study of Race and Ethnicity" *Journal of Communication Inquiry* 10.2 (1986): 5–27.

11. But not everyone crosses, or needs to. Certain members of the group become especially adept at crossing the border, and others cross vicariously because of them. "Border keepers" often embody the importance of tradition and community identity, and "border crossers" embody change and individual otherness. Border crossers reap the benefits of being able to transgress, and the group gains from the sure line of citizenry and culture.

Border crossers and border keepers both stand as popular subjects of tales. Border crossers create unusual identities, and the creation often requires violent eruptions and culture shocks. These crossers possess two bodies, two heads, two lives—one in the old land and one in the new.

12. The challenging or changing of a cultural structure offers a fascinating sort of folklore. Many folklorists have considered folklife's role in expressing social conflicts or cultural stresses. In "Personal Power and Social Restraint in the Definition of Folklore" published in *Towards New Perspectives in Folklore* (Austin: U of Texas P, 1972), Roger Abrahams discusses folklore's usefulness in dealing with community problems, personal and interpersonal anxieties, and social conflicts.

13. However, the violence surrounding border folklife has a purpose. The brutality occurring on the border is often an unfortunate means to a much-needed end. Eruptions and shocks may prove necessary for some important change to occur. In "Compromised Narratives along the Border," Castronovo explains, "The misrecognition of domination for hegemony allows for a narrative that begins with the rebellion of an unruly underdog against 'hegemonic culture' and concludes with a glimpse of a landscape whose geographic and psychic dimensions outstrip traditional categories" (200).

14. As the cultural landscape dictates, Smith comes from across the river, which accounts for his meanness and makes him an outsider. Even though these residents may celebrate the toughness engendered by the Neutral Zone, none of them wants to embrace a life of complete anarchy and chaos. As an outsider, he can occupy this position. In addition, Smith exists for a defined period to represent the common man's frustrations within the current economic system, and then is gone. In a sense, Smith embodies border consciousness, angst caused from economic disparity, and the xenophobia brought on by witnessing outsiders reap profit from local resources.

15. Author's notes, interview with a librarian from Beauregard Parish Library, June 2003.

16. Author's notes, June 2003.

17. Ralph Ramos, "Leather Britches Smith Didn't Fear Nothin,' Folks Say," *Beaumont Enterprise Journal*, Beaumont, TX, Aug. 13, 1972, p. 2.

18. In "The Outlaw: A Distinctive American Folktype" (*Journal of the Folklore Institute* 17:94–124), Richard Meyer claims that outlaw legends possess a certain number of identifiable traits. The second of these explains that the heroic-outlaw figure must be driven to commit his first crime (99).

19. The panel discussion, held on June 6, 2000, at the library in DeRidder, Louisiana, consisted of four people, including myself. One was a local folk artist who has contributed much to compilations of local histories. One was an older man who knew a great deal about a lost silver mine and other local legends. One was a woman who worked extensively in preservation and local history.

20. Mrs. Ester Terry was a Newton before she married. Goob Newton's sister, she was a young child when Leather Britches was in the area. Known as an expert in the area's history,

Mrs. Terry, like her brother, could tell stories adeptly. Also like her brother, she seemed to enjoy a crowd when telling stories and knew how to entertain audience members.

21. In Ester Terry's version, Smith's place on death row is taken by another man: "Kind of like the story of Jesus and the crucifixion and all that going on, . . . they were going to let this drunk other man out; instead, they let him [Smith] out."

22. Webb and Gregory claim even the indigenous people of the region considered it a rough place (18).

23. For a version of this story, see Mildred Gleason, *Caddo: A Survey of the Caddo Indian in Northeast Texas and Marion County, 1541–1840* (Jefferson, TX: Marion County Historical Commission, 1981), 27.

24. Webb and Gregory's *The Caddo Indians of Louisiana* discusses the Caddo people, and much of this information about the Caddo comes from that source.

25. Webb and Gregory's work offers an excellent discussion of this topic.

26. In *No Man's Land* (Gretna, LA: Firebird Press-Pelican Publishing, 1998), Louis Nardini spends a significant amount of time in his work discussing these and other interactions. In his historical summary, he enumerates the region's early activity and its clashing cultures (3–44).

27. See Webb and Gregory.

28. For one source considering the function of neutral zone as political maneuver, see Scott Michaelson and David E. Johnson, *Border Theory: The Limits of Cultural Politics* (Minneapolis, U of Minnesota P, 1997).

29. Perhaps the best historical source on the Louisiana's Neutral Zone is J. Villasana Haggard, "The Neutral Ground Between Louisiana and Texas, 1806–1821," *Louisiana Historical Quarterly* 28.4:1001–1128.

30. Light Townsend Cummins, "By the Stroke of a Pen: Louisiana Becomes Spanish," *Louisiana: A History*, ed. Bennett H. Wall, 2nd ed. (Arlington Heights, IL: Forum Press, 1984), 52–70.

31. The dispute concerned the exact southern boundary between Spanish territory and the United States territory. The United States argued that the thirty-first geographic parallel acted as boundary, and Spain claimed the geographic line was thirty-two degrees twenty-eight minutes, near Natchez, Louisiana.

32. William M. Malloy, *Treaties, Conventions, International Acts, Protocols and Agreements between the United States of America and Other Powers, 1776–1909,* qtd. in Evelyn Turk, "Adams-Onís Treaty," *Handbook of Texas Online*, <http://www.tsha.utexas.edu/handbook/online/articles/view/AA/nba1.htm>.

33. See Haggard, "The Neutral Ground between Louisiana and Texas, 1806–1821," 1001–1053.

34. One can find information concerning the formation of the Louisiana Neutral Ground in a variety of sources. In addition to J. V. Haggard's "The Neutral Ground between Louisiana and Texas, 1806–1821," see Lawrence E. L'Herisson, "The Evolution of the Texas Road and the Subsequential Settlement Occupancy of the Adjacent Strip of Northwestern Louisiana: 1528–1824," Master's thesis (Louisiana State University, Shreveport, 1977). Much of the information concerning the events leading to the signing of the Adams-Onís Treaty comes from Haggard's work.

35. His design never came to fruition. Wilkinson died in Mexico City in 1825 and not in battle on the Louisiana frontier.

36. Varying opinions exist on General Wilkinson. For one side, see John Francis Bannon, *The Spanish Borderlands Frontier, 1513–1821* (Albuquerque: U of New Mexico P, 1974). For the other side, see Don C. Marler, *The Neutral Zone: Backdoor to the United States* (Woodville, TX: Dogwood, 1995).

37. See Haggard, "The Neutral Ground between Louisiana and Texas, 1806–1821," 1001–1053.

38. Ibid.

39. Carolyn Ericson's *Natchitoches Neighbors in the Neutral Strip* (Nacogdoches, TX: Ericson Books, 1993) covers this information.

40. Malloy, *Treaties, Conventions*.

41. Joe Gray Taylor, "The Territorial Period," in *Louisiana: A History*, ed. Bennett H. Wall, 2nd ed. (Arlington Heights, Il: Forum Press, 1984), 91–109.

42. William B. Glover, "A History of the Caddo Indians," *Louisiana Historical Quarterly* 18.4:872–946. Reprinted and formatted for the World Wide Web by Jay Salsburg, <ops.tamu.edu/x075bb/caddo/Indians.html>.

43. Qtd. in Cecile Elkins Carter, "Caddo Voices," *Texas Beyond History*, <www.texasbeyondhistory.net>.

44. In "Sha'chahdínnih," located at the *Beyond Texas History* website, Molly Gardner and Mark Parsons describe an interesting piece of collected material: "Many years later, anthropologist Dayna Bowker Lee recorded Lowell 'Wimpy' Edmonds, a member of the Caddo Nation of Oklahoma, singing some 'riding songs.' Mr. Edmonds is a descendent of a Caddo woman and Larkin Edwards, the Caddos' white interpreter during the time of Timber Hill, the last village of the Caddo people in the original Caddo homeland. He said the riding songs were sung while traveling on horseback, and he thought two of them related to his people's removal to Oklahoma, when they rode at night to avoid antagonistic Texas soldiers. In this song, a redbird warns them that daylight approaches." <http://www.texasbeyondhistory.net/timberhill/treaty.html>.

45. Intimate and invisible, a cultural landscape is difficult to define, but certain basic factors seem responsible for a region's cultural landscape. First, the geography of the region provides the foundation of the relationship between these people and their environment. In particular, the prominence and characteristics of the Sabine River and its function as a border shaped the development of the region and the residents' perception of it and themselves. Second, the specific historical events of No Man's Land direct the formation of the cultural landscape. This history includes the settlement of the region, some key historical events, and the interpretation of these events. Finally, the residents' knowledge of these two stimuli and their reactions to them create and recreate the region's cultural landscape. Often evidenced in the expression of folklore, the residents control what stories are told, how they are told, and who usually tells them. Residents maintain or eliminate traditions, determine the aesthetics of the community, and constantly project or reject notions of their own identity. Clear in residents' minds, Louisiana's Neutral Strip clearly exists as a particular place, and even though drawing specific boundaries of the region proves problematic since much of the place relies on mental boundaries, people know what lies in and out of the Neutral Zone. Today, though long removed from the Louisiana Purchase, people readily reconnect to that moment in the past.

CHAPTER 3

1. Shelley is at the end of a long line of Whiddons in the area. Her grandfather was known as a talented gunsmith and the Whiddon family has lived as a tight bunch near the Sabine.

2. Legends often communicate popular cultural myths of a region in a concrete and identifiable manner. Legends attach belief to the physical world. Simultaneously, legend offers the persons, places, and activities of the local environment a means of transcending the ordinary. For instance, the region's border consciousness fueled by isolationism and rugged individualism manifests itself in local legends of actual tough pioneers and outlaws who roamed the local landscape and shaped the history here.

3. For a discussion of this idea, see Alan Dundes, "Folk Ideas as Units of Worldview,"

Toward New Perspectives in Folklore, eds. Américo Paredes and Richard Bauman (Austin: U of Texas P, 1972).

4. For an excellent discussion of this topic, see John Francis Bannon, *The Spanish Borderlands Frontier, 1513–1821* (Albuquerque: U of New Mexico P, 1974).

5. Don Marler, *The Neutral Zone Backdoor to the United States* (Woodville, TX: Dogwood, 1995), 41.

6. It is believed that some of Burr's men did meet with Wilkinson in October of 1806 to discuss the planned attack.

7. Others have different opinions of the act. Bannon claims Wilkinson had "decided to break with Burr and turn patriotic" (210). Marler claims Wilkinson to be "perhaps the most corrupt man in American public life" (42).

8. Matthew L. Davis, *Memoirs of Aaron Burr, 1836,* vol. 2 (Freeport, NY: Books for Libraries, 1970), 327.

9. *Filibusters and Expansionists* (Tuscaloosa: U of Alabama P, 1997), by Frank Owsley and Gene Smith, provides a brief remark about Burr's plans for Texas, including the argument proving whether he had any plans at all. The work explains that in 1806 Burr, backed by a large force and in partnership with General Wilkinson, headed for New Orleans. Burr's plans remain unclear, as well as his intentions for the area upon victory. Regardless, Wilkinson thought that his best future lay in exposing Burr to President Jefferson. Jefferson charged Burr with treason and, for all intents and purposes, rendered him powerless. The case did spark the interest of other filibusters and opened the floodgates of strife for Spain.

10. In *The Neutral Zone,* Marler devotes many pages to Burr's personal history, his filibustering expedition attempt, and the settlement of the town that still bears his name. The town's name is Burr Ferry, Louisiana (33–49, 62–73).

11. Ibid., 62–73.

12. For one example, see John Francis Bannon's *The Spanish Borderlands Frontier.*

13. Marler states that "perhaps no other public figure has been so consistently and falsely accused and abused by politicians, teachers, and historians" (33).

14. Owsley and Smith provide a general overview of the history of filibustering expeditions and of the mind-set and motivations behind the activity.

15. This particular attempt threw Spanish officials into a panic, until a Spanish rout in the battle of the Medina in 1813 settled the matter for good.

16. A few books exist on this subject. For two, see Augustus Q. Walton, *A History of the Detection, Conviction, Life and Designs of John A. Murel, The Great Western Land Pirate: Together with His System of Villainy, and Plan of Exciting a Negro Rebellion also, a Catalogue of the Names of Four Hundred and Fifty-five of his Mystic Clan Fellows and Followers, and a Statement of Their Efforts for the Destruction of Virgil A. Stewart, the Young Man Who Detected Him, To Which is Added a Biographical Sketch of V. A. Stewart 1834* (rpt. Woodville, TX: Dogwood, 1994) and Ross Phares, *Reverend Devil: Master Criminal of the Old South* (Gretna, LA: Pelican Publishing Company, 1974). (John A. Murrell is the accepted spelling today.)

17. Richard Briley III, *Nightriders: Inside Story of the West and Kimbrell Clan* (Woodville, TX: Dogwood, 1992).

18. Even though the book was published in 1993, the editors, Don C. Marler and Jane P. McManus, share the opinion that Crawford's work was written shortly after 1932.

19. Webster Talma Crawford, *The Cherry Winche Country: Origins of the Redbones and the Westport Fight,* eds. Don C. Marler and Jane P. McManus (Woodville, TX: Dogwood, 1993).

20. Manie White Johnson, *The Colfax Riot of April, 1873* (Woodville, TX: Dogwood, 1994).

21. W. T. Block, *Schooner Sail to Starboard: Confederate Blockade-Running on The Louisiana-Texas Coast Lines* (Woodville, TX: Dogwood, 1997).

22. Crawford, 21.

23. Joe Gray Taylor, "The Territorial Period," in *Louisiana: A History*, ed. Bennett H. Wall, 2nd ed. (Arlington Heights, IL: Forum Press, 1984), 95.

24. Qtd. in Nola Mae Wittler, *Pioneers of Calcasieu Parish: Memories of Early Calcasieu*, vol. 1, (Lake Charles, LA: Knight Manufacturing, 1987), 51.

25. Marler, 2.

26. Louis R. Nardini, *No Man's Land: A History of El Camino Real* (Gretna, LA: Firebird Press-Pelican Publishing, 1998), 83.

27. Luther Sandel, *The Free State of Sabine and Western Louisiana* (Many, LA: Jet Publication, 1982), 16.

28. Velmer B. Smith, *The Best of Yesterday, ... Today: A History of the Sabine River and "No Man's Land"* (DeRidder, LA: VBS Enterprises, 1994), 6.

29. Academic scholars also have written a few academic history books or, at least, chapters on the region—works considering the Caddo, early settlers, sawmills and the old times. Even these books on the Neutral Strip's history always seem to demarcate the region's lawlessness and strife as its most significant moment. Each book, also, has its own ideas about what notions have remained in the cultural consciousness. Rugged individualism, the harsh environment, the clannishness, the indescribable mood—different writers embrace these sorts of ideas to one degree or another, but all turn to the area's brief period as a Neutral Zone as a defining moment.

CHAPTER 4

1. This information comes from "Come See an Empire" located at <http://www.arthurstilwell.com/kcpg/>.

2. For a reprint of January 7, 1836, testimonies outlining the many land grants between the Rio Hondo and the Sabine, see Carolyn Ericson, *Natchitoches Neighbors in the Neutral Strip* (Nacogdoches, TX: Ericson Books, 1993).

3. See Steven Smith, *A Good Home for a Poor Man: Fort Polk and Vernon Parish, 1800–1940*. (Legacy Resource Management Program, Washington, DC, and the National Park Service, Southeast Regional Office, Tallahassee, FL, 1999), 218–225.

4. Luther Sandel in *The Free State of Sabine and Western Louisiana* (Many, LA: Jet Publication, 1982) explains that "many of these people obtained land grants, but some just found a likely spot and simply squatted. Later they homesteaded in most cases" (17).

5. Ibid.

6. See Fred B. Kniffen, "Material Culture in the Geographic Interpretation of the Landscape," in *The Human Mirror: Material and Spatial Images of Man*, ed. Miles Richardson (Baton Rouge: Louisiana State UP, 1974), 252–267.

7. Barry Ancelet, Jay Edwards, and Glen Pitre's *Cajun Country* (Jackson: UP of Mississippi, 1991) lists the three major zones of development of the southern portion of the Sabine River: the banks of the major rivers and bayous [Mississippi River, Bayou Lafourche, Bayou Teche], the swamps and marshes, and the great western prairies [Faquetique, Mamou, Calcasieu, Sabine, Vermilion, and others]. The Sabine Prairie and the Little Calcasieu Prairie (the prairie west of the Calcasieu River) provided two of the early westernmost regions of Cajun settlement. Eventually, the settlement of Cajuns would spread even farther west into Texas.

8. Growing in parishes like Calcasieu, Beauregard, Allen, and Evangeline, the pinewoods (the piney woods as some call it) became a cultural dividing line, a geographic boundary. On this line, Cajun met Anglo-American and Redbone as prairie and pinewoods collided, and the meeting often resulted in tension. One example is the Westport Fight, a battle between an entrenched Redbone community and an encroaching Cajun settlement. A complete account of this fight—the reasons behind it and its participants—appears in Webster Crawford's *The Cherry Winche Country: Origins of the Redbones and the Westport Fight* (Woodville, TX: Dogwood, 1993).

9. Ester Terry, personal interview, Jan. 17, 2000.

10. Charlotte Todes, in *Labor and Lumber* (New York: International Publishers, 1931), includes statistics of the industry at the time. The statistics include the land devoted around the world for lumber production, number and size of mills in several states, ownership of forestland in different regions, and other information. Steven Smith's *A Good Home for a Poor Man* offers similar statistics (113–138).

11. Joe V. Warren, Jr., *A History of the Long-Bell Lumber Co. and "The Family" at Longville, La. 1906–1934* (n.p.: Curtis Media, 1997), 42.

12. Roger W. Shugg, *Origins of Class Struggle in Louisiana* (Baton Rouge: Louisiana State UP, 1939), 15.

13. Charles V. Holbrook et al., "Early Sawmills," in *History of Beauregard Parish Louisiana*, compiled by Beauregard Parish Historical Society (Dallas: Curtis Media Corporation, 1986), 21.

14. See C. Vann Woodward, *Origins of the New South, 1877–1913* (Baton Rouge: Louisiana State UP, 1951).

15. Ibid., 22.

16. Several works discuss the establishment of area towns connected to sawmills. See Carolyn Ericson, *Natchitoches Neighbors in the Neutral Strip* (Nacogdoches, TX: Ericson Books, 1993); Roy McDaniel, Jr., *Kurthwood, Louisiana: "The Sawmill Town that Refused to Die"* (Woodville, TX: Dogwood, 1997); Erbon W. Wise, *Tall Pines: The Story of Vernon Parish* (Sulphur, LA: West Calcasieu Printers, 1971); Joe V. Warren, Jr., *A History of the Long-Bell Lumber Co. and "The Family" at Longville, La. 1906–1934* (n.p.: Curtis Media, 1997); and Ethelinda J. Andrus and Grace H. Cornish, eds. *Looking Back at Kinder* (Lake Charles, LA: Calcasieu Printing, 1985). Of these, some also include discussions of the lumber industry's effects on parishes and towns in the region. A few interesting examples are *Tall Pines*; *Looking Back at Kinder*; and *Kurthwood, Louisiana*.

17. Ralph Ramos, "Leather Britches Smith Didn't Fear Nothin', Folks Say," *Beaumont Enterprise Journal,* Aug. 13, 1972, p. 1.

18. Ibid.

19. For folklorists, the classification of a story as a legend becomes crucial because it facilitates the folklorist's ability to anticipate the legend's functions. As a result, folklorists have developed an extensive classification system to define *legend* and to determine the sub-genres of the form, each with a unique set of characteristics. First, people believe the story, at least a portion of it, to be true. It contains true events, a real-world setting, and real characters., Bound by the identifiable and immediate past, legends follow the rules of reality and deal in historical fact. With their primary characters being humans and their settings usually local or known, legends—especially historical legends—often supplement or counter "official" history. As a result, tellers emphasize content and getting it right. This is not to say the legend does not reach beyond the immediate and tangible. Of course, tellers often weave values and beliefs into a legend's text of facts and history.

A great many folklorists have offered definitions of these forms. Even though William Bascom's notions are now challenged, his "The Forms of Folklore" (*Journal of American Folklore* 78:3–21) offers a beginning for the discussion of legend.

20. The kernel narrative, regardless of the amount of deviation surrounding it, remains true to certain important cultural beliefs. Too much deviation and at some point the legend ceases any longer to be a legend and embody its basic ideas. A teller usually seeks to demonstrate that he possesses the basic knowledge of the legend and its surrounding history. While hearing a legend, people expect a certain amount of truth and expect the legend to be believable, but not everyone who tells or hears the legend believes in the legend's veracity to the same degree. He or she does expect to participate in the act of accepting or rejecting portions of what happened.

For some time, experts on the legend form have stressed the importance of tellers believing in the legend as it is being told, but other recent scholars have explained that belief is often unconscious and that the setting and style of the legend make it a realistic genre. For a pertinent discussion, see Linda Dégh, "The 'Belief Legend' in Modern Society: Form, Function, and Relationship to Other Genres," in *American Folk Legend: A Symposium*, ed. Wayland D. Hand (Berkeley and Los Angeles: U of California P, 1971), 55–69.

21. A legend also relies on its flexibility. Built upon a malleable form and engendering creativity in the tellers, a legend requires constant modification in order to express personal desires and serve the needs of the community. It must be able to adapt in order to comment on the issues at hand and remain connected to history. As an individual presents his version of the legend, he must balance how conservative the telling will be with how much deviation will occur. When a person tells a legend, it cannot be unrecognizable; likewise, the telling cannot be so rigid that it does not meet the needs of the current situation. A teller may need to cut out something in the interest of time or audience, or emphasize something so the story applies to a current verbal exchange. Variation in legend exists as a critical part of its form.

For a discussion of this idea, see Linda Dégh, "Folk Narrative," in *Folklore and Folklife* (Chicago: U of Chicago P, 1972). Dégh includes four tentative categories of legends drawn by an international committee, based on available collections, and listed in Wayland Hand's "Status of European and American Legend Study" in *Current Anthropology*. These categories are (1) Etiological and Eschatological Legends, (2) Historical Legends and Legends of the History of Civilization, (3) Supernatural Beings and Forces of Mythical Legends, and (4) Religious Legends or Myths of Gods and Heroes.

22. The tendency for a certain legend to exist in so many versions and to exist in ambiguity (as is the case with Smith's role as outlaw or hero) derives from the construction of legends—the way they are told and their functions for the community. One rarely hears a legend in its complete form in one telling. One may hear a performer's unique details, additional incidents, or corrections to other versions in a single telling, but usually not the entire legend. Moreover, most people tell legends in a communal fashion. As a legend's popularity grows, its communal composition and its incompleteness grow as well. At this point, each version contains the broad general ideas, but varies in details and specifics. Varying a legend can also be a status symbol for an individual. The addition of certain changes and the skill to do so adeptly can pronounce or can reaffirm a teller's belonging and status. The interplay between the fixed and varied aspects of the legend can transmit a teller's inside knowledge—knowledge about the community, history, locale, or even cultural beliefs. Besides, the act of believing requires participation, and participation is an act of identity.

Though often told casually, the legend may sometimes be a form reserved for more ceremonious occasions—something to be told at an initiation, a story to tell at a funeral, a lesson around a holiday dinner. Regardless of when it's told, the legend goes beyond merely recounting a local community's past (even though that is quite important) and grasps at cultural values and notions of right and wrong, good and evil, vengeance and justice. Its presence can intensify the importance of an occasion. It can mark and re-mark identity, reestablish bonds of community and place, and offer an opportunity to participate in a verbal ritual of belonging. For a discussion of this, see Dégh's "The 'Belief Legend' in Modern Society," which offers an excellent discussion of legend and its identifying characteristics.

23. Gussie Townsley, personal interview, Oct. 3, 1998

24. Ester Terry, personal interview, Jan. 17, 2000.

25. Ralph Ramos, "Leather Britches Smith Didn't Fear Nothin,' Folks Say," 3.

26. Gussie Townsley, personal interview, Oct. 3, 1998.

27. The sixth trait explained by Meyer is "the outlaw-hero frequently outwits and confounds his opponents through a variety of 'trickster'-type tactics" (106). This specific quality provides the opportunity for humor. With irony, elaborate guises, and scenes reminiscent of

the Keystone Cops, outlaw legends contain scenes showcasing the figure's unique form of rebellion, which includes the outlaw-hero's victories over lawmen and symbolic overthrows by the common man (106–107). Meyer also notes that this certain characteristic can manifest itself in the form of a "miraculous escape, most frequently from a jail which is supposedly escape-proof" (107).

28. Robert Carmen, personal interview, Dec. 12, 1999
29. Ralph Ramos, "Leather Britches Smith Didn't Fear Nothin,' Folks Say," 2.
30. Ester Terry, personal interview, Jan. 17, 2000.
31. Frontier exaggerations are evidence of this idea. The humor of these tall tales and jokes usually arises from an outsider lacking enough common sense to disbelieve these stories.
32. Mody Boatright, "The Myth of Frontier Individualism," in *Mody Boatright, Folklorist: A Collection of Essays* (Austin: U of Texas P, 1973), 13–38
33. In the seventh trait, Meyer writes that "during his career the outlaw-hero is helped, supported, and admired by his people" (107). Meyer cites the lines "And Pretty Boy found a welcome / At many a farmer's door" in the ballad "Pretty Boy Floyd" as a brief and perfect example (108). Richard Meyer cites his source for this song as Richard E. Lingenfelter, Richard A Dwyer, and David Cohen, eds., *Songs of the American West* (Berkeley and Los Angeles: U of California P, 1928).
34. Ester Terry, personal interview, Jan. 17, 2000.
35. Goob says that this occurred at his Uncle Seab Collins's home.
36. See Ralph Ramos, "Arch Slaydon," *Rocking Texas' Cradle* (Beaumont, TX: The Enterprise Company, 1974).
37. Information about the region's plethora of hideouts can be found in many books. See Richard Briley III, *Nightriders: Inside Story of the West and Kimbrell Clan* (Woodville, TX: Dogwood, 1992); Don Marler, *The Neutral Zone* (Woodville, TX: Dogwood, 1995); Louis R. Nardini, *No Man's Land: A History of El Camino Real* (Gretna, LA: Firebird Press-Pelican Publishing, 1998); and Augustus Q. Walton, Esq., *The Life and Adventures of John A. Murel: The Great Western Land Pirate*, 1834. (Rpt. Woodville, TX: Dogwood, 1994).
38. See Alan Dundes, "Defining Identity through Folklore," in *Folklore Matters* (Knoxville: U of Tennessee P, 1989); Edward H. Spicer, "Persistent Cultural Systems: A Comparative Study of Identity Systems That Can Adapt to Contrasting Environments" *Science* 174 (1971): 795–800; Richard Bauman, "Differential Identity and the Social Base of Folklore" *Journal of American Folklore* 85 (1971): 31–41; Max Weber, *Economy and Society*, vol. 1, (New York: Bedminster, 1968); and George De Vos, "Ethnic Pluralism: Conflict and Accommodation," in *Ethnic Identity: Cultural Continuities and Change*, eds. George De Vos and Lola Romanucci-Ross (Palo-Alto: Mayfield Publishing, 1975), 5–41.
39. In "The Family Saga as a Form of Folklore" (in *Mody Boatright, Folklorist: A Collection of Essays*, Austin: U of Texas P, 1973), Boatright claims that these stories developed from the long history of it being "assumed by the conservative well-to-do that anybody who left for the frontier did so for a good but hardly laudable reason"; thus, the "tradition that the frontiersman was a fugitive became intensified and localized" (127).
40. For a detailed discussion, see Mark T. Carleton and William Ivy Hair, "Bourbonism, Populism, and a Little Progressivism, 1892–1924," in *Louisiana: A History*, ed. Bennett H. Wall, 2nd ed. (Arlington Heights, IL: Forum Press, 1984), 231–251, and "The Struggle to Catch Up, 1877–1935," in *Louisiana: A History*, ed. Bennett H. Wall, 2nd ed. (Arlington Heights, IL: Forum Press, 1984), 269–87.
41. See J. F. Duggar, "Areas of Cultivation in the South," in *South in the Building of the Nation: Economic History, 1865–1901*, ed. J. C. Ballagh, vol. 6 (Richmond, VA: Southern Historical Publication Society, 1909–1913). See also C. Vann Woodward, *Origins of the New South, 1877–1913* (Baton Rouge: Louisiana State UP, 1951), 118.
42. For a description of the timber bust in Merryville, see Judy Wood, Opal Moore, Lena

Robberson, Virginia Patton, Margaret Krasso, and Joy Hudson, "Merryville Louisiana" in *History of Beauregard Parish Louisiana* (Compiled by Beauregard Parish Historical Society, Dallas: Curtis Media Corporation, 1986), 104.

CHAPTER 5

1. Richard Meyer, "The Outlaw as a Distinctive American Folktype," *Journal of the Folklore Institute* 17 (1980), 97.

2. Ibid., 97–99.

3. George T. Morgan, "No Compromise-No Recognition: John Henry Kirby, the Southern Lumber Operators' Association, and Unionism in the Piney Woods, 1906–1916," *Labor History* 10 (Spring 1969): 196.

4. Qtd. in Morgan, 196. Pulled from a speech entitled "The Duties of Citizenship," in *Proceedings, Eighth Annual Meeting of the Subscribers to the Southern Pine Association, March 20–21, 1923,* located in the Southern Pine Association Papers, Department of Archives and Manuscripts, Louisiana State University.

5. Description comes from portrait in Mitchell C. Harrison, "John Henry Kirby," *Prominent and Progressive Americans: An Encyclopedia of Contemporaneous Biography*, vol. 1 (New York: New York Tribune, 1902), 196–198.

6. Information concerning Kirby can be found in various sources.

7. Harrison, 198.

8. Ibid.

9. This description of timber work is based on Steven Smith, *A Good Home for a Poor Man: Fort Polk and Vernon Parish, 1800–1940* (Legacy Resource Management Program, Washington DC, and the National Park Service, Southeast Regional Office, Tallahassee, FL, 1999); Laurence C. Walker, *The Southern Forest* (Austin: U of Texas P, 1991); Otis Dunbar Richardson, "Fullerton, Louisiana: An American Monument," *Journal of Forest History* 27.4:192–201; and Robert S. Maxwell and Robert D. Baker, *Sawdust Empire* (College Station: Texas A&M P, 1983).

10. George T. Morgan's "No Compromise-No Recognition: John Henry Kirby, the Southern Lumber Operators' Association, and Unionism in the Piney Woods, 1906–1916" offers excellent information concerning Kirby's philosophy.

11. James E. Fickle, "The Louisiana-Texas Lumber War of 1911–1912," *Louisiana History* 16 (Winter 1975): 62.

12. Morgan, 197.

13. Ibid., 198.

14. In *Louisiana Labor: From Slavery to "Right-to-Work"* (Lanham, MD: UP of America, 1976), Bernard Cook and James Watson explain that "rapid industrialization also caused painful dislocations . . . [as] Louisiana found itself confronted by a work force whose cultural traditions were at odds with the modern mode of production" (126–128).

15. In his "The Brotherhood of Timber Workers" (*Past and Present*, August 1973), James Green explains this relationship between residents of the piney woods and the lumber company owner. He also connects this latent hostility to the area's eventual "organized resistance to industrial capitalism" (169).

16. C. Vann Woodward, *Origins of the New South, 1877–1913* (Baton Rouge: Louisiana State UP, 1951), 223.

17. Qtd. in Green, 171. *The Rebel* was the Texas paper of the Socialist party from 1911 to 1917.

18. Qtd. in Vernon H. Jensen, *Lumber and Labor* (New York: Farrar & Rinehart, 1945), 79.

19. See George Creel, "The Feudal Towns of Texas," *Harper's Weekly*, Jan. 23, 1915, pp. 76–78.

20. Through the work of his journalistic endeavors, Creel gained such a reputation that he earned the head position of Woodrow Wilson's United States Committee on Public Information in order to promote the WWI war effort. The work of journalists prompted other government action. The 1912–1915 Commission on Industrial Relations (sometimes referred to as the Walsh Report), created by the U.S. Congress to study work conditions throughout the United States, collected evidence on the possible existence of an authoritarian system in the South.

For a discussion of this evidence, see James R. Green, "The Brotherhood of Timber Workers 1910–1913: A Radical Response to Industrial Capitalism in the Southern U.S.A," *Past and Present* 86 (August 1973): 161–200. Green cites extensively from the David Saposs reports conducted during his work with the Commission on Industrial Relations. Saposs interviewed several people in Louisiana. For the report, see National Archives, Commission on Industrial Relations Papers, Department of Labor, Record Group 174.

21. Creel, 76.

22. William Haywood, *Bill Haywood's Book: The Autobiography of William D. Haywood* (Westport, CN: Greenwood P, 1983. Rpt. New York: International Publishers, 1929), 242–243, and Charlotte Todes, *Labor and Lumber* (New York: International Publishers, 1931), 12.

23. Frederic Meyers, "The Knights of Labor in the South," *Southern Economic Journal* 6, no. 4 (1940): 479–487.

24. Green, 175.

25. Green, 175. See also Philip Sheldon Foner, *History of the Labor Movement in the United States* (New York: International Publishers, 1966), 236.

26. Todes, 171; Jensen, 87; and Foner, 236.

27. For information on the SLOA, see Morgan, "No Compromise—No Recognition: John Henry Kirby, the Southern Lumber Operators' Association, and Unionism in the Piney Woods, 1906–1916"; Fickle, "The Louisiana-Texas Lumber War of 1911–1912"; and the Kurth Papers, Box 102 in the Forest History Collections, Stephen F. Austin State University Library, Nacogdoches, Texas.

28. This information about the development of the BTW comes from a variety of sources, which seem to agree on key portions of the organization's history. Many of these sources have been referenced prior to this point. For one of the earliest and best records of the BTW's history, see Charles McCord, *A Brief History of the Brotherhood of Timber Workers*, (Master's thesis, University of Texas, 1958). For some of the discussion on A. L. Emerson, McCord turns to William D. Haywood, "Timber Workers and Timber Wolves," *International Socialist Review,* 13 (August 1912): 105–110. See also Connie Elizabeth Berry, *The Brotherhood of Timber Workers and The Grabow Incident in Southwest Louisiana* (Master's thesis, McNeese State University, 1958).

29. I think Ester Terry means Ed Fussell, the vice-president of the Brotherhood, and confuses the last name with that of the coroner at the time.

30. Connie Elizabeth Berry's *The Brotherhood of Timber Workers and The Grabow Incident in Southwest Louisiana* offers a localized discussion of the Grabow War. She claims that Arthur Lee Emerson, a past member of a local IWW union formed by Pat O'Neill who ended up in Leesville as the editor of the union paper *The Toiler*, teamed with Jay Smith, a fellow southern-born lumber worker.

31. In *Louisiana Labor: From Slavery to "Right-to-Work"* (Lanham, MD: UP of America, 1976), Bernard Cook and James Watson offer a detailed discussion of this event (127–134).

32. The AFL ridiculed Kirby's attempts to use the AFL to vilify other unions.

33. "Eight Lumber Mills Close Monday," *New Orleans Times Picayune,* July 20, 1911, p. 6.

34. "Shut Mills to Fight Union," *New York Times*, August 25, 1911, special to *New York Times*.

35. "Fourteen of the Big Sawmills of Louisiana Are Now Idle," *Lake Charles American Press*, August 25, 1911, p. 1.

36. Morgan, 200–201.
37. McCord, 56.
38. Robert Carmen, personal interview, Dec. 12, 1999.
39. For a view of Merryville's situation at the time, see Ella Windham Lewis, "America's First Union Strike," copied from Lewis' original writings by Joy Hudson in *History of Beauregard Parish Louisiana*, compiled by Beauregard Parish Historical Society (Dallas: Curtis Media Corporation, 1986).
40. While taking pictures of a section of the Sabine River forty miles south of Merryville, I made a casual acquaintance with a man who knew of Leather Britches. Though during our entire conversation he claimed that he really knew nothing at all about the outlaw, he did know who Leather Britches was and knew about Smith's reputation for meanness. He also knew that he was an outsider from Texas and knew that he was connected to the union.
41. Though many versions of the Smith legend present him simply as a notorious badman, other versions do cast Smith as a righteous do-gooder. He does not hold up stagecoaches, rob banks, destroy deeds and liens, or steal from a dictator, but he does in essence burgle away huge profits and unopposed growth by helping to organize the cheap labor force and to demand fair wages, which in turn reduced profit. In fact, the outlaw's actions become more beneficial to ordinary citizens than to him. In this way, Leather Britches acts as counterbalance for the financial inequity that existed in Merryville and throughout the region. In this way, Smith stands against the encroaching outsider lumber mills that cared little for the local residents, especially compared to their concern for profits.
42. See Ralph Ramos, "Leather Britches Rides Again," *Beaumont Enterprise Journal*, Sept. 24, 1972.
43. I am not sure if this Whidden is misspelled. I do not doubt that the last name has alternate spellings, but the vertical file does contain other typing errors. Whiddon is a well-known last name in the area, and, as Shelley Whiddon's interviews indicate, the family had contact with Leather Britches Smith.
44. Even his acts against local families or women with chickens are counterbalanced with tales that say the families were willing to cook for him, that the women were wives of men not home (thus at work and not striking), or that the families were against him or the union.
45. Cook and Watson, 125.
46. Jensen, 80.
47. Green, 169.
48. Ibid., 164.
49. Robert Carmen, personal interview, Dec. 12, 1999.
50. The Galloway family, owners of the mill in Grabow, sponsored the historical marker commemorating the fight between union members and mill workers occurring at Grabow Mill in 1912. Mrs. Terry does make a direct statement about Kirby's mills. She says that "John Henry Kirby was out of Houston, his company. They bought up a lot of timber, a lot of cheap land, twenty-five cents an acre. All the land from Merryville to Oakdale sold for twenty-five cents an acre back in those days, so of course he had to have his mill so he could cut the timber. Stripped the land . . . that's what happened. I was grown in high school when . . . Kirby Lumber Company. . . . Mr. John Henry Kirby was paying a dollar a day to Hamp Yan's father in Merryville. . . . So I know they didn't give them anything, they didn't make anything, but you had to trade with the commissary."
51. Granny Cat, personal interview, Nov. 14, 1998. Granny Cat made this comment while trying to place Grabow's importance in the town's history.

Chapter 6

1. Gussie Townsley's paintings often have accompanying prose pieces. Many of these have been published along with images of her paintings in Velmer Smith's *The Best of Yesterday,*

.... *Today: A History of the Sabine River and "No Man's Land"* (DeRidder, LA: VBS Enterprises, 1994). During one of our interviewing sessions, Gussie Townsley read from her descriptive sketch about Grabow.

2. Obviously, depending on the biases of the author or speaker, the name of the event changes to indicate the aggressor, which side was right and innocent, and the political sides of the speaker. The name "Grabow Riot" makes the union man crazed and the mill owner a minister of order. The name "Grabow Massacre" makes the owner a militant economic tyrant and the union man a lamb. The name "Grabow War" perhaps lands somewhere in the middle.

3. "The Grabow Riot," *Lake Charles American Press*, July 8, 1912.

4. Anne Iles, "The Grabow Riot," *History of Beauregard Parish Louisiana* (Dallas: Curtis Media Corporation, 1986).

5. Charles McCord, A *Brief History of the Brotherhood of Timber Workers*, (Master's thesis, University of Texas, 1958), 58.

6. This description of the Grabow Riot comes from reports included in the *Lake Charles American Press*, July 8, 1912–July 12, 1912.

7. All of the following speakers and their stories of the events that day come from reports included in the *Lake Charles American Press*, July 8, 1912–July 12, 1912. All of the quotations come from what was reported in the papers.

8. This exchange and description comes from Harvard's explanation that appeared in the paper.

9. "Coroner's Jury Hold John Galloway Responsible for 'Cate' Hall's Death," *Lake Charles American Press*, July 12, 1912. The paper would go on to write, "This was probably because about that time Gibbon remembered an important business engagement at DeRidder and left for that place in a hurry."

10. "Three Killed, Twenty Wounded in the Sawmill Men's Conflict at Grabow," *Lake Charles American Press*, July 12, 1912.

11. Ester Terry, personal interview, Jan. 17, 2000.

12. Like many other oral accounts of events, the specifics of the Grabow Riot vary from one teller to the next. Others would disagree about how many men were killed that day by Leather Britches and that anyone would try to keep their identities hidden.

13. Ralph Ramos spells this mill as Greybo.

14. Ralph Ramos, "A Preacher Recalls Violence. . . . Dave Burge," in Rocking Texas' Cradle (Beaumont, TX: The Enterprise Company, 1974), 167–175.

15. "Grand Jury Began Investigation Today of the Riot at the Galloway Mill," *Lake Charles American Press*, July 19, 1912. All of Overton's statements come from this source.

16. The sixty-five were L. F. Johnson, C. C. Holley, G. H. Gibson, George Green, Jack Payne (alias Charles Gibbon), Ed Hollingsworth, W. Davis, A. L. Emerson, Robert Burge, Alf Burge, Henry Simpson, Wiley Green, Leon Zebeau, Will Smith, Joe A. Green, Charles Woodward, W. A. Chatman, F. E. Ezell, W. Colley (alias Alabama), Walter Delcour, John Bowers, Tom Cooper, Jeff Cooper, Charles Smith, Claude Hatley, George Lacy, Alf Cryer, Ed Lehman, W. M. Brown, C. LeBleu, Doc Havens, Will Estes, J. Pennington, Bud Stacy, Sam Slaydon, L. Perry, Harvey Hennigan, Joe Rodgers, Will Coleman, Robert Parham, Bruce Collier, Charles Zebeau, John Killen, J. M. "Red" Reichley, A. A. Budreaux, W. A. Mathis, J. F. McBride, J. M. Moore, A. F. Creed, N. A. Hammond, Walden Cooley, W. R. Jones, James Sturgis, C. A. Jones, Louis Brown, Bennett Lee, Jim Bailey, Rile Perry, John Hilton, John Perry, Andy Denby, Josh Perkins, Pat Perkins, Frank Farr, and Philip Fazeral. The spelling of their names varies between the court records and the October 18, 1912 *Lake Charles American Press* article.

17. *New Orleans Daily Picayune*, July 10, 1912. Located in the Western Historical Manuscript Collection-Columbia, University of Missouri.

18. Qtd. in McCord, 65 (from *The Rebel*, July 20, 1912, p. 1).

19. Ibid.

20. Qtd. in McCord, 66 (from *The Rebel*, July 20, 1912, p. 1).

21. *Lake Charles American Press*, Sept. 5, 1912–Oct. 7, 1912.

22. "Grabow Defense Refused a Delay," *New Orleans Daily Picayune*, Oct. 8, 1912.

23. Evidence entered into the case record. Located in the Calcasieu Parish Courthouse, Case nos. 6021–6023, *State of Louisiana v. L. F. Johnson et al.*

24. Some of the words here were inaudible, and an ellipsis marks their omission.

25. A great deal of information comes from several files located in "Grabow Pamphlet File, Archives and Special Collections Department, Frazar Memorial Library, McNeese State University." Many of the files used in this chapter can be found there.

Chapter 7

1. See Richard Meyer, "The Outlaw as a Distinctive American Folktype," *Journal of the Folklore Institute* 17 (1980): 94–124.

2. Meyer states that "authorities are unable to catch the outlaw-hero through conventional means;" thus, "ultimate success" comes "through other means" (108). He numbers this element as the eighth distinctive trait of the outlaw legend.

3. Meyer explains that continual failures in conventional attempts lead to the "outlaw-hero's death" being "brought on through a betrayal by a former confederate or friend" (108). As Meyer adeptly demonstrates in his many examples (108–110), this theme, captured in "That dirty little coward that shot Mr. Howard," remains an obvious and important component in various outlaw legends. In fact, for Meyer the universality of this theme (what he terms the "Judas" theme) ranks in importance second only to the "Robin Hood" theme.

4. Frank Hennigan, "Folklore of Louisiana's Neutral Ground" (panel discussion, Beauregard Parish Library, DeRidder, LA, June 15, 2000).

5. "Chas. Smith Killed by Del Charlan," *Lake Charles American Press*, Sept. 25, 1912.

6. The description of the event comes from "Chas. Smith Killed by Del Charlan," *Lake Charles American Press*, Sept. 25, 1912.

7. Ibid.

8. Imperial Calcasieu Parish would soon be split into Allen, Beauregard, Calcasieu, and Jefferson Davis parishes. In fact, one of Judge Hunter's rejected appeals argued that the Calcasieu jury would soon have no jurisdiction over the events of Grabow located in Beauregard Parish. The appeal was rejected.

9. Ralph Ramos, "The Last Violent Days of Leather Britches," Beaumont Enterprise, Sept. 13, 1972, p. 2.

10. Ibid., 2. Much like the debate about who fired the first shot at Grabow, whose shot actually killed Leather Britches stands as a point of contention.

11. Ralph Ramos, *Rocking Texas' Cradle*, (Beaumont, TX: The Enterprise Company, 1974), 120.

12. William Lynwood Montell's *Killings: Folk Justice in the Upper South* (Lexington: UP of Kentucky, 1986) addresses the Upper South region and the disposition to violence that scholars have attributed to it. John Shelton Reed's *The Enduring South* (Lexington: Lexington Books, 1972) and *One South* (Baton Rouge: Louisiana State UP, 1982) also address the issue of southern violence.

13. In fact, in many of the versions I have heard, few remember the deputy's name.

14. Robert Carmen, personal interview, March 7, 2002.

15. Citing that Pretty Boy Floyd's and John Dillinger's funerals were each attended "by upwards of twenty thousand persons," Richard Meyer claims that the tenth feature is "the outlaw-hero's death provokes great mourning on the part of the people" (110).

16. Richard Meyer numbers this trait as the eleventh element of the outlaw folktype. Meyer explains that after his death and burial and after the exhibition of mourning by his

local constituency, "the outlaw-hero manages to 'live-on' in one or a number of ways" (110). After hearing that of the outlaw's death and even after seeing his body on display, many claim the man continues to live, that some mistake occurred identifying him, or that someone else's body has been confused with the outlaw's. Meyer also explains that the outlaw may "live-on" in "supernatural rather than natural fashion" or in the many ballads and folklore items that carry on his name (110–111).

17. "Five Witnesses Agree That the First Shot Came from Galloway Mill Office," *Lake Charles American Press*, Oct. 29, 1912. Spelling is as printed.

18. Melanie Carmen, personal interview, Oct. 3, 1998.

19. Many people say the same or that he might claw his way out.

20. See Tadashi Nakagawa, *The Cemetery as a Cultural Manifestation: Louisiana Necrogeography* (Ph.D. diss., Louisiana State University, 1987).

21. See Jerome S. Handler, "A Prone Burial from a Plantation Slave Cemetery in Barbados West Indies: Possible Evidence for an African-type Witch or other Negatively Viewed Person," *Historical Archaeology* 30:76–86. Handler reads the positioning of the body in the burial as he examines a burial mound in Newton Cemetery in southern Barbados and combines a variety of mortuary evidence, including the positioning of the body facedown, to read the community's comment on that person. Handler focuses on one woman buried facedown. He explains that dying from what seems to be extreme lead poisoning, the woman must have exhibited visible signs of pain, which her community would mark as bizarre. Next, Handler views certain aspects of this woman's burial as evidence of her position in the community. Her solitary burial, the lack of goods within the site, the type of coffin, and, especially, her body's positioning indicate low status within the community. In "A Prone Burial," Handler also cites Edwin Ardener's "Coastal Bantu of the Cameroons," an ethnographic survey conducted in Africa. Ardener's work deals with "Kpe and other coastal Bantu people in the western Cameroons" (qtd. in Handler, 82). The work describes people who practiced "a special form of witchcraft" and were "buried face downward so that if they attempt to come out of their graves they will move in the wrong direction" (qtd. in Handler, 90, 105).

22. Meyer outlines his final characteristic as "the outlaw's actions and deeds do not always provoke approval and admiration, but may upon occasion elicit everything from mild stated criticisms and moral warnings to outright condemnation and refutation of any and all of the previous eleven elements" (111).

Usually, a portion of any outlaw legend, maybe the last few sentences of a teller's version, passes judgment on the figure. People can't seem to help themselves. They want to tell how this figure lived and how and why he died. Almost inevitably, a moral scratches its way through the dirt and climbs up out of the ground to haunt the story. People know his reputation as a dangerous community member, even if they never stood facing the dangerous end of his weapon. Some warn that the life of an outlaw inevitably ends in death. Some question whether the outlaw ever exhibited any behavior that could be considered admirable. Really, the moral stands as the reason for the story. Outlaws can't last; they shouldn't, and even their supporters know this; as a result, in any outlaw legend several reports about the figure will not be positive. As people pass these judgments, they use the outlaw to pass judgments on a host of social issues. In the end, providing the community with something complex to judge and use as a symbol might be the true raison d'être of any outlaw, and the act of passing judgment might be proof enough of the outlaw's worth.

23. Since a cemetery's design fills no biological need of those who are buried there, the cemetery is formed primarily through belief and certain other mitigating factors, such as economy, ethnicity, and religion. A cemetery, as a result, can exist as an elaborate means of cultural communication. Thus, by employing a systematic analysis of a cemetery, one can understand how it reflects cultural beliefs and mentifacts of a region. See Ricardas Vidutis

and Virginia A. P. Lowe, "The Cemetery as a Cultural Context," *Kentucky Folklore Record: A Regional Journal of Folklore and Folklife* 26.3–4 (July–Dec. 1980): 103–13. The authors approach certain cultural details of Fulda, a German-Catholic culture area of southern Indiana, through the arrangement of the cemetery. These authors read the cemetery as a cultural text and establish criteria, syntactic and semantic, on which a cemetery can be read, explaining that understanding begins by examining syntactic meaning, "the cemetery's location in relation to the rest of town" and "its internal structurings—the placement of the stones themselves" (104–105). For example, certain sections of this particular cemetery seemed designed for certain groupings (e.g., children in one area). One particular section that "lies outside the cemetery-proper" seems designed to hold those of "social or moral outcast and of unnatural death" (106).

24. Nakagawa's work outlines specific elements that classify Louisiana cemeteries under these groups.

25. The marker records the outlaw's name, his death, and the year. Its scant information teases onlookers and promises a tantalizing legend waiting for discovery. The stone's simplicity and inconspicuousness belie its complexity, especially in terms of its communicative ability. Though these details might be easy to ignore, many scholars argue that the characteristics of individual markers communicate a great deal about the person buried in a site and the community that buried that person.

26. Vidutis and Lowe stress that cultural beliefs and ideologies drive the creation and arrangement of certain sections. In fact, they explain that current interactions with the cemetery reflect current beliefs. Thus, suicides, for example, are buried near the rest of the community.

27. The design of the entire cemetery and the position of Leather Britches's grave in relation to that design exist as starting points for a better understanding of the community's view of Smith and his place in its cultural system. Such permanent markers make a public statement about the figure inside the grave, and they make pronouncements about community ideas and values about death, the afterlife, morality, and status. For example, sometimes an individual's social status can be determined by the time and money expended on making and maintaining a gravesite or by interpreting the symbolism latent in a gravesite's marker, epitaph, and any other surrounding additions, especially when in comparison to surrounding sites.

See Paula J. Fenza, "Communities of the Dead: Tombstones as a Reflection of Social Organization," *Markers: Annual Journal of the Association for Gravestone Studies* 6 (1989): 136–157. In the work, the author explains that low-status burials usually involve plain, small, low-maintenance stones; contain plain and sparse epitaphs; and rest in undesirable or remote locations: "There is no variation or complexity among low-status burials. They represent the barest minimum expenditure necessary to inter individuals according to legal and social mores of society" (147).

28. In his work on Louisiana necrogeography, Tadashi Nakagawa notes that for Protestants, the cemetery "is a resting place for sacred bodies" (262); as a result, the placement of the body during burial is all-important: "Protestants place considerable significance on the resurrection of the dead, showing that desire by arranging the burial along an east-west axis, with the feet pointing toward the east" (262). In effect, the body remains positioned for the Second Coming, since the Protestant belief relies in this case on a literal interpretation of the Bible.

29. See Ralph Ramos, "Leather Britches: Hero and Benefactor? Or Murderer? Tale of Horror Recalled" Beaumont Enterprise Journal, Oct. 8, 1972, p. 1, and Ralph Ramos, "Legend of Leather Britches Untold" *Beaumont Enterprise Journal*, Nov. 24, 1972, p. 1.

30. Ralph Ramos, "Leather Britches: Hero and Benefactor? Or Murderer?, Tale of Horror Recalled," 3.

31. Vidutis and Lowe would term these qualities the semantic meanings that must be understood.

Chapter 8

1. "Veteran of Grabow Battle Led Murderous Band of Smugglers," *Lake Charles American Press*, Sept. 19, 1913.

2. Maxine Condit, "Beauregard Historical Society," in *History of Beauregard Parish Louisiana* (Dallas: Curtis Media Corporation, 1986).

3. The blossoming of cultural awareness that occurred in Beauregard Parish and Merryville align with a national trend emerging in the late 1960s and throughout the 1970s, during which time the entire United States experienced an increased effort in celebrating local folklife. For example, in 1967 the Smithsonian Institution established the Festival of American Folklife, which focused on local culture. Though established in 1888, in the 1970s the American Folklore Society, propelled by the force of several prominent members, concentrated its efforts to emphasize public sector folklore (festivals, public demonstrations, community outreach, etc.). Founded in 1974, the National Endowment for the Arts Folk Arts Program began to support local endeavors to collect and disseminate folklife. Through the American Folklife Preservation Act, the Library of Congress established the American Folklife Center in 1976, and created several state and local agencies to document and display local examples of folklife and to use this knowledge to educate local residents about their own traditions. Created in 1977, the Louisiana Division of the Arts became our local manifestation. An agency in the Office of Cultural Development, Department of Culture, Recreation, and Tourism, the Louisiana Division of the Arts established its goals of supporting local artists and stimulating public participation in the arts. One important section of the agency, the Folklife Division, focused on traditional arts and culture.

4. This pamphlet was created by the Beauregard Historical Society.

5. Condit.

6. Joy Hudson, "Merryville Historical Society," in *History of Beauregard Parish Louisiana* (Dallas: Curtis Media Corporation, 1986).

7. Ibid.

8. See Shawn Martin, "Battle Re-Enactment Kicks off with 'Bang.'" *Lake Charles American Press*, March 5, 2000, B6; "Get Ready to Travel Back in Time with Merryville History Programs," Lake Charles American Press, Feb. 18, 2000, D6; and "Students Get Firsthand Look at Civil War Years," Lake Charles American Press, March 4, 2000, B2.

9. Instead of burdening itself with long discussions of folklore theory, this chapter proceeds with the idea that many of its ideas about festivals have been thoroughly discussed by several scholars. These conclusions about festivals appear to be quite established opinions about the workings of festivals. For some discussions on the structure of the festival and its special traits, see Harvey Cox, *The Feast of Fools*, (Cambridge: Harvard UP, 1969); Alessandro Falassi, ed., *Time Out of Time: Essays on the Festival* (Albuquerque: U of New Mexico P, 1987); Falassi, Alessandro, "Festival," in *Folklore: An Encyclopedia of Beliefs, Customs, Tales, Music, and Art*, ed. Thomas Green, (Santa Barbara: ABC-Clio, 1997); Beverly Stoelje, "Festival in America," in *Handbook of American Folklore*, ed. Richard Dorson, (Bloomington: Indiana UP, 1983).

10. Mandy Goodnight, "Heritage Tourism Can Be Tapped for Even More Economic Growth," *Alexandria (LA) Town Talk*, Feb. 23, 2003, Jan. 1, 2006, <http://www.thetowntalk.com/html/210BB8E0-E8BE-4E3B-AF78-29B21009FD59.shtml>.

11. Ibid.

12. Taken from the Merryville Museum's electronic posting of scheduled events.

13. As is the case with many festivals, the schedule constantly changes; as a result, this description does not follow a specific year. Instead, it describes an amalgamated version of the festival from the years 2001–2008.

14. The description of this festival comes from the 2005 program. However, the events of the program do not differ significantly from one year to the next.

15. As a means of demarcating not only the start of a festival but also the end of normal

time and ordinary space, opening ceremonies in festivals, through a process known as valorization, frame the activities as events occurring in a time and space free of typical constraints and outside ordinary activities and rules. Through this process, community members can perform actions that would not be appropriate in their everyday lives. The separation of the festival from ordinary time also creates a space and time laden with meaning and significance. Actions during the festival become symbolic actions.

16. Reversal affords individuals the opportunity to relieve the tension created by adhering to the accepted societal confines and limitations. Second, it comments on the transitory nature of life and the special qualities of festival time. Finally, by inverting social roles and community behavior during festival time, which is considered different from normal time and which is marked as opposite from real time, the townspeople solidify customary behavioral expectations and roles.

17. In addition to the rites of reversal, rites of conspicuous display and conspicuous consumption are meant to celebrate the culture in an overt manner. In these rites, cultural artifacts and other symbolic elements are conspicuously displayed to reference specific aspects of group identity.

18. In any culture, the festival is a periodic celebration meant to mark social norms and values, even if it does so through exaggeration, role reversal, or ritualistic buffoonery. Including many events and affecting, indirectly or directly, large segments of the community, festivals represent and effectively communicate a group's worldview, and the various components of a festival create a larger communicative structure.

APPENDIX B

1. William Bascom, "The Four Functions of Folklore," *Journal of American Folklore* 67 (1954): 333–349.

2. Richard E. Meyer identifies this trait as the third characteristic of the American outlaw folktype. Robbing from the rich and giving to the poor, the outlaw, "in this and other ways functioning as one who serves to 'right wrongs.'" Meyer states that this "Robin Hood" theme is "probably the most pervasive element in the lore of outlawry" and that these figures "rectify economic and social imbalances" (101).

3. Richard E. Meyer provides an overview of the outlaw tradition and a delineation of the most prolific characteristics of American outlaw tales in "The Outlaw: A Distinctive American Folktype" (*Journal of the Folklore Institute* 17:94–124). When considering the story, characteristics, and reputation of each outlaw, Meyer employs written accounts, collected ballad texts, and collected oral tales. He claims that Ramon F. Adams's *Six-Guns and Saddle Leather: A Bibliography of Books and Pamphlets on Western Outlaws and Gunmen* is "central to any investigation of the historical authenticity of outlaw biography. Other important and reliable references for Meyer include William A. Settle, *Jesse James Was His Name*; Homer Croy, *Jesse James Was My Neighbor*; Albert Hilliard Hughes, "Jesse James: Outlaw with a Halo"; Wayne Gard, *Sam Bass*; Walter Prescott Webb, "Sam Bass: Texas' Beloved Bandit" in *The Texas Rangers: A Century of Frontier Defense*; J. Frank Dobie, "The Robinhooding of Sam Bass"; Helena Huntington Smith, "Sam Bass and the Myth Machine"; J. C. Dykes, *Billy the Kid: The Bibliography of a Legend*; Ramon F. Adams, *A Fitting Death for Billy the Kid*; Robert N. Mullin and Charles E. Welch, "Billy the Kid: The Making of a Hero"; John O. West, "Billy the Kid: Hired Gun or Hero" in *The Sunny Slopes of Long Ago*; Kent Ladd Steckmesser, *The Western Hero in History and Legend*; Paul Wellman, *A Dynasty of Western Outlaws*; and Kent L. Steckmesser, "The Oklahoma Robin Hood." For full bibliographic references for these sources, see the bibliography at the end of this work.

4. In *American Folklore* (Chicago: U of Chicago P, 1959), Richard Dorson attributes the popularity of the most notable "American Robin Hoods," like Jesse James, Billy the Kid, and

Sam Bass, to exposure in the mass media. Moreover, as these stories swept the nation, they prompted dime novels and newspaper stories about other legends, which in turn spawned even more interest in similar local legends. As a result, when telling stories about their local legends, they may have borrowed, intentionally or unintentionally, structural elements or details from the most popular legends, such as Jesse James, Billy the Kid, and so on.

5. Eric Hobsbawm's *Bandits* (London: Abacus, 1969) offers an extensive comparative discussion of the outlaw figure.

6. In *Bandits*, Hobsbawm identifies nine basic characteristics of the outlaw: (1) he begins his outlawry as the victim of injustice, punished for breaking an official law but not a custom; (2) he "rights wrongs"; (3) he "takes from the rich to give to the poor"; (4) he kills only in self-defense or just revenge; (5) he returns to his people as a hero; (6) he is supported by the community; (7) he dies through treason; (8) he is "invisible and innumerable"; (9) he is not the "enemy of the king" since "he is the fount of justice, but only of the local gentry, clergy, or other oppressors" (35–36).

7. In "The Outlaw," Meyer points out that most outlaw legends contain portions praising "the outlaw-hero [as] good-natured, kind-hearted, and frequently pious" and emphasizes that "the religious and 'God-fearing' aspects are present in some degree throughout the spectrum of American outlaw lore" (105). Meyer also claims that other portions detail the outlaw-hero's "audacity, daring and sheer stupendousness of his exploits" (105) and that "tales of incredible shooting prowess by outlaws and other western gunmen are not uncommon in American folklore" (106).

8. In *From Memory to History* (Nashville: American Association for State and Local History, 1981), Barbara Allen and William Lynwood Montell remind that "When people talk about local history, they draw on a number of sources: firsthand observations of changes in the community's physical and social make-up across the years; personal experiences; conversations with other members of the community; and knowledge gleaned from all sorts of written documents and printed materials. Such a variety of sources—an enumeration by no means exhaustive—produces a broad range of topics that make up orally communicated history" (47).

9. Frank Richard Prassel's *The Great American Outlaw* (Norman: U of Oklahoma P, 1993) expands on this very topic. Providing "an outlaw chronology" documenting figures from Hereward the Wake in 1071 to William Munny in Clint Eastwood's *Unforgiven* in 1992 and grouping these outlaws as "bandit, pirate, highwayman, desperado, rebel, bugheway [a desperado terrorizing a town], hoodlum, gunman, gangster, renegade, moll, patrio [patriot], mobster, badman, and fugitive" (5–10), Prassel uses travel accounts, local histories, and images in mass media to document the enduring presence of the outlaw in the world and in our minds.

BIBLIOGRAPHY

Abrahams, Roger. "The Complex Relations of Simple Forms." *Genre* 2 (1969): 105.

———. "Personal Power and Social Restraint in the Definition of Folklore." In *Towards New Perspectives in Folklore*, edited by Américo Paredes and Richard Bauman. Austin: U of Texas P, 1972.

Adams, John Quincy. *The Diary of John Quincy Adams, 1794–1845*. Edited by Allan Nevins. New York: Scribner's, 1951.

Adams, Ramon F. *A Fitting Death for Billy the Kid*. Norman: U of Oklahoma P, 1960.

———. *Six-Guns and Saddle Leather: A Bibliography of Books and Pamphlets on Western Outlaws and Gunmen*. 2nd ed. Norman: U of Oklahoma P, 1960.

Allen, Barbara. "The Genealogical Landscape and the Southern Sense of Place." In *Sense of Place: American Regional Cultures*. Lexington: UP of Kentucky, 1990. 152–163.

Allen, Barbara, and Thomas J. Schlereth, eds. *Sense of Place: American Regional Cultures*. Lexington: UP of Kentucky, 1990.

Allen, Barbara, and William Lynwood Montell. *From Memory to History: Using Oral Sources in Local Historical Research*. Nashville: American Association for State and Local History, 1981.

Ancelet, Barry Jean, Jay Edwards, and Glen Pitre. *Cajun Country*. Jackson: UP of Mississippi, 1991.

Anderson, Perry. "Components of the National Culture." *New Left Review* 38 (1968): 50–67.

Andrus, Ethelinda J., and Grace H. Cornish, eds. *Looking Back at Kinder*. Lake Charles, LA: Calcasieu Printing, 1985.

Anzaldúa, Gloria. *Borderlands/La Frontera: The New Mestiza.* San Francisco: Aunt Lute, 1987.

Bannon, John Francis. *The Spanish Borderlands Frontier, 1513–1821.* Albuquerque: U of New Mexico P, 1974.

Barth, Fredrik. Introduction. In *Ethnic Groups and Boundaries: The Social Organization of Cultural Difference.* Edited by Fredrik Barth. Boston: Little, 1969.

Bascom, William. "The Forms of Folklore: Prose Narratives." *Journal of American Folklore* 78 (1965): 3–21.

———. "The Four Functions of Folklore." *Journal of American Folklore* 67 (1954): 333–349.

Baum, Willa K. *Oral History for the Local Historical Society.* 2nd. ed. Nashville: American Association for State and Local History, 1969.

Bauman, Richard. "Differential Identity and the Social Base of Folklore." *Journal of American Folklore* 85 (1971): 31–41.

———. "The Field Study of Folklore in Context." In Dorson, *Handbook of American Folklore.*

———, ed. *Folklore, Cultural Performances, and Popular Entertainments.* New York: Oxford UP, 1992.

———. *Verbal Art as Performance.* Prospect Heights, IL: Waveland, 1977.

Beauregard Parish Historical Society, compilers. *History of Beauregard Parish Louisiana.* Dallas: Curtis Media Corporation, 1986.

Beck, Horace P. "The Making of the Popular Legendary Hero." In Hand, *American Folk Legend,* 121–33.

Ben-Amos, Dan. "Toward a Definition of Folklore in Context." *Journal of American Folklore* 84 (1971): 10.

Berry, Connie Elizabeth. *The Brotherhood of Timber Workers and the Grabow Incident in Southwest Louisiana.* Master's thesis, McNeese State University, 1958.

Bible, Jean Patterson. *Melungeons: Yesterday and Today.* Rogersville, TN: East Tennessee Printing Co., 1975.

Block, W. T. *Cotton Bales, Keelboats and Sternwheelers: A History of the Sabine and Trinity River Cotton Trades, 1837–1900.* Woodville, TX: Dogwood, 1995.

———. "*Schooner Sail to Starboard:*" *Confederate Blockade-Running on the Louisiana-Texas Coast Lines*. Woodville, TX: Dogwood, 1997.

Boatright, Mody C. "The Family Saga as a Form of Folklore." In *Mody Boatright, Folklorist: A Collection of Essays*, edited by Ernest B. Speck. Austin: U of Texas P, 1973. 124–44.

———. *Folklore of the Oil Industry*. Dallas: Southern Methodist UP, 1963.

———. "The Myth of Frontier Individualism." In *Mody Boatright, Folklorist: A Collection of Essays*, edited by Ernest B. Speck. Austin: U of Texas P, 1973. 13–38.

Briley, Richard, III. *Nightriders: Inside Story of the West and Kimbrell Clan*. Woodville, TX: Dogwood, 1992.

Bronner, Simon J. *American Material Culture and Folklife: A Prologue and Dialogue*. Ann Arbor: UMI Research Press, 1985.

———. *Grasping Things*. Lexington: UP of Kentucky, 1986.

Brooks, Philip Coolidge. *Diplomacy and the Borderlands: The Adams-Onís Treaty of 1819*. New York: Octagon Books, 1970.

Brown, Clair A. *Louisiana Trees and Shrubs*. Rpt. of Louisiana Forestry Commission, Bulletin No. 1, 1945. Baton Rouge: Claitor's Publishing Division, 1972.

———. *Wildflowers of Louisiana and Adjoining States*. Baton Rouge: Louisiana State UP, 1972.

Brunvand, Jan Harold. "Modern Legends of Mormondom, or, Supernaturalism is Alive and Well in Salt Lake City." In *American Folk Legend: A Symposium*, edited by Wayland D. Hand. Berkeley and Los Angeles: U of California P, 1971. 185–203.

Burr, Aaron. "Letter to Joseph Alston on 13 July 1804." In *Memoirs of Aaron Burr with Miscellaneous Selections from his Correspondences*. Vol. 2. Edited by Matthew L. Davis. Freeport, NY: Books for Libraries, 1970.

Burt, Olive Woolley, ed. *American Murder Ballads and Their Stories*. New York: Oxford UP, 1958.

Carleton, Mark T., and William Ivy Hair. "Bourbonism, Populism, and a Little Progressivism, 1892–1924." In Wall, *Louisiana*, 231–51.

———. "The Struggle to Catch Up, 1877–1935." In Wall, *Louisiana*, 269–87.

Carmen, Eloise. Personal interview. March 1, 2000.

Carmen, Marshall. Personal interview. Feb. 20, 2000.

Carmen, Melanie. Personal interview. Oct. 3, 1998.

Carmen, Robert. Personal interview. Oct. 3, 1998.

———. Personal interview. Dec. 12, 1999.

———. Personal interview. March 7, 2002.

Carter, Cecile Elkins. "Caddo Voices" *Texas Beyond History*. <www.texasbeyondhistory.net>.

Castronovo, Ross. "Compromised Narratives along the Border: The Mason-Dixon Line, Resistance, and Hegemony." In *Border Theory: The Limits of Cultural Politics*, edited by Scott Michaelson and David E. Johnson. Minneapolis: U of Minnesota P, 1997.

Clifford, James. "Introduction: Partial Truths." In *Writing Culture: The Poetics and Politics of Ethnography*, edited by James Clifford and George E. Marcus. Berkeley: U of California P, 1986. 1–26.

Coffin, Tristam Potter, and Hennig Cohen. *The Parade of Heroes: Legendary Figures in American Lore*. Garden City, NY: Anchor Press, 1978.

Colorado Folksong Bulletin 2. 1963.

Condit, Maxine. "Beauregard Historical Society." In Beauregard Parish Historical Society, *History of Beauregard Parish Louisiana*.

Cook, Bernard A., and James R. Watson. *Louisiana Labor: From Slavery to "Right-to-Work."* Lanham, MD: UP of America, 1976.

Cox, Harvey. *The Feast of Fools*. Cambridge, MA: Harvard UP, 1969.

Crawford, Webster Talma. *The Cherry Winche Country: Origins of the Redbones and the Westport Fight*. Edited by Don C. Marler and Jane P. McManus. Woodville, TX: Dogwood, 1993.

Creel, George. "The Feudal Towns of Texas." *Harper's Weekly* (Jan. 2, 1915): 76–78.

Croy, Homer. *Jesse James Was My Neighbor*. New York: Duell, Sloan and Pearce, 1949.

Cummins, Light Townsend. "By the Stroke of a Pen: Louisiana Becomes Spanish." In Wall, *Louisiana*, 52–70.

———. "The Final Years of Colonial Louisiana." In Wall, *Louisiana*, 71–86.

Davis, Matthew L. *Memoirs of Aaron Burr, 1836.* Vol. 2. Freeport, NY: Books for Libraries, 1970.

De Caro, Frank. *Folklife in Louisiana Photography.* Baton Rouge: Louisiana State UP, 1990.

Dégh, Linda. "The 'Belief Legend' in Modern Society: Form, Function, and Relationship to Other Genres." In *American Folk Legend: A Symposium,* edited by Wayland D. Hand. Berkeley and Los Angeles: U of California P, 1971. 55–69.

———. "Folk Narrative." In Dorson, *Folklore and Folklife,* 53–85.

———. *Folktales and Society: Storytelling in a Hungarian Peasant Community.* Bloomington: U of Indiana P, 1969.

Del Sesto, Steven, and Jon L. Gibson, edited by *The Culture of Acadiana: Tradition and Change in South Louisiana.* Lafayette: U of Southwestern Louisiana, 1975.

De Vos, George. "Ethnic Pluralism: Conflict and Accommodation." In *Ethnic Identity: Cultural Continuities and Change,* edited by George De Vos and Lola Romanucci-Ross. Palo-Alto: Mayfield Publishing, 1975. 5–41.

Dobie, J. Frank, ed. *Legends of Texas.* 2 vols. Gretna, LA: Pelican Publishing, 1975.

———. "The Robinhooding of Sam Bass." *Montana: The Magazine of Western History* 5 (1955): 34–41.

———, ed. *Texas and Southwestern Lore.* 1927. Vol 6. Austin: Texas Folklore Society, 1934.

Dorson, Richard M. "American Cultural Myths." In Dorson, *American Folklore,* 57–59.

———. *American Folklore.* Chicago: U of Chicago P, 1959.

———. *Bloodstoppers and Bearwalkers: Folk Traditions of the Upper Peninsula.* Cambridge: Harvard UP, 1952.

Dorson, Richard M., ed. *Folklore and Folklife: An Introduction.* Chicago: U of Chicago P, 1972.

———. *Handbook of American Folklore.* Bloomington: Indiana UP, 1983.

———. "How Shall We Rewrite Charles M. Skinner Today?" In Hand, *American Folk Legend,* 69–97.

———. Introduction. In Dorson, *Folklore and Folklife,* 1–50.

———. *Land of the Millrats.* Cambridge, MA: Harvard UP, 1981.

———. "A Theory for American Folklore." *Journal of American Folklore* 72 (1959): 197–215.

Dundes, Alan. "Defining Identity through Folklore." In *Folklore Matters.* Knoxville: U of Tennessee P, 1989.

———. "Folk Ideas as Units of Worldview." In *Toward New Perspectives in Folklore*, edited by Américo Paredes and Richard Bauman. Austin: U of Texas P, 1972.

———. "On the Psychology of Legend." In Hand, *American Folk Legend*, 21–37.

———. "Texture, Text, and Context." *Southern Folklore Quarterly* 28 (1964): 251–65.

Dundes, Alan, and E. Ojo Arewa. "Proverbs and the Ethnography of Speaking Folklore." *American Anthropologist* 66 no. 6 part 2 (1964): 78.

Duggar, J. F. "Areas of Cultivation in the South." In *South in the Building of the Nation: Economic History, 1865–1901*, edited by J. C. Ballagh. Vol. 6. Richmond, VA: Southern Historical Publication Society, 1909–1913.

Dykes, J. C. *Billy the Kid: The Bibliography of a Legend.* University of New Mexico Publications in Language and Literature no. 7. Albuquerque: U of New Mexico P, 1952.

"Eight Lumber Mills Close Monday." *New Orleans Times Picayune*, July 2, 1911, p. 6+.

Ericson, Carolyn. *Natchitoches Neighbors in the Neutral Strip.* Nacogdoches, TX: Ericson Books, 1993.

Falassi, Alessandro, ed. *Time out of Time: Essays on the Festival.* Albuquerque: U of New Mexico P, 1987.

Falassi, Alessandro. "Festival." In *Folklore: An Encyclopedia of Beliefs, Customs, Tales, Music, and Art*, edited by Thomas Green. Santa Barbara, CA: ABC-Clio, 1997.

Fenza, Paula J. "Communities of the Dead: Tombstones as a Reflection of Social Organization." *Markers: Annual Journal of the Association for Gravestone Studies* 6 (1989): 136–157.

Fickle, James E. "The Louisiana-Texas Lumber War of 1911–1912." *Louisiana History* 16 (Winter 1975): 59–85.

Fife, Austin E., and Alta S. Fife, eds. *Cowboy and Western Songs: A Comprehensive Anthology*. New York: Clarkson N. Potter, 1969.

Foner, Philip Sheldon. *History of the Labor Movement in the United States*. Vol. 4: *The Industrial Workers of the World, 1905–1917*. New York: International Publishers, 1966.

Fortier, Alcée. *Louisiana Folk-Tales in French Dialect and English Translation*. Memoirs of the American Folklore Society 2. Boston: Houghton Mifflin, 1895.

Foucault, Michel. *The History of Sexuality: An Introduction*. Vol 1. Translated by Alan Sheridan-Smith. New York: Random, 1978.

"Fourteen of the Big Sawmills of Louisiana Are Now Idle." *Lake Charles American Press*, Aug. 25, 1911, daily ed., p. 1+

Friedman, Albert B. "The Usable Myth: The Legends of Modern Mythmakers." In Hand, *American Folk Legend*, 37–47.

Gard, Wayne. *Sam Bass*. Boston: Houghton Mifflin, 1936.

Gardner, Molly, and Mark Parsons. "Sha'chahdínnih" *Beyond Texas History*. <http://www.texasbeyondhistory.net/timberhill/treaty.html>.

Gaudet, Marcia. "Mississippi Riverlore and Customs." *Louisiana Folklore Miscellany* 5.2 (1982): 26–33.

———. *Tales from the Levee: The Folklore of St. John the Baptist Parish*. Lafayette: Center for Louisiana Studies, University of Southwestern Louisiana, 1984.

Georges, Robert A. "The General Concept of Legend: Some Assumptions to be Reexamined and Reassessed." In Hand, *American Folk Legend*, 1–21.

———. "Toward an Understanding of Storytelling Events." *Journal of American Folklore* 82 (1969): 317.

Glassie, Henry. *All Silver and No Brass*. Philadelphia: U of Pennsylvania P, 1975.

Gleason, Mildred. *Caddo: A Survey of the Caddo Indian in Northeast Texas and Marion County, 1541–1840*. Jefferson, TX: Marion County Historical Commission, 1981.

Glover, William B. "A History of the Caddo Indians." *Louisiana Historical Quarterly*. 18.4:872–946. Reprinted and formatted for the World Wide Web by Jay Salsburg. <ops.tamu.edu/x075bb/caddo/Indians.html>.

Goldstein, Kenneth E. "The Induced Natural Context: An Ethnographic Field Technique." In *Essays in the Verbal and Visual Arts*, edited by June Helm. Seattle: University of Washington Press for the American Ethnological Society, 1967.

Goodnight, Mandy. "Heritage Tourism Can Be Tapped for Even More Economic Growth." *Alexandria (LA) Town Talk*, Feb. 23, 2003, Jan. 1, 2006. <http://www.thetowntalk.com/html/210BB8E0-E8BE-4-E3B-AF78-29B21009FD59.shtml>.

"Grabow Defense Refused a Delay." *New Orleans Daily Picayune*, Oct. 8, 1912.

"The Grabow Riot." *Lake Charles American Press*, July 8, 1912.

"The Grabow Riot." *Lake Charles American Press*, Oct. 23, 1962. Rpt. of "The Grabow Riot." *Lake Charles American Press,* July 8, 1912.

Green, James. "The Brotherhood of Timber Workers, 1910–1913: A Radical Response to Industrial Capitalism in the Southern U.S.A." *Past and Present* 60 (August 1973).

Hadnot, Jack. "Lumbering Brought Prosperity to Vernon." In *Tall Pines: The Story of Vernon Parish*, ed. Erbon W. Wise. Sulphur, LA: West Calcasieu Printers, 1971. 12–13.

Haggard, J. Villasana. "The Neutral Ground Between Louisiana and Texas, 1806–1821." *Louisiana Historical Quarterly* 28.4:1001–1128.

Hall, Stuart. "Gramsci's Relevance for the Study of Race and Ethnicity." *Journal of Communication Inquiry* 10.2 (1986): 5–27.

Halpert, Herbert. "Definition and Variation in Folk Legend." In Hand, *American Folk Legend*, 47–55.

Hand, Wayland D., ed. *American Folk Legend: A Symposium*. Berkeley and Los Angeles: U of California P, 1971.

Hand, Wayland. "The Index of American Folk Legends." In Hand, *American Folk Legend*, 213–21.

———. Preface. In Hand, *American Folk Legend*, v–vi.

———. "Status of European and American Legend Study. *Current Anthropology* 6 (1965): 439–46.

Handler, Jerome S. "A Prone Burial from a Plantation Slave Cemetery in Barbados, West Indies: Possible Evidence for an African-type

Witch or other Negatively Viewed Person." *Historical Archaeology* 30:76–86.

Harrison, Mitchell C. "John Henry Kirby." In *Prominent and Progressive Americans: An Encyclopedia of Contemporaneous Biography* Vol. I. New York: New York Tribune, 1902. 196–198.

Haywood, William. *Bill Haywood's Book: The Autobiography of William D. Haywood*. Westport, CN: Greenwood, 1983. Rpt. New York: International Publishers, 1929.

———. "Timber Workers and Timber Wolves." *International Socialist Review* 13 (August 1912): 105–110.

Hennigan, Frank. "Folklore of Louisiana's Neutral Ground." Panel discussion, Beauregard Parish Library, DeRidder, LA, June 15, 2000.

Hobsbawm, Eric. *Bandits*. London: Abacus, 1969.

Holbrook, Charles V., et al. "Early Sawmills." In Beauregard Parish Historical Society, *History of Beauregard Parish Louisiana*.

Hudson, Arthur Palmer, ed. *Folksongs of Mississippi and their Background*. Chapel Hill: U of North Carolina P, 1936.

Hudson, Joy. "Merryville Historical Society." In Beauregard Parish Historical Society, *History of Beauregard Parish Louisiana*.

Hughes, Albert Hilliard. "Jesse James: Outlaw with a Halo." *Montana: The Magazine of Western History* 17 (1967): 60–75.

Iles, Anne. "The Grabow Riot." In Beauregard Parish Historical Society, *History of Beauregard Parish Louisiana*.

———. "The Grabow Riot." Apr. 1, 1981. Listed as thesis in Beauregard Public Library Vertical File.

Jacobs, James Ripley. *Tarnished Warrior: Major-General James Wilkinson*. New York: Macmillan, 1938.

Jenson, Vernon H. *Lumber and Labor: Labor in Twentieth Century America*. New York: Farrar & Rinehart, 1945.

Johnson, David E., and Scott Michaelson. "Border Secrets: An Introduction." In *Border Theory: The Limits of Cultural Politics*, edited by Michaelson, Scott and David E. Johnson. Minneapolis: U of Minnesota P, 1997.

Johnson, Manie White, B.A. *The Colfax Riot of April, 1873*. Woodville, TX: Dogwood, 1994.

Jones, Mike. "The Legend of Leather Britches Smith." *Lake Charles American Press*, May 23, 1993, p. 13+.

Jones, Suzi. "Regionalization: A Rhetorical Strategy." *Journal of the Folklore Institute* 13 (1976): 105–20.

Jordan, Terry G. *Texas Graveyards: A Cultural Legacy*. Austin: U of Texas P, 1982.

Kennedy, N. Brent. *The Melungeons: The Resurrection of a Proud People*. Rev. ed. Macon, GA: Mercer UP, 1997.

Kniffen, Fred B. "Material Culture in the Geographic Interpretation of the Landscape." In *The Human Mirror: Material and Spatial Images of Man*, edited by Miles Richardson. Baton Rouge: Louisiana State UP, 1974. 252–267.

Lake Charles American Press, July 11, 1912–Sept. 13, 1913.

Lafargue, Reba. "Cagle, Christian Keener." In Beauregard Parish Historical Society, *History of Beauregard Parish Louisiana*, 212.

"Leather Britches Smith." In Beauregard Parish Historical Society, *History of Beauregard Parish Louisiana*.

Lewis, Ella Windham. "America's First Union Strike." Copied from Lewis's original writings by Joy Hudson. In Beauregard Parish Historical Society, *History of Beauregard Parish Louisiana*.

L'Herisson, Lawrence E. "The Evolution of the Texas Road and the Subsequential Settlement Occupancy of the Adjacent Strip of Northwestern Louisiana: 1528–1824." Master's thesis, Louisiana State University, Shreveport, 1977.

Liebling, A. J. *The Earl of Louisiana*. Baton Rouge: Louisiana State UP, 1961.

Lightfoot, William. "Regional Folkloristics." In Dorson, *Handbook of American Folklore*, 183–93.

Lindahl, Carl, Maida Owens, and C. Renée Harvison, eds. *Swapping Stories: Folktales from Louisiana*. Jackson: UP of Mississippi, 1997.

Lingenfelter, Richard E., Richard A Dwyer, and David Cohen, eds. *Songs of the American West*. Berkeley and Los Angeles: U of California P, 1928.

Lippard, Lucy. *The Lore of the Local*. New York: New York P, 1997.

Littleton, C. Scott. "A Two-Dimensional Scheme for the Classification of Narratives." *Journal of American Folklore* 78 (1965): 21–28.

Lomax, John A., and Alan Lomax, eds. *American Ballads and Folk Songs*. New York: Macmillan, 1959.

———. *Cowboy Songs and Other Frontier Ballads*. Revised and enlarged. New York: Macmillan, 1952.

Louisiana Regional Folklife Program. Newsletter, April 1999. Baton Rouge: Office of Cultural Development, Louisiana Division of the Arts, 1999.

Lugo, Alejandro. "Reflections on Border Theory, Culture, and the Nation." In *Border Theory: The Limits of Cultural Politics*, edited by Scott Michaelson and David E. Johnson. Minneapolis: U of Minnesota P, 1997.

Maginnis, John. *The Last Hayride*. Baton Rouge: Gris Gris Press, 1984.

Malloy, William M. *Treaties, Conventions, International Acts, Protocols and Agreements between the United States of America and Other Powers, 1776–1909*, qtd. in Turk, "Adams-Onís Treaty," *Handbook of Texas Online*.

Marcus, George E. *Perilous States: Conversations on Culture, Politics, and Nation*. Chicago: U of Chicago P, 1993.

Marler, Don C. *The Neutral Zone: Backdoor to the United States*. Woodville, TX: Dogwood, 1995.

Martin, Shawn. "Battle Re-Enactment Kicks off with 'Bang.'" *Lake Charles American Press*, March 5, 2000, B6

———. "Get Ready to Travel Back in Time with Merryville History Programs." *Lake Charles American Press*, Feb. 18, 2000, D6.

———. "Students Get Firsthand Look at Civil War Years." *Lake Charles American Press*, March 4, 2000, B2.

Marx, Leo. *The Machine in the Garden: Technology and the Pastoral Ideal in America*. Oxford, UK: Oxford UP, 1964.

Maxwell, Robert S., and Robert D. Baker. *Sawdust Empire*. College Station: Texas A&M P, 1983.

McCarty, Jerry. *Louisiana-Mississippi Treasure Leads*. New Orleans: Treasure Publishers, 1966.

McCord, Charles. *A Brief History of the Brotherhood of Timber Workers*. Master's thesis, University of Texas, 1958.

McDaniel, Roy, Jr. *Kurthwood, Louisiana: "The Sawmill Town that Refused to Die."* Woodville, TX: Dogwood, 1997.

McNeill, Gerald Thomas. *Necrogeography: Material Cultural Elements in Modern Upland South Cemeteries of Louisiana and Mississippi.* Master's thesis, University of New Orleans, 1998.

Meyers, Frederic. "The Knights of Labor in the South" *Southern Economic Journal* 6, no. 4 (1940): 479–487.

Meyer, Richard E. "Image and Identity in Oregon's Pioneer Cemeteries." In *Sense of Place: American Regional Cultures,* edited by Barbara Allen and Thomas J. Schlereth. Lexington: UP of Kentucky, 1990.

———. "The Outlaw: A Distinctive American Folktype." *Journal of the Folklore Institute* 17 (1980): 94–124.

Michaelson, Scott, and David E. Johnson, eds. *Border Theory: The Limits of Cultural Politics.* Minneapolis, U of Minnesota P, 1997.

Mims, Sam. *Rio Sabinas.* Northport, AL: American Southern, 1964.

———. *Toledo Bend.* Gretna, LA: Pelican Publishing Company, 1972.

Mira, Manuel. *The Forgotten Portuguese.* Franklin, NC: Portuguese-American Historical Research Foundation, 1998.

Montell, William Lynwood. *Don't Go Up Kettle Creek: Verbal Legacy of the Upper Cumberland.* Knoxville: U of Tennessee P, 1983.

———. *Killings: Folk Justice in the Upper South.* Lexington: UP of Kentucky, 1986.

———. *The Saga of Coe Ridge: A Study in Oral History.* Knoxville: U of Tennessee P, 1970.

Moore, Opal. "Early Merryville Schools." In Beauregard Parish Historical Society, *History of Beauregard Parish Louisiana,* 144.

———. "History of High School Education in Merryville." In Beauregard Parish Historical Society, *History of Beauregard Parish Louisiana,* 144.

———. "Merryville Agricultural High School." In Beauregard Parish Historical Society, *History of Beauregard Parish Louisiana,* 145.

———. "Merryville Elementary School." In Beauregard Parish Historical Society, *History of Beauregard Parish Louisiana,* 143.

Morgan, George T. "No Compromise-No Recognition: John Henry Kirby, the Southern Lumber Operators' Association, and Unionism in the Piney Woods, 1906–1916," *Labor History* 10 (Spring 1969): 193–204.

Morrison, Steven J. "Downhome Tragedy: The Blues and the

Mississippi River Flood of 1927." *Southern Folklore* 51 (1994): 265–84.

Mullen, Patrick B. *I Heard the Old Fisherman Say: Folklore of the Texas Gulf Coast.* Austin: U of Texas P, 1978.

Mullin, Robert N., and Charles E. Welch, Jr. "Billy the Kid: The Making of a Hero" *Western Folklore* 32 (1973): 104–11.

Nakagawa, Tadashi. *The Cemetery as a Cultural Manifestation: Louisiana Necrogeography.* Ph.D. diss., Louisiana State University, 1987.

Nardini, Louis R. *No Man's Land: A History of El Camino Real.* Gretna, LA: Firebird Press-Pelican Publishing, 1998.

Odum, Howard W., and Harry Estill Moore. *American Regionalism: A Cultural-Historical Approach to National Integration.* Gloucester, MA: Peter Smith, 1966.

Oring, Elliot, Barbara Kirshenblatt-Gimblett, and Henry Glassie. "The Arts, Artifacts, and Artifices of Identity with Specific Discussions: On Difference (Kirshenblatt-Gimblett), On Identity (Glassie), The Interests of Identity (Oring)." *Journal of American Folklore* 107 (Spring 1994): 211–47.

Owsley, Frank Lawrence Jr., and Gene A. Smith. *Filibusters and Expansionists: Jeffersonian Manifest Destiny, 1800–1821.* Tuscaloosa: U of Alabama P, 1997.

Paredes, Américo. "Mexican Legendry and the Rise of the Mestizo: A Survey." In Hand, *American Folk Legend*, 97–107.

———. *"With His Pistol in His Hand": A Border Ballad and Its Hero.* Austin: U of Texas P, 1958.

Pavie, Theodore. *Tales of the Sabine Borderlands: Early Louisiana and Texas Fiction.* College Station: Texas A&M P, 1998.

Post, Lauren C. *Cajun Sketches from the Prairies of Southwest Louisiana.* Baton Rouge: Louisiana State UP, 1962.

Prassel, Frank Richard. *The Great American Outlaw: A Legacy of Fact and Fiction.* Norman: U of Oklahoma P, 1993.

Propp, V. *Morphology of the Folktale.* 2nd ed. Translated by L. Scott. Austin: U of Texas P, 1968.

Pricer, Tensey. "Lady Panthers: Pride of Merryville, Girls Basketball Team Gives Town Plenty to Cheer About." *Lake Charles American Press,* Feb. 6, 2000, C8.

Pruitt, Sam. "Leather Britches." *Something Old—Something New*. Warner Robins, GA: Pruitt Productions, n.d.

Ramos, Ralph. "The Last Violent Days of Leather Britches." *Beaumont Enterprise Journal*, Sept. 13, 1972, p. 1.

———. "Leather Britches: Hero and Benefactor? Or Murderer?," and "Tale of Horror Recalled." *Beaumont Enterprise Journal*, Oct. 8, 1972, p 1.

———. "Leather Britches Rides Again." *Beaumont Enterprise Journal*, Sept. 24, 1972, p. 1.

———. "Leather Britches Smith Didn't Fear Nothin,' Folks Say." *Beaumont Enterprise Journal*, Aug. 13, 1972, p. 1.

———. "Legend of Leather Britches Untold." *Beaumont Enterprise Journal*, Nov. 24, 1972, p. 1.

———. *Rocking Texas' Cradle*. Beaumont, TX: The Enterprise Company, 1974.

Reed, John Shelton. *The Enduring South: Subcultural Persistence in Mass Society*. Lexington: Lexington Books, 1972.

———. *One South: An Ethnic Approach to Regional Culture*. Baton Rouge: Louisiana State UP, 1982.

Relph, E. C. *Place and Placelessness*. London: Pion, 1976.

Richardson, Otis Dunbar. "Fullerton, Louisiana: An American Monument." *Journal of Forest History* 27.4:192–201.

Robe, Stanley L. "Hispanic Legend Material: Contrasts Between European and American Attitudes." In Hand, *American Folk Legend*, 109–21.

Rosaldo, Renato. *Culture and Truth: The Remaking of Social Analysis*. Boston: Beacon, 1989.

Ryden, Kent C. *Mapping the Invisible Landscape: Folklore, Writing, and the Sense of Place*. Iowa City: U of Iowa P, 1993.

Sandel, Luther. *The Free State of Sabine and Western Louisiana*. Many, LA: Jet Publication, 1982.

Santino, Jack. *All Around the Year: Holidays and Celebrations in American Life*. Urbana and Chicago: U of Illinois P, 1995.

Sayers, Brian. *On Valor's Side: Tom Green and the Battles for Early Texas*. Hemphill, TX: Dogwood, 1999.

Schoemaker, George H., ed. Glossary. *The Emergence of Folklore in Everyday Life*. Bloomington, IN: Trickster, 1990. 231–41.

Schwartz, Delmore. *Summer Knowledge: New and Selected Poems.* Garden City, NY: Doubleday, 1959.

Settle, William A., Jr. *Jesse James Was His Name.* Columbia: U of Missouri P, 1966.

Shugg, Roger W. *Origins of Class Struggle in Louisiana.* Baton Rouge: Louisiana State UP, 1939.

"Shut Mills to Fight Union." *New York Times*, Aug. 25, 1911, special to *New York Times*.

Simonson, Harold P. Introduction. *The Significance of the Frontier in American History*, by Frederick Jackson Turner. New York: Frederick Ungar, 1963.

Slaydon, Arch. Interview with Ralph Ramos. *Rocking Texas' Cradle.* Beaumont, TX: The Enterprise Company, 1974. 119–25.

Slotkin, Richard. *Regeneration through Violence: The Mythology of the American Frontier, 1600–1860.* Middletown, CT: Wesleyan UP, 1973.

Smith, Helena Huntington. "Sam Bass and the Myth Machine." *The American West.* 7 (1970): 31–35.

Smith, Henry Nash. *Virgin Land: The American West as Symbol and Myth.* Cambridge, MA: Harvard UP, 1970.

Smith, Steven. *A Good Home for a Poor Man: Fort Polk and Vernon Parish, 1800–1940.* Legacy Resource Management Program, Washington DC, and the National Park Service, Southeast Regional Office, Tallahassee, FL, 1999.

Smith, Velmer, B. *The Best of Yesterday, ... Today: A History of the Sabine River and "No Man's Land."* DeRidder, LA: VBS Enterprises, 1994.

Spicer, Edward H. "Persistent Cultural Systems: A Comparative Study of Identity Systems That Can Adapt to Contrasting Environments." *Science* 174 (1971): 795–800.

Stanbery, V. B. *An Approach to Regional Planning.* Portland: Oregon State Planning Board, Oct. 25, 1935.

Stark, Catherine. Personal interview. Nov. 14, 1998.

Steckmesser, Kent Ladd. "The Oklahoma Robin Hood." *American West* 7 (1970): 38–41.

———. *The Western Hero in History and Legend.* Norman: U of Oklahoma P, 1965.

Stoelje, Beverly. "Festival in America." In Dorson, *Handbook of American Folklore*.

———. "Making the Frontier Myth: Folklore Process in a Modern Nation." *Western Folklore* 46 (1987): 235–53.

Taylor, George Rogers, ed. *The Turner Thesis Concerning the Role of the Frontier in American History*. Rev. ed. Boston: D. C. Heath, 1956.

Taylor, Joe Gray. "The Territorial Period." In Wall, *Louisiana*, 91–109.

Taylor, Julie. "The Outlaw State and the Lone Rangers." In *Perilous States: Conversations on Culture, Politics, and Nation* edited by George E. Marcus. Chicago: U of Chicago P, 1993. 283–305.

Terry, Ester. "Folklore of Louisiana's Neutral Ground." Panel discussion, Beauregard Parish Library, DeRidder, LA, June 15, 2000.

Terry, Ester. Personal interview. Jan. 17, 2000.

Todes, Charlotte. *Labor and Lumber*. New York: International Publishers, 1931.

Toelken, Barre. "*Ma'i Joldloshi*: Legendary Styles and Navaho Myth." In Hand, *American Folk Legend*, 203–13.

Townsley, Gussie. "Folklore of Louisiana's Neutral Ground." Panel discussion, Beauregard Parish Library, DeRidder, LA, June 15, 2000.

Townsley, Gussie. Personal interview. Oct. 3, 1998.

Tuan, Yi-Fu. *Space and Place: The Perspective of Experience*. Minneapolis: U of Minnesota P, 1977.

Turner, Frederick Jackson. *The Frontier in American History*. 1920. New York: Holt, 1962.

Turk, Evelyn. "Adams-Onís Treaty." *Handbook of Texas Online*. <http://www.tshaonline.org/handbook/online/articles/AA/nba1.html> (accessed July 5, 2010).

United States Committee on Public Works. Letter from the Secretary of the Army Transmitting a Letter from the Chief of Engineers. *Sabine River and Tributaries, Texas and Louisiana*. Washington: U.S. Government Printing Office, 1970.

Vance, Rupert B. "Concept of Region." *Social Forces* 8 (Dec. 1929): 202–218.

"Veteran of Grabow Battle Led Murderous Band of Smugglers." *Lake Charles American Press*, Sept. 19, 1913.

Vidal de la Blanche, Paul. *Principles of Human Geography*. Edited by Emmanuel de Martonne. Translated by Millicent Todd Bingham. New York: Holt, 1926.

Vidutis, Ricardas, and Virginia A. P. Lowe. "The Cemetery as a Cultural Context." *Kentucky Folklore Record: A Regional Journal of Folklore and Folklife*. 26.3–4 (July–Dec. 1980): 103–13.

Von Sydow, C. W. *Selected Papers on Folklore*. Copenhagen: Rosenkilde and Bagger, 1948.

Walker, Laurence C. *The Southern Forest*. Austin: U of Texas P, 1991.

Walker, Tony. "Dust Not Ashes: The American Preference for Burial." *Landscape* 32.1 (1993): 42–48.

Wall, Bennett H. *Louisiana: A History*. 2nd ed. Arlington Heights, IL: Forum Press, 1984.

Walls, Robert E. "Chapter 12: Folklife and Material Culture." In *The Emergence of Folklore in Everyday Life*, edited by George H. Schoemaker. Bloomington, IN: Trickster, 1990.

Walton, Augustus Q., Esq. *The Life and Adventures of John A. Murel: The Great Western Land Pirate*. 1834. Woodville, TX: Dogwood, 1994.

Warren, Joe V., Jr. *A History of the Long-Bell Lumber Co. and "The Family" at Longville, La*. 1906–1934. N.p.: Curtis Media, 1997.

Webb, Clarence H., and Hiram F. Gregory. *The Caddo Indians of Louisiana*. 2nd ed. Louisiana Archaeological Survey and Antiquities Commission Anthropological Study, no. 2, 1978. Baton Rouge: State Printing, 1990.

Webb, Walter Prescott. "Sam Bass: Texas' Beloved Bandit." *The Texas Rangers: A Century of Frontier Defense*. Austin: U of Texas P, 1965.

Weber, Max. *Economy and Society*. Vol. 1. New York: Bedminster, 1968.

Wellman, Paul. *A Dynasty of Western Outlaws*. New York: Bonanza Books, 1961.

West, John O. "Billy the Kid: Hired Gun or Hero." In *The Sunny Slopes of Long Ago*, edited by Wilson M. Hudson and Allen Maxwell. Publications of the Texas Folklore Society, no. 33. Dallas: Southern Methodist UP, 1966.

Whiddon, Shelley. Personal interview. Dec. 13, 1999.

Wilgus, D. K. "The Individual Song: 'Billy the Kid'." *Western Folklore*. 30 (1971): 227–230.

Wilgus, D. K., and Lynwood Montell. "Beanie Short: A Civil War Chronicle in Legend and Song." In Hand, *American Folk Legend: A Symposium*, 133–57.

Williams, T. Harry. *Huey Long*. New York: Vintage Books, 1969.

Wise, Erbon W. *Tall Pines: The Story of Vernon Parish*. Sulphur, LA: West Calcasieu Printers, 1971.

Wittler, Nola Mae. *Pioneers of Calcasieu Parish: Memories of Early Calcasieu*. Vol. 1. Lake Charles, LA: Knight Manufacturing, 1987.

Wood, Judy, Opal Moore, Lena Robberson, Virginia Patton, Margaret Krasso, and Joy Hudson. "Merryville Louisiana." In Beauregard Parish Historical Society, *History of Beauregard Parish Louisiana*.

Woodward, C. Vann. *Origins of the New South, 1877–1913*. Baton Rouge: Louisiana State UP, 1951.

Yoder, Don. "The Saint's Legend in the Pennsylvania German Folk-Culture." In Hand, *American Folk Legend*, 157–85.

INDEX

American Lumber Company, 91
Atakapa, 32–33, 161
Beaumont Enterprise, 19, 68, 154
Beauregard Parish Historical Society, 31, 136
   sesquicentennial celebration, 158–163
Brotherhood of Timber Workers, 86–88, 96–98, 114–115
   Grabow War, 99–103, 107–108, 116
   Leather Britches Smith, 89, 102
   oath, 111–112
Burr, Aaron, 53–54
   Burr Ferry, Louisiana 54
Backdoor to the United States, 13, 56
   See also Free State of the Sabine, Neutral Ground, Neutral Strip, Neutral Zone, No Man's Land

Caddo, 32–34, 35, 41–43
Carmen, Eloise (Grand), 4–7, 10, 15, 25, 50, 94, 130, 133
Carmen, Robert (Bobby), 120, 124, 129
Charlan, Del (Deputy), 103, 120–124

DeRidder, Louisiana, 60–62
   DeRidder Daily News, 154
   Grabow War, 103–105, 108
   History of Beauregard Parish Louisiana, 162
   photos, 142

Emerson, Arthur Lee, 86–88, 92, 96, 97–98
   jail, 105, 108
   Grabow War, 99–103, 117

Free State of the Sabine, 13, 56
   Festival, 157, 158
   See also Backdoor to the United States, Neutral Ground, Neutral Strip, Neutral Zone, No Man's Land
Fuller, Ocelean, 59, 62, 75

Galloway
   Grabow trial, 109–114
   Jim, 114
   John, 103–104, 106, 113, 114
   Martin, 113, 114
   Mill, 92, 95–101, 105, 107
   Paul, 103, 106, 114
Grabow, 51, 84, 120, 125, 128, 134, 172
   Incident, 159, 161
   Leather Britches Smith, 22
   Massacre, 97
   mill, 132
   Riot 56, 78, 95–106, 115, 162
   trial, 108–115, 154
   See also Grabow War
Grabow War, 94–106, 115, 116–117, 118, 135, 137
   Leather Britches Smith, 155, 170
Grand (Eloise Carmen), 4–7, 10, 15, 25, 50, 94, 130, 133
Granny Cat (Catherine Stark), 19–20, 30–31, 82, 118, 131
   Leather Britches Smith grave, 129–133, 135

Hall, Covington, 107, 109
Haywood, "Big Bill," 84, 107
Herrera, Don Simón (Lieutenant Colonel), 37–40
Hickman, Bud, 96, 101, 103, 112–113
Hieronymus, Darrell, 14, 15
Hunter, E. G. (Judge), 109–111, 115

Industrial Workers of the World, 47, 84
   See also IWW
IWW, 85, 87, 96, 98, 154
   Grabow War, 106–107

Kirby, John Henry, 78–79, 86, 91–92
   Kirby Lumber Company, 79–80, 83
   obligation, 82
   SLOA, 87–88

220 | INDEX

Kirbyville, Texas, 80, 83–84

Lafitte, Jean, 24, 45, 52, 54, 58, 157
Lake Charles American Press, 68, 121–122, 127, 145
Leather Britches Smith
   ambush, 120–128
   Ben Myatt, 19, 20, 27, 28, 122, 127, 145
   Brotherhood of Timber Workers, 89–90
   crime, 27, 29–31, 114
   Grabow War, 96, 116–117, 118, 135, 137, 155, 170, 173
   grave, 4, 19, 128–130, 132–137, 170
   gun skills, 29, 48, 68–70, 116, 126
   song, 21–24, 137
   See also Smith, Charles
Louisiana Territory, 13, 35–37, 39
   Adams-Onís Treaty of 1819, 41, 62
   Louisiana Purchase, 13, 36, 165
   See also Sabine River Valley

Merryville Historical Society, 158–159, 162–163
Merryville, Louisiana, 1–3, 5, 66, 67
   Cemetery, 3–4, 133
   Heritage Festival photos 147, 151
   Historical Society, 158–159, 162–163
   Leather Britches Smith death 126
   mills, 10–11, 74
Merryville Museum, 163–168, 170, 172
Murrell, John A. (The Reverend Devil), 55, 56, 73

Neutral Ground, 13, 51, 56
   See also Backdoor to the United States, Free State of the Sabine, Neutral Strip, Neutral Zone, No Man's Land
Neutral Strip, 13, 14, 35, 40, 94, 156
   Leather Britches Smith, 70, 75, 178
   legends, 24, 43, 49, 52–55
   Ralph Ramos, 18–19
   residents, 170, 171
   settlers, 63–65, 74, 159
   See also Backdoor to the United States, Free State of the Sabine, Neutral Ground, Neutral Zone, No Man's Land
Neutral Zone, 13, 56–57, 62–63, 157
   Leather Britches Smith, 23, 71, 73–74
   legends, 52, 54
   residents, 49
   See also Backdoor to the United States, Free State of the Sabine, Neutral Ground, Neutral Strip, No Man's Land
Newton, Goob, 16–19, 50, 124
   Leather Britches Smith legend, 29, 67–70, 72, 126, 129
   Leather Britches Smith grave, 132, 133, 136
No Man's Land, 13, 14, 18, 26, 158, 159, 161
   Gussie Townsley, 94, 95
   Leather Britches Smith, 75, 155, 170–171, 172
   legends, 45, 49–56, 58, 73
   Merryville Historical Society, 165, 167, 168
   residents, 93, 125

   See also Backdoor to the United States, Free State of the Sabine, Neutral Ground, Neutral Strip, Neutral Zone
No Man's Land Gang, 156, 165–167, 169
   photos, 148–150, 152

Overton, Winston (Judge), 104, 106, 109, 114
   portrait, 144

Pujo, Arsène (Congressman), 109, 111

Ramos, Ralph, 16, 18–21, 154
   Beaumont Enterprise, 68
   Leather Britches Smith articles, 90, 102–103, 116, 123, 124–125, 137
   Rocking Texas' Cradle, 19, 56
Reid, Henry (Sheriff), 103–104, 108, 122
Reverend Devil, The (John A. Murrell), 55, 56, 73
Rice Land Lumber Company, 2

Sabine River, 8–10, 13–24, 33, 38, 40–41, 59
   border, 27, 31–32, 37
   description, 25–26
   No Man's Land, 45, 48, 52, 54, 57, 68, 95
Sabine River Valley, 34, 47
   See also Louisiana Territory
sawmill towns, 10–11, 66–67, 95, 161
SLOA, 86–88, 96, 97
   Grabow War, 105–106, 107, 116
Southern Lumber Operations Association, 86
   See also SLOA
Smith, Charles, 106–107
Stark, Catherine (Granny Cat), 19–20, 30–31, 82, 118, 131
   Leather Britches Smith grave, 129–133, 135

Terry, Ester, 155, 163
   Grabow War, 98, 102, 115–117
   Leather Britches Smith ambush, 121, 123, 125–128
   grave, 133, 137
   past, 31–32, 69, 76, 78
   mills, 84, 92
   No Man's Land, legend, 49–56, 58
   union men, 88
Townsley, Gussie, 85, 94–96, 116–117, 155

unions, 14, 83, 84, 85–86, 91–93
   Emerson, A. L., 87, 97–98
   Grabow trial, 110–111, 114–115
   Grabow War, 78, 96, 99–102, 106–107
   Kirby, John Henry, 82, 87–88
   Leather Britches Smith, 19, 47, 72, 76, 89–90, 113, 116–117
   photos, 144, 145
   SLOA, 86

Whiddon, Shelley, 46–47, 123–124, 128
Wilkinson, James (General), 37, 38–40, 53